Making Sense of
Grammar

David Crystal

Cartoons by Edward McLachlan

PEARSON
Longman

Contents

The noun phrase

Pronouns

Adjectives

Adverbs and adverbials

Introduction

They say a week can be a long time in politics; well, a decade is a short time in educational linguistics.

In the past few years, the study of grammar, in an educational context, has come of age. From being a topic of marginal interest, beloved by a few, hated by many, and ignored by most, it has moved into the centre of pedagogical attention. You may still love it, or hate it, but you can no longer ignore it. And as it is not going to go away, it is well worth while getting to grips with it. The crucial question is: How?

This book is a sequel to *Rediscover Grammar*, which first appeared in 1988, well before the current renaissance of interest in grammatical matters. The conclusions of various government reports were pointing the way towards a brave new linguistic world, but the English National Curriculum was still five years off. Few people were seriously interested in grammar then.

The situation was nicely captured in cartoon form by McLachlan at the very front of *Rediscover Grammar*. We see a man begging in the street, holding out his hat for donations. Around his neck there is a card which says: 'Grammar Explained: Thank You'. But the passers-by are ignoring him, and his hat is empty. Today, such a person would need an appointment book, and his hat would be full.

Why has there been such a dramatic change, in such a short time? Why have people suddenly become so interested?

Grammar helps

The answer lies in developments in thinking about the nature of language which became widely known during the 1990s. These enabled people to see that the study of grammar has a point. In a word, it helps.

Helps what? To improve a person's language abilities. There are four core linguistic domains which need to be attended to, if children are to reach their full potential as communicating human beings: listening, speaking, reading, and writing. And in each of these, grammar has a fundamental role to play.

The key is to appreciate how grammar relates to meaning. Nobody would ever doubt the importance of meaning in educational practice. Meaning is at the heart of communication. It is why we communicate – in order to understand each other. We need to follow and interpret what other people do when they talk or write, and make ourselves clear and effective when we carry out these tasks ourselves.

It is sometimes thought that meaning is nothing to do with grammar – that it is just a matter of vocabulary. When we say we are going to 'look the meaning of a word up in a dictionary', we give this impression. But it is a misleading impression. A word on its own conveys little meaning, as this brief experiment shows.

Write the meaning of the following word on the line below.
charge

....

If meaning lives 'in a word', you will be able to do this.

But of course you cannot do this, because you do not know which of the several possible meanings of *charge* I had in mind. Did I mean *charge* in the sense of electricity, or economics, or military science, or criminology, or one of its other meanings? You have no way of knowing.

'Give us some context,' you would argue, 'and then we will be able to carry out the task.' Quite right. That is a prerequisite. But how am I to give you some context? You could rephrase: 'Put the word into a sentence, and then we will know what you mean.'

Precisely. If I put the word into a sentence, then you will know what I mean. That is the key principle. Only by using words in sentences are we able to 'make sense' of them. That is what sentences are for. They are there, quite literally, to 'make' – create – sense. Without sentences, words are vague, ambiguous things.

So:
    I ordered the troops to charge.
    I need to charge the battery.
    I'm going to charge him with an offence.
    The bank want to charge extra interest.
By putting *charge* into a sentence, we relate it to other words, and thus convey a particular meaning.

If I repeated the experiment now, you would be able to make some headway with it.

Write the meaning of the word in bold on the line below.
*I ordered the troops to **charge**.*

....

Introduction

Grammar is the study of how sentences mean. And that is why it helps. If we want to understand the meaning conveyed by sentences, and to develop our ability to express and respond to this meaning, then the more we know about grammar, the better we will be able to carry out these tasks.

'Knowing about grammar' means studying how we construct sentences, and in particular how we manipulate the parts of a sentence in order to give satisfactory expression to whatever meaning we have in mind. It also means studying how we use sentences, and how our choice of sentence affects other people.

People sometimes worry about grammar because it seems so complicated. But there is a good reason for the complexity: we are beings who need to express complex thoughts. If we wanted to express only the most primitive ideas, then grammar would be very simple. But no human society is like that.

Grammar has evolved to enable us to express the most profound and subtle nuances of meaning. It can make all the difference to the meaning of a sentence if we make a slight change in word order, alter a word ending, put an extra word in, or leave one out. So often, the exact point being made lies in the detail.

Grammar is all about how we handle any kind of meaning, on any occasion, in any subject. Whatever the nuance we want to express, we need grammar in order to express it. Whatever the nuance someone else expresses, we need grammar in order to understand it. There is no other way.

Grammar is the structural foundation of our ability to express ourselves. The more we are aware of how it works, the more we can monitor the meaning and effectiveness of the way we and others use language. It can help foster precision, detect ambiguity, and exploit the richness of expression available in English. And it can help everyone – not only teachers of English, but teachers of anything, for all teaching is ultimately a matter of getting to grips with meaning.

Theory into practice

It all sounds fine in theory. But how do we get from theory to practice? How do we get our knowledge of grammar to improve our performance, so that we become better listeners, speakers, readers, and writers? We have to build a bridge, and this means introducing a new dimension to the approach of *Rediscover Grammar*. The bridge needs two spans, and that book built only the first.

The first span: description

Naming of parts

All scientific investigations begin by noticing something which intrigues us, and which makes us want to talk about it. In the case of grammar, we notice the particular way someone speaks or writes — perhaps because we like the effect of it and want to copy or adapt it in some way, or perhaps we think it is an error and want to avoid it or draw attention to it. Either way, we need to identify what we have noticed, and that means *naming* it.

This was the primary purpose of traditional grammar: to provide us with terms to label things. Once we have such labels as 'sentence', 'word', 'noun', and 'adjective', then we can talk about 'a word at the end of a sentence' or 'an adjective going after the noun'. It is an essential first step. Terminology is intrinsic to grammar, as it is to chemistry, geography, and all other subjects which describe things. And a major aim of *Rediscover Grammar* was to introduce a core set of grammatical terms.

Analysis

But noticing and naming a feature of grammar is not an isolated exercise. It is not enough to say, 'Hedgehog? Aha, that is a singular noun'. If we are bold enough to identify hedgehog as a noun, this means that we must also have noticed that it is not some other part of speech – a verb, say, or an adjective. To say that it is singular means we must have noticed that it is not plural.

In grammar, one observation is always part of a network of other observations. We learn about concepts in clusters – often clusters of two, such as singular / plural or positive / negative, but also larger clusters, such as subject – verb – object. We begin to understand grammar only when we see how an observation fits into the total scheme of things. When we analyse sentences, we are developing our sense of how the whole grammatical system works.

The second major aim of *Rediscover Grammar* was, accordingly, to introduce a way of analysing English sentences so that all the important patterns could be described. Along the way, I pointed to some of the difficulties in doing grammatical analysis (under the heading of **Caution**) and some of the variations in the way people use grammar (under the heading of **Usage**). But the thrust of the book was, in a nutshell, to describe.

So, at the end of *Rediscover Grammar*, a survivor would be able to look at (or listen to) a text, identify an interesting feature of grammar, name it, and relate it to other features. 'There are six instances of the passive in the opening paragraph.' 'The passage is written entirely in the present tense.' 'The writer uses many adjectives, but no adverbs.' This is a descriptive ability, which in an exam might get a few marks – but probably not very many. Why not?

Any examiner will tell you. Because the descriptive skill, on its own, is not very informative. In an educational context, it is sometimes called 'feature-spotting'. It is a facility that computers have, and the skill shows a similar mechanical-mindedness in humans. Accurate as such descriptive statements may be, we feel that they are somehow missing the point. They invite the reaction: 'So what?'

What point is being missed? Underneath all such observations lurks the crucial question: **Why?** Why is the speaker or writer using the passive? Why the present tense? Why so many adjectives? We need explanations, and feature-spotting does not explain anything.

The second span: explanation

There are two answers to the 'why' questions, and both are important. One answer explains the usage in terms of the meaning it expresses – a **semantic** explanation. The other explains the usage in terms of the effect it conveys – a **pragmatic** explanation.

Meaning

As we have seen in the Introduction, the semantic issue is the heart of the matter. Every time we encounter a grammatical feature, we need to ask: what does it mean? Every time we study a grammatical contrast, we need to ask: what meaning difference does the contrast express?

Sometimes the answer will be obvious: *singular* expresses the notion of 'one' and *plural* 'more than one'. Sometimes the answer is more complex: tense forms do more than just 'tell the time'. It is often quite difficult to put the 'meaning' of a grammatical feature into words. But always we must bear meaning in mind. After all, that is why we are speaking or writing in the first place.

Effect

The second way in which we can explain the use of a grammatical feature is by pointing to the effect it conveys. There are many kinds of effect. Some features convey an informal tone, others a formal tone. Some give an impression of elegant care, others of casual spontaneity. Some elicit a reaction of humour, respect, or admiration. Some establish rapport, antagonize, or persuade.

Often, the effect produced by a grammatical usage is a sense of appropriateness or inappropriateness. All subject areas have norms of expression, and we need to conform to these norms if we do not want to mislead, irritate, or simply appear inept. Certain grammatical features are associated with scientific English, for example; others with advertising English, or the English of the Internet, or the English we use in everyday conversation. Sometimes – as with legal or religious language – the norms have been sanctioned by centuries of tradition. In other cases – as with the Internet – they are still evolving. But always we need to think about the kind of grammar which will suit the circumstances.

The point applies equally to the various domains of the curriculum. These have their norms too, often explicitly recognized by exam boards. There may be recommended ways of writing up a scientific experiment, for instance, or of writing a history essay, or providing a commentary on a piece of literature. Some domains allow flexibility in grammatical expression; others are much stricter in maintaining a consistent and conventional style.

It is always a matter of **choice**. Whether in school or society, we have in our heads a wide range of grammatical constructions available for our use, and it is up to us to choose which ones will work best to express what we want to say and to achieve the desired effect.

DEED

The bridge between the theory and the practice of grammar requires two spans: Description and Explanation. *Rediscover Grammar* dealt with the descriptive part of the exercise. *Making Sense of Grammar* deals with the explanatory part.

Both spans are needed to complete our appreciation of English grammar. We regularly cross the bridge in both directions, depending on the linguistic task we perform.

- **D>E** If we are listening and reading, we begin with Description and proceed to Explanation. We notice how someone else is using a grammatical feature, and want to explain its meaning and effect.

- **E>D** If we are speaking and writing, we begin with Explanation and proceed to Description. We reflect on the meaning we want to convey or the kind of effect we want to achieve, and then choose the features of grammar which will enable us to communicate our intentions effectively.

This two-way approach is reflected in its acronym: DEED. The DEED palindrome suggests the mutual dependence of the relationship between Explanation and Description. It is very important that we should be able to move easily from one dimension of awareness to the other. The chapters in the present book therefore correspond, topic by topic, to those in *Rediscover Grammar*.

Each chapter of this book begins with a summary of the essential descriptive point made in its predecessor, so that it is possible to read *Making Sense of Grammar* as a self-contained exercise. Those who have already read *Rediscover Grammar* can use this summary by way of revision, before proceeding to the semantic and pragmatic perspectives. Those who have not will find in the earlier book a greater depth of descriptive detail, as well as discussions of tricky points of analysis and everyday usage.

Crossing the bridge

Once both spans of the DEED bridge are in place, then the core information we need to improve our grammatical abilities is available, ready to be put to active use. The final step, of course, is to do just that: to put it to use, and (in the case of teachers) to entice others to put it to use.

The long-term aim must be to get into the habit of crossing the DEED bridge routinely, so that it becomes second nature – a process which operates without our needing to think about it, but which can be brought to the surface when occasion demands. Grammar is a means to an end, as the next chapter illustrates, and once we have mastered it we can, for most purposes in life, stop consciously reflecting upon it. At that point we have become alert to its expressive potential, capable of capitalizing on its strengths and avoiding its pitfalls.

But to get to that stage, we need to cross the DEED bridge regularly and often. Our crossing has to be a smooth one, so that we do not find ourselves collapsing in the middle under the weight of terminology, or being led to do analyses where we fail to see the point. We have to find the crossing so illuminating and enjoyable that we want to keep making it. This is what best practice in grammar teaching is able to do.

There are as many opportunities here as teachers can create and timetables allow, but we have to recognize that we are still at an early stage in the development and dissemination of the appropriate educational techniques. Grammar books need to be followed up by lesson-plans, self-help materials, and other teaching aids. There is still much to be done, by way of selecting and grading topics to meet the needs of students at various ages and levels of ability. We do not always know the best ways of crossing the grammar bridge, from either end. But at least now we have a grammar bridge to cross.

Grammar and vocabulary

The educational climate of the last few years has brought a renewed interest in the study of grammar, and the nature of the subject – especially its abstract character and awe-inspiring terminology – has caused it to loom large in the vision of language that many people hold. The danger, of course, is that the special focus on grammar makes them fail to pay comparable attention to other aspects of language which are also important in fostering intelligible, appropriate, and effective communication.

Grammar is not the whole story. It is just one dimension – a crucially important dimension, but a single dimension nonetheless – within the network of properties which make up spoken and written language. When we listen, speak, read, and write, we are doing much more than attending to grammar. And when we want to improve abilities in listening, speaking, reading, and writing, we need to foster much more than grammatical skills.

As I suggested in the opening section, grammar is the structural foundation of our ability to express ourselves meaningfully and effectively. But to continue the metaphor: if language is a skyscraper, and grammar is its foundation and structural skeleton, which we cannot easily see, what constitutes its visible bulk?

Words, words, words. In a word: vocabulary – the content words of the language. Whatever our linguistic aims are – to achieve precision, avoid ambiguity, express ourselves appropriately ... – we cannot succeed without a good command of vocabulary. Content words without grammar, as we have seen, convey very little sense; but grammar without content words does not convey much sense either. We are left with a meaning-less shell. Only the combination of both dimensions, grammar and vocabulary, gives us a meaningful result.

> Content words without grammar
> *guide, wait, car, six*
>
> Grammar without content words
> *The — will be —ing with a — at —.*
>
> Content words and grammar combined
> *The guide will be waiting with a car at six.*

The use of language always requires us to make simultaneous choices in both grammar and vocabulary. And these choices must be compatible, if we want our language to be intelligible, acceptable, and effective. For example, it is anomalous (unless we are making a comic point) to use formal grammar with informal vocabulary:

Notwithstanding our respective sizes, I approached the geezer with whom I had previously had a barney.

And it is even more anomalous to use informal grammar with formal vocabulary – as the Heineken copy-writers well knew when they ended one television advertisement with this variant of their famous slogan:

Heineken refreshes the parts wot other beers cannot reach.

Grammar is a means to an end – the confident production and comprehension of meaningful and effective expression. The systematic study of grammar is a crucial step in attaining this end, though it needs to be accompanied by a corresponding interest in vocabulary. Ironically, vocabulary – part of the study of semantics – has received even less attention than grammar. But that is another story.

1 The sentence

DESCRIPTIVE SUMMARY

Grammar is the study of how sentences are structured and how they connect with each other. It is not feasible to give at the outset of a grammar book a summary account of the range of structural choices available in a language for the formation of sentences, because there are far too many possibilities. It takes an entire book to do that. But it is certainly possible to make some general observations about the meaning and effect of sentences, at the same time taking account of their important but neglected counterparts – non-sentences.

EXPLANATION

Why do we need sentences at all? The point has already been made in the Introduction (p.8). Sentences are the only way in which we can, quite literally, 'make' sense. Words alone are not enough. We need to put words into sentences in order to know what they mean. This principle applies equally to all modes of communication: speech, writing, signing, and electronic interaction.

A sentence is an active, dynamic entity. Every structure conveys a particular sense, and it is up to us, as sentence-makers, to find the right structure for what we want to say. Similarly, as sentence-receivers, we interpret the sentences of others by assuming that the users mean what they say. When we hear somebody complaining, 'That's not what I meant', something has gone very wrong.

Jabberwocky

We can show the way we use sentences to create sense by reflecting on how a piece of nonsense verse works, such as Lewis Carroll's 'Jabberwocky'. Its opening lines are:

'Twas brillig, and the slithy toves
Did gyre and gimble in the wabe.

Why do we think we can make sense of this utterance? Because we recognize the English sentence structure, and can relate it to other structures in the language. We know intuitively that the mother of one of the slithy toves would be able to tell her offspring to 'stop gimbling at once!', or that one of the toves could tell its schoolmates that 'We gyred and gimbled yesterday'. We could not do this if we did not recognize the utterance as a possible English sentence. If Carroll had written his first lines in the following way, we would be able to make nothing at all of them:

Slithy the and brillig toves gyre
'Twas did the in gimble wabe and.

Completeness

For a sentence to 'make sense', it needs to be complete. No crucial element must be missing from its structure, and when we reach the end it must feel finished. We are able to recognize this even without punctuation.

These sentences feel complete:
    our cat is asleep in its basket
    give me a chance to explain
    where are you going
Even though this last sentence is asking for information, we know that the question has come to an end. It is now the listener's turn to speak.

By contrast, these utterances feel incomplete:
    gone to town   (who has?)
    the policeman put   (put what where?)
    she gave   (gave what to whom?)

Some of these fragments might turn up in English, but something else needs to be present before we can make sense of them.
• Something in the social situation can make clear what is missing. If someone leaves a scribbled note saying *Gone to town*, we can read in the missing element.
• Something in the linguistic context can make clear what is missing. If someone asks us *Where's Mary?*, a reply *Gone to town* now makes sense.

Quite a wide range of expressions rely on situation or context in this way (see Chapter 2). Authors differ as to whether they should be called 'sentences' or not, or whether some such term as 'abbreviated sentence' would be better (Chapter 62). But from a semantic point of view, this is a side-issue. The central point is that communication relies on our ability to distinguish between expressions which are complete and those which are not, even if we need to rely on the situation or context to do so.

How do we show completeness?

In writing, a capital letter and three punctuation marks have come to mark the beginning and end of a complete unit: the full-stop, question mark, and exclamation mark.

The train was on time.   The train was on time?
The train was on time!

In some special circumstances, other symbols can be used to mark beginning and end, such as the use of angle brackets in an e-address.

<crystal@rhubarb.com>

In e-communication, full-stops are part of the identity of a site-name, as this example shows; so a final full-stop would be ambiguous. We wouldn't know if it was part of the e-address or not.

Punctuation marks are also available to show lack of completeness. Formal usage employs a single dash or a series of three dots ('ellipsis dots' or 'suspension dots'):

The train was on time –   The train was on time ...

The dash suggests an abrupt break; the dots a trailing away. The size of the dash, whether an 'en-dash' (–) or an 'em-dash' (—) is a matter of publishing practice (p.384). In informal usage, the number of dots and dashes varies:

The train was on time ....   The train was on time – – –

If a piece of language ended with a comma, colon, or semi-colon, we would also think it to be unfinished:

The train was on time,   The train was on time:
The train was on time;

Such punctuation marks have no status as sentence markers in standard English.

The lack of end-punctuation is ambiguous: it *can* show incompleteness, but in many settings it is simply part of conventional graphic design – as in a book title. Some examples are mentioned on p.28. Punctuation is discussed further in Chapter 76.

The problem of speech

It is easy to show the difference between complete and incomplete in writing. In speech, it is more difficult, because a combination of melody (intonation), rhythm, tone of voice, and pause is used to mark sense-units, and these features are not as clear-cut as punctuation marks (Chapter 75).

The problem usually doesn't arise when people are reading aloud. In a broadcast news-reading, you can 'hear the full-stops'. But in spontaneous speech, the boundaries between sentences are much more difficult to detect, as any transcription of a piece of spoken English quickly shows. (Pauses are shown by –; rhythm-units by /)

their football grounds are purpose built for modern conditions /
– whereas ours aren't / – and every time someone gets trampled
in a crush / this highlights it / and they sort of patch it up / and
it's botched / you know ...

Is this one sentence or two? If you were turning this into a play dialogue, would you choose a comma or a full-stop after *aren't*? In writing, you have to make decisions of this kind. In speech you don't.

Why is completeness important?

It is easy to see why sentences need to be complete. Completeness makes it more likely that a sentence will make sense and be clear, intelligible, and unambiguous.

This is the bare minimum, of course. We can still produce nonsense or ambiguity, even in a sentence which has all its crucial elements present, if we do not pay attention to vocabulary and to all the other features of the structure. For example, this one looks complete, but it is still ambiguous:

The police were told to stop drinking at midnight.

(Who's doing the drinking? And what was happening at midnight? Stopping the drinking, or the telling?)

The uses of incompleteness

More interesting, from a pragmatic point of view, is why we might ever want our sentences to be incomplete. Completeness is what speakers and writers usually try to achieve. But sometimes it is crucial to the nature of the interaction that a sentence remains unfinished.

Withholding information

The police burst into the room. Murphy lay on the floor, his chest covered with blood. Branson went over to him. 'Who did it, Murphy?' Branson put his ear next to the dying man's lips. 'Who did it?' Murphy's eyes flickered. 'It was ... It was ...' His head fell sideways. Branson cursed. Their last lead had gone.

Branson's problem was that Murphy didn't finish his sentence. But if Murphy had, there would have been no crime novel. It can be essential to the plot to leave a sentence incomplete.

Interrupting

In Shakespeare's *Henry IV Part 1* (I.iii.185), Hotspur has been haranguing his noble colleagues about the English political situation. But after 30 lines, Worcester has had enough.

HOTSPUR: ... this proud King, who studies day and night
To answer all the debt he owes to you,
Even with the bloody payment of your deaths
Therefore, I say –
WORCESTER: Peace, cousin, say no more.

Although it is nice to think of conversation as being an elegantly cooperative activity, in which everyone politely waits for speakers to finish before reacting, the reality is very different. Interruptions are commonplace. Indeed, in television soaps, where plots are driven by domestic disputes, and multi-party dialogue is routine, it is sometimes difficult to find anyone being allowed to speak a complete sentence!

Evading

In conversations dealing with an intimate or awkward subject, we can leave the tricky part of a message unsaid, often acknowledging the difficulty with a hesitation noise or comment. The listener can either take the unsaid element for granted and move on, or get us to spell it out, or even spell it out for us:

A: I think you should – er, you know ...
B: Tell him, you mean?

Topics which give rise to some degree of embarrassment often remain unfinished:

A: Where's the er ...
B: First on the right upstairs.

Advertising

Advertisements commonly leave a sentence incomplete, allowing the listener or reader to draw the desired conclusion from a brand-name or from the accompanying images or sounds:

You're feeling ... mmmm ...
[image of person eating the product]
For the cat who knows what's best ...
[image of cat eating a brand of cat-food]
For you this summer ...
[image of a holiday destination]
Does she ... or doesn't she?
[image of a woman's hair, with a hair colourant]
Simply the best. Bloggo.
[image of the product]

If we try to complete these sentences, we find there is no obvious single way to do so. Nor is this necessary. The auditory or visual context is enough to make the meaning clear, and the unstated or understated conclusion can add a sense of intrigue or empathy. After all, if we are the intelligent owners of an intelligent cat we do not have to be told to 'buy Catto'. We can draw that conclusion for ourselves.

Taking for granted

For many television viewers, if *It's* is spoken in a low, husky tone of voice, no more need be said: what follows is *Monty Python's Flying Circus*. The usage developed a life of its own outside the series, and became a jocular catch-phrase used to announce someone's arrival.

Well-known utterances, such as catch-phrases and quotations, are often left unfinished if they are at all lengthy. Because they are recognizable, the rest of their content is usually taken for granted:

It takes all sorts ...   When in Rome ...
If at first you don't succeed ...

Indeed, the end of the sentence may not be known:

The best laid schemes o' mice an' men ...
(... *gang aft a-gley*: Robert Burns, 'To a Mouse')

Even nonstandard English can be used:

Greater love hath no man ...   If it ain't broke ...

And sometimes the unstated element is not predictable, so that the listener has to apply the utterance to the situation:

I didn't get where I am today ...
Meanwhile, back at the ranch ...
... as the actress said to the bishop [and variants]

Mentally lapsing

Probably the most basic reason for not finishing a spoken sentence is that, through ignorance, inattention, or forgetfulness, we lose track of what we want to say. Even Owl got out of his depth (in A.A. Milne's *The House at Pooh Corner*). Describing a 'Backson', he begins:

'Well,' said Owl, 'the Spotted or Herbaceous Backson is just a –'
'At least,' he said, 'it's really more of a – '
'Of course,' he said, 'it depends on the – '
'Well,' said Owl, 'the fact is,' he said, 'I don't know *what* they're like,' said Owl frankly.

Cooperating in dialogue

Towards the end of Tom Stoppard's *Rosencrantz and Guildenstern Are Dead*, the two heroes discuss Hamlet:

> GUIL: His play offended the king –
> ROS: – offended the king –
> GUIL: – who orders his arrest –
> ROS: – orders his arrest –
> GUIL: – so he escapes to England –
> ROS: On the boat to which he meets –
> GUIL: Guildenstern and Rosencrantz taking Hamlet –
> ROS: – who also offended the king –
> GUIL: – and killed Polonius –
> ROS: – offended the king in a variety of ways –
> GUIL: – to England. *(Pause.)* That seems to be it.

Such sequences of incomplete sentences always generate special effects, and alter the dynamic of an interaction. In the first part of this example, the repetition of sentence fragments rather suggests that Rosencrantz is having some trouble keeping up. But he then 'gets the point', and the pace increases as he enthusiastically takes up the story. Stoppard makes the most of the effect, introducing a pause in the last line followed by a stolid understatement. It always gets a laugh.

This technique is widely used in drama and the novel, for it simulates a common practice in conversation, where people 'chip in' with information, or one person takes advantage of a pause to finish off a sentence. It can build a rhetorical climax, as in these lines from Shakespeare's *Troilus and Cressida* (II.iii.232), where three people are talking Ajax into fighting Hector:

> NESTOR: What a vice were it in Ajax now –
> ULYSSES: If he were proud –
> DIOMEDES: Or covetous of praise –
> ULYSSES: Ay, or surly borne –
> DIOMEDES: Or strange, or self-affected.

Characterizing

Some people have a habit of leaving sentences hanging in the air. In *Thank You For Having Me*, Maureen Lipman describes someone nicknamed 'The Birdman of Alcatraz' on the grounds that he never finishes a sentence':

'What I'm gonna – what I'm planning – all things being – ' *(thirty-second meaningful pause)* 'I mean, anything could happen, right?'

Literature is full of such characters, comical and serious.

In Harold Pinter's *The Caretaker*, unfinished sentences characterize Davies the tramp. Indeed, a string of incomplete sentences from him actually ends the play:

Listen ... if I ... got down ... if I was to ... get my papers ... would you ... would you let ... would you ... if I got down ... and got my ...

And earlier on, the use of incompleteness helps to create an atmosphere of unease and 'unspoken threat'. Davies is being asked if he wants to be caretaker:

ASTON: How do you feel about being one, then?
DAVIES: Well, I reckon ... Well, I'd have to know ... you know ...
ASTON: What sort of ...
DAVIES: Yes, what sort of ... you know ...
(Pause)
ASTON: Well, I mean ...
DAVIES: I mean, I'd have to ... I'd have to ...
ASTON: Well, I could tell you ...
DAVIES: That's ... that's it ... you see ... you get my meaning?
ASTON: When the time comes ...

In this book, we shall be studying complete sentences. But we can always sharpen our sense of what counts as 'complete' by comparing complete and incomplete sentences, thereby highlighting the properties of each.

Sentence punctuation

Punctuation always, as it were, has a point (Chapter 76). And we can see the point only if we grasp the contrast of meaning or use which it expresses. An individual punctuation mark should never be studied in isolation, therefore, but always in contrast with some other mark – or, of course, with its absence. This principle applies to sentences as much as to any other area of grammar.

Something or nothing

We expect a sentence to end with a mark of 'final' punctuation (p.21). Something is evidently missing if a sentence fails to have such a mark at the end

This is not just a matter of convention. Such cases make us uncomfortable because we are unsure whether information has been inadvertently lost. Is it just a typographical error (a 'typo'), or something more serious?

On the other hand, when the context makes it clear that nothing is missing, we can view punctuationless sentences with equanimity. In fact they are all around us, as the contemporary graphic fashion is to leave public signage as 'uncluttered' as possible (p.385). We are unlikely to find end-punctuation in such settings as these:
• newspaper headlines and subheadings
• public signs, such as *SLOW*, *EXIT*, and *No Smoking*
• advertising slogans and brand-names
• titles of books, films, programmes, etc.
• product-names and summary descriptions
• addresses on envelopes and in letters.

Then, once we opt for end-punctuation, we have two further choices:
• choosing between final and non-final marks
• choosing the appropriate mark from within each set.
For non-final choices, see p.21; for final choices, see pp.58, 76.

A pragmatic distraction

Writers have been reflecting on the nature of good stylistic practice for over two thousand years, and there is no shortage of recommendations. But what counts as 'good style' changes, partly because language itself changes, and partly because literary fashions change. It is therefore essential to view all stylistic 'rules' with caution, especially as they are often made by writers who have a very narrow view of what counts as 'good' style. If you were to follow their prescriptions, you would exclude a significant amount of English literature.

One of the most famous of these prescriptions applies to the way sentences begin.

Never begin a sentence with a conjunction.

This maxim achieved some popularity in the nineteenth century, and has stayed in the minds of some pundits ever since. It chiefly attacks sentences beginning with *and, or,* or *but.* However, starting a sentence – or even a paragraph – with one of these conjunctions is at the heart of English literary tradition. It was a major feature of Old English texts, and usage has continued without a break to the present day.

• Here is Chaucer's Wife of Bath getting back to the point after a long digression, and beginning a fresh section of her Prologue (line 711):
  But now to purpos, why I tolde thee
  That I was beten for a book, pardee!

• Here is Shakespeare's Hamlet, reacting to his first vision of his dead father (I.v.92):
  O all you host of heaven! O earth! What else?
  And shall I couple hell? O, fie! Hold, hold, my heart.
  And you, my sinews, grow not instant old ...
  Two examples in two lines. And there are dozens more throughout the play.

- Here is Charles Dickens, describing the world of fashion at the beginning of *Bleak House* (Chapter 2):
  There is much good in it; there are many good and true people in it; it has its appointed place. But the evil of it is, that it is a world wrapped up in too much jeweller's cotton and fine wool ...

- And here is Winston Churchill, beginning a new paragraph in the Preface to *A History of the English-Speaking Peoples*:
  But this youthful, flourishing, immature civilization lacked any solid military defence.

The effects are plain. A conjunction at the beginning of a sentence can mark a turning point in the narrative. It can make a dramatic contrast. The use of an opening monosyllable increases a sentence's narrative pace. None of these effects would be possible if the texts were rewritten as single sentences, or if the conjunctions were omitted or replaced by adverbs such as *however*.

We can sense the available effects even in a short sequence. Which of these two examples would be the more dramatic way of describing an impending railway disaster?
  Jo saw the train coming, but it was too late.
  Jo saw the train coming. But it was too late.
Most people opt for the second. The full-stop breaks the flow, and the new short sentence introduces a fresh pace and rhythm. The effect is to reinforce the unexpected, unpredictable nature of the event. During that brief pause at the full-stop, there is just a hint that Jo might have been able to do something to stop the accident.

By contrast, the comma binds the two parts together, making the meaning of the second part follow smoothly on from the first. The effect is to reduce the dramatic contrast, making the event more expected and matter-of-fact. There was no time for Jo to do anything here. The accident was inevitable.

The other alternatives offer further possibilities, but do not always help. To omit the conjunction loses the contrast in meaning conveyed by *but* – a meaning we might paraphrase as 'and yet'. Also, in this example, the omission introduces an unwelcome ambiguity – that the train was not on time.

Jo saw the train coming. It was too late.

To replace the *but* by a connecting adverb completely alters the tone and pace.

Jo saw the train coming. However, it was too late.

This would be more likely in a formal, unemotional account of the events, such as a police report.

As always, with features of grammar where we have a choice, the overuse of any one option can reduce or eliminate the effectiveness of the stylistic contrast. It is the hallmark of an immature style to overuse a feature – something typical of young children's writing:

Last week we went to the beach. And I saw a donkey. And I went for a ride. And I got an ice-cream ...

A maturing writer learns the value of alternative strategies for sentence connectivity (see p.368).

Incompleteness within sentences

This chapter has been devoted to the idea of completeness in relation to the beginnings and ends of sentences. As a final observation, we should also note the fact that incompleteness can occur *inside* a sentence. Here are some contexts:

- In science, dots mark the omission of obvious data:
  In the sequence 1, 3, 5, ... 17, 19, 21
- In quotations, dots show an omitted portion:
  To be ... is the question
- In puzzles, a dash can mark a challenge to be solved:
  7 Down 'To be or — to be' (3 letters)

Sentences fall into two types, based on whether they are
constructed in a regular or irregular way. Most sentences are
regular, or **major**, in type: we build up their structure using
established rules, producing repeated patterns:

| Jean | found | the cat | in the garden. |
| The cat | was drinking | its milk | greedily. |

Irregular or **minor** sentences do not follow these rules, and often
look as if they have little or no structure:

Hello.   Shhh!   Taxi!   How do?

There are very few types of minor sentence, so grammar books
can list them and analyse them quite quickly. By contrast, the
structural range and complexity of major sentences is
considerable, and their study comprises most of a grammar. This
chapter, accordingly, deals only with minor sentences; subsequent
chapters will explore major sentence patterns. The most complex
kinds of major sentence (**multiple** sentences) are discussed in
Chapter 63.

Why do we have minor sentences at all? Why aren't all sentences
regular? The answer is to do with the kind of meaning that we
want to express. Major sentences exist to enable us to express a
complex, potentially infinite range of meanings, such as 'who did
what to whom, when, where, and why'. The range of meanings
expressed by minor sentences is much more simple and limited in
character.

What minor sentences express

The term **minor** relates only to the grammatical structure of sentences. It has nothing to do with the 'importance' of what is said. Minor sentences have an important communicative role, and often perform a more effective job than their major counterparts. On hearing a noise, *Shhh!* is much more likely to elicit the desired immediate response than *I would appreciate silence while we listen!*

Minor sentences tend to be short, sharp, and to the point, usually single words or succinct phrases, or longer utterances with a fixed shape and rhythm. Most have either a very simple grammatical structure:

Good Lord!   Nice day!   For sale.

or no structure at all:

Gosh!   Eh?   Hello.   Hush!

and when they do appear to be structurally complex, the appearance is deceptive, because the sentence is learned and used as a single invariable unit:

Least said, soonest mended.   How are you?

Minor sentences lack complexity because they do not need it. In some cases, the meaning they express is cognitively simple or lacks the potential to change. In others, their social use is very restricted. From a semantic viewpoint, their meaning can be expressed without the use of the language's grammatical resources. From a pragmatic viewpoint, further structure is unnecessary or undesirable, as it would impede effective communication.

We can group minor sentences, accordingly, into three types.
• Sentences which express little or no cognitive meaning.
• Sentences which express the bare minimum of cognitive meaning, but little or no possibility for varying it.
• Sentences which express a more complex cognitive meaning, but which allow no variation at all.

Little or no content: interjections

Grammar has to allow us the option of expressing sentences with no (or virtually no) cognitive content. Emotional noises fall into this category:

   Ugh! Ouch! Oh! Gee! Ahem! Wow! Hey!

In grammars, such noises are often called **interjections**, because they are inserted into or between sentences without the surrounding grammar being affected. They are plainly sentence-like in function, though, because we can relate their meaning to major sentences:

   Ugh! = 'I don't like this' Ouch! = 'I am hurt'.

Why do we use interjections? Plainly, an immediate emotional response to a situation demands a kind of language which is short, satisfying, and acoustically prominent. Several interjections therefore use sounds which are not part of the usual English system, such as the click sound in *Tut-tut!* A huge range of emotions have their associated noises: among the examples in these pages are pleasure, pain, approval, disapproval, surprise, shock, recognition, impatience, attention-seeking, and silence-requesting.

Interjections are common only in speech, though of course they will be found in written representations of conversation. However, they do occasionally appear in non-conversational writing where the aim is to establish a particular emotional association in the reader's mind. *WOW!* might appear in an advertisement. *YUK!* or *OOPS!* in a tabloid newspaper headline. *Alas!* is hardly ever found outside of (older) literature.

Interjections can also vary over place, occupation, genre, and social level. *Cor!* is typically British, *Cooee!* Australian. *Ahoy!* is nautical, *Gee-up!* equestrian. Forms such as *yikes* and *yipes* are found only in comics and cartoons. Indeed, comic-book writers are renowned for their exclamatory inventiveness.

Interjections are typically informal, and some are subject to social sanctions, as any child who says *Eh?* knows ('Don't say *Eh*, say *Pardon!*'). But formal settings have their interjections too, and it is important to develop a sense of appropriate usage. Listening to a formal speech, we might expect, as an expression of approval, *Hear, hear!* (from earlier *Hear him!*) but not *Yippee!* And there is something distinctly odd about the following:

Oho, your majesty!   Psst, brigadier!

Shhh, m'lud!   Oy, headmaster!

Interjections also change over time. Literature provides many instances, such as *fie*, *faugh*, and *pshaw*. Here is an angry and disgusted Othello (Shakespeare, *Othello*, IV.i.41):

It is not words that shakes me thus! Pish!

And here is Horatio, disparaging the claim of Marcellus and Barnardo that they have seen a ghost (Shakespeare, *Hamlet*, I.i.29):

Tush, tush, 'twill not appear.

It is often difficult to know exactly what sounds a spelling is supposed to represent. What noise is Hamlet making when he says *foh!* (*Hamlet*, II.ii.585) and *pah!* (V.i.197)? Actors produce quite a range of sounds.

Little or no content: expletives

Closely related to interjections is the range of taboo items ('swear words') whose primary purpose is emotional release. They are not mere noises, however, but recognizable words which also have a literal meaning, usually sexual, religious, or excretory in character. A substitute for aggressive bodily responses, they can be used privately, to let off steam, or publicly, aimed at anyone or anything that the speaker feels needs or deserves an outburst.

Even though swearing uses words which have a literal meaning, its function is not at all to make sense but to make a social impact. Indeed, several of the expressions, such as *holy shit* and *fucking hell*, are literally nonsense. But whatever the words, whether mild or strong, softened or explicit, when used alone they are all minor sentences. To take some milder examples:

Golly! Sugar! Damn it! Lord! Bloody hell!

When someone says *Damn it!* the sentence does not follow the normal grammatical rules. We cannot adapt it to say ~~Don't damn it!~~ or ~~You damn it!~~ And the same applies to all expletives, which make maximum use of the succinctness and rhythmical impact inherent in the minor sentence in order to carry out their function.

Expletives, whether mild or severe, also have an important rapport-building function. People who belong to a particular social milieu tend to swear in the same kind of way, and newcomers to the group learn to adopt the same behaviour if they want to feel included. As a result, swearing changes over time:

dash it   my gosh   golly   ruddy well   lawks ...

These expletives are what some of P.G. Wodehouse's characters say when they are roused. Common enough in the early twentieth century, they sound dated today.

Little or no content: social formulae

Several minor sentences consist of a word or phrase which has little or no meaning. Their function is purely pragmatic (the term **phatic** is often used), to provide a routine way of initiating, maintaining, or breaking off a commonly occurring social interaction. It does not make much sense to ask 'What is the meaning of *Hi*?' But we can easily see how to answer the question 'When or why do we use *Hi*?'.

Here are some of the common situations which elicit minor sentences:

- Greeting someone
  Hello   Hi   Hey there   Yo   (Good) morning
- Saying farewell
  Goodbye   Bye(-bye)   Cheerio   See you   All the best
- During introductions
  How do (you do)?   How are you?   Pleased to meet you
- Apologising
  (I'm) sorry   So sorry   (I beg your) pardon   My mistake
- Responding to an apology
  That's OK   Don't mention it   No problem   Never mind
- Thanking
  Thank you (very much)   Ta   Thanks   Cheers

There are several other types of situations. In each case, the sentences are short or abbreviated. If they consist of several words, the stereotyped nature of the interaction gives them a formulaic character.

- They do not follow the usual rules of the language. From *Don't mention it* we cannot derive ~~Mention it~~ or ~~Don't mention them~~. And there is no opposite to *Good health*: we do not say ~~Bad health~~. These sentences are learned and used as single idiomatic units.
- If we take the sentences literally, something goes wrong with the interaction. The proper response to *How are you?* is not: 'Thank you for asking. My temperature is normal, my pulse a little fast, and my boils are better'.

A minimum of content: constrained by time

Constraints of time and space often force us to reduce what we want to say to the bare minimum. We have a clear meaning in mind, but circumstances demand that we express this as succinctly as possible. If we wasted time or space by elaborating, it could lead to a communicative failure. Here are some typical examples:

Taxi!	All aboard!	Action stations!
Lights!	Phone!	Fire!
On your feet!	At ease!	Off with his head!

Notice that these are not shorter forms of a major sentence. It is not possible to say what words might have been omitted. We could expand such sentences in many different ways:

I want a taxi.
Will you come over here, O taxi?
A taxi is at last in sight.

It is a pointless exercise. The sentences are complete in their own right, and capable of performing their function. Most of them are directives expressing urgency or admitting no refusal (p.72). But they are all minor sentences, and do not follow the rules of the language. *Taxi* is a singular noun, but we do not pluralize it, or add adjectives to it:

~~Taxis!~~   ~~Black taxi!~~

though I did once hear a desperate home-goer, on a dark London street at 2 a.m., call forlornly *Nice taxi!*

Several other time-constrained situations make use of minor sentences. When rushing people don't want to talk, they usually use them in a rapid exchange:

A: Nice day.   B: Rain later.

And we all use them in the reaction signals we send in a conversation, when supplying the speaker with feedback – the *mhm*s and *yeah*s which we add at regular intervals, and without which no conversation can succeed.

A minimum of content: constrained by space

Constraints of space elicit minor sentences in any situation where
there is a minimal meaning to be expressed and a physical limit on
what can be written. So, TAXI appears on the cab's roof or side.
EXIT appears above a door. And, in various sizes and typefaces,
we see graphic minor sentences all around us:

No entry   Exit   50 mph   For Sale   Danger

The need to make a rapid semantic impact is critical, in such
cases. Driving round a bend, I can react quicker to a sign saying
ACCIDENT than I can to one which reads *An accident has taken
place further along the road*. Even if the message could fit on the
sign, it would be absurd to attempt it. I do not need a major
sentence to get the point.

Any page, by definition, constrains space, so all written material
will use minor sentences from time to time, usually appearing as
'blocks' of text. Newspapers have headlines and headings. Books
have titles, chapter heads, and running heads. Labels have product
names and prices. Picture postcards have place-names and often
a verbal wave, such as *Greetings*. On the reverse, the message
might be all minor or abbreviated (Chapter 62) sentences.

Promised greetings! Weather warm. All well.

The same principle applies to computer 'pages'. The space
constraints of a screen means that Web pages usually contain several
minor sentences, often identifying hypertext links. Sometimes we
cannot even say which word-class is being used: is *Help* a noun or a
verb? Such questions are beside the point. These are minor
sentences, and the normal properties of the language do not apply.

Programmers also have a strategy of keeping common messages
short. So you will not usually receive a major sentence alerting
you to a problem or asking you to carry out a command. Minor
sentences are enough:

Fatal error   Print abort   Time out
OK   Cancel   Contact

A minimum of content: constrained by genre

There are several genres of speaking or writing in which a small number of activities occur repeatedly, and can be assumed to be common knowledge by the listener or reader. In such cases, there is a natural tendency to replace time- or space-consuming major sentences by minor ones. Elliptical constructions are also used (see Chapter 62).

Such situations include sports commentaries, instruction manuals, model-building kits, and cooking recipes. In this last domain, for example, the more intricate instructions, expressed as major sentences, will be interspersed by lists of ingredients, a note of relevant utensils, and routine directions, usually presented as minor sentences, either in a horizontal sequence or in a vertical list:

```
1 onion, chopped        5 fl oz milk
8" round cake tin       Mix well        Stir 5 mins
```

Lay-out, rather than punctuation (see p.380), identifies each separate sentence in a list of ingredients.

Minor sentences are also common in tables, diagrams, matrices, and other kinds of reading where we do not follow the words in a single, linear, left-to-right, top-to-bottom manner. Posters, menus, catalogues of all descriptions, and tables of results all work in this way.

In a football league table, for example, we usually find the names of the teams on the left, followed by a series of columns telling us how many games the teams have played, whether home or away, whether they have won, drawn, and lost, and how many points they have accumulated. There are no major sentences here:

		HOME		
	Played	Won	Drawn	Lost
Man. Utd.	6	4	1	1 ...
Liverpool	6	3	2	1 ...

A minimum of content: constrained by situation

We often find ourselves in situations where there is, quite literally, nothing much we can say or write. Formulaic language has a real role to play in such settings. It expresses a single thought which meets a need, fills a silence, or captures the mood of the moment.

   Oh for a bus!   No news?   Drink?
   No luck?   So sorry.   Of all the ...

In the last example, we have the interesting case of an incomplete minor sentence (p.23).

Longer sentences can also be used in this way:

   The things they get up to!   You and your CDs!

Although superficially resembling major sentences, these are actually minor – formulaic items. We cannot alter their grammar and say, in a similar exclamatory style,

   ~~The thing I got up to!~~ or ~~You and my CDs!~~

The superficial complexity can extend much further than an individual phrase or clause. In these next examples, a coordination linked by *or* (Chapter 64) is being used as a stereotyped expression:

Your money or your life! [supposedly said by highwaymen when robbing passers-by]
Trick or treat! [a similar notion, said by American – and increasingly by British – children at Hallowe'en]

In fiction, characters are often given utterances to say which have a fixed form and a minimal content, though the inexplicitness of the utterance can carry an extra meaning. Utterances such as *false alarm* or *no big deal* can be used in situations to refer to many possible events. We hear shots, and a gangster walks in saying *some unfinished business*. We do not need a major sentence to work out what he means.

More complex content: wishes

'Wishes' cover a wide range of notions, from mild expressions of hope and goodwill to forceful prayers and threats. They can be expressed by some complex-looking types of minor sentence. In each case, though, the structures involved are wholly or partly formulaic in character, allowing none of the options available when we express a wish in a major sentence.

USING THE SUBJUNCTIVE

In major sentences, in the present tense, a statement containing a singular subject, such as *she*, *it*, or *our cat*, would be followed by a verb ending in -*s* (p.116):

She live**s** in London.   Our cat eat**s** twice a day.

When the verb lacks the -*s* ending, the usage is called the **subjunctive** (Chapter 21), and this is one of the ways in which minor sentences express wishes:

God save the Queen!
Lord help you if ...
Long live the Duke!

The verb *be* is also used in this way:

Far be it for me to ...
So be it.

Restoring the major-sentence grammar totally alters the meaning of these sentences:

God saves the Queen.   The Lord helps you ...

And in some cases there is no natural major sentence. We do not say:

~~Long lives the Duke.~~   ~~Far is it for me...~~   ~~So is it.~~

USING *MAY* AND *WOULD*

The *may* construction is used when we want to adopt a formal tone:

Long may they live!   May all problems be solved!

The use of *would* is more old-fashioned in tone, and in the second case is really quite literary or archaic:

Would to God he'd go!   Would that I'd never gone.

More complex content: universal utterances

English contains thousands of pithy sayings which go under various headings – maxims, old saws, aphorisms, dictums, proverbs. Their meaning ranges from the simplest of observations about daily living to reflections of gnomic profundity. But in all cases they have a fixed grammatical structure, and thus fall into the category of minor sentence.

Many of these sentences are effective because they use a parallel structure, the balanced rhythm – often supported by alliteration – helping to make them memorable.

The sooner the better.   Out of sight, out of mind.

Easy come, easy go.   Like father, like son.

It is often impossible to relate these to any major sentence construction.

Longer proverbial sayings likewise display a fixed structure:

Too many cooks spoil the broth.

A rolling stone gathers no moss.

The wise (gnomic) meaning resides in the sequence of words as given. As soon as we change them, we lose any possible proverbial interpretation, and the sentence sounds bizarre:

〻 ~~Very few cooks have spoiled the broth~~.

Although minor sentences are limited in their grammatical structure and variability, they have an essential role to play in everyday communication. They are frequently used, conveying a wide range of semantic and pragmatic functions in speech, writing, and computer-mediated language. Informal conversation would be impossible without them, but so would a great deal of formal, ritualized speech behaviour; and they have come to be one of the most visible manifestations of graphic interaction – in the form of neon signs (see the cover of this book) – in a modern literate society.

3 Clause elements

DESCRIPTIVE SUMMARY

The most basic kind of major sentence is known as a **simple** sentence, and this can be analysed into a specific pattern of elements called a **clause**. More complex kinds of sentence (**multiple** sentences) are presented in Chapter 63. That is also where we discuss why we need both notions – clause and sentence – in a grammar.

Up to five elements can be found in a clause. In this grammar they are identified as **subject (S)**, **verb (V)**, **object (O)**, **complement (C)**, and **adverbial (A)**. All five can be seen in this sentence:

I / always / find / the hotel / comfortable.
S   A   V   O   C

The main types of clause are discussed in Chapter 4. The meaning and use of the individual elements are dealt with in Chapters 8 to 12.

EXPLANATION

Grammar uses clause elements in order to express the chief notions we need in order to talk about ourselves and our world. Things happen. We make things happen. We have experiences. Events affect objects. Events happen at different times and places, and in different ways.

If we are going to talk intelligibly about the world, we need units of language which clearly identify basic notions of this kind. That is what clause elements do. And the rules governing clause structure (Chapter 4) ensure that each unit clearly relates to the others.

Opinions vary about the relative importance of clause elements. An ancient tradition singles out the subject, and groups everything else under a separate heading, the **predicate**. Another approach singles out the verb, and sees the other elements as supplementing the meaning of the verb in some way. A third suggests that some elements are more central than others: in particular, the adverbial is seen as an 'extra'. Grammar books differ greatly in the way they present the structure of the clause.

From the viewpoint of semantics and pragmatics, it is important to stress that a clause element is used because it adds a meaning which makes a communication intelligible and effective. Omitting an element can make a sentence ambiguous or incomplete (Chapter 1). Adding extra elements can make it cumbersome or tautologous.

Depending on what we want to say, and the situation in which we say it, any clause element can express a crucial point. So, in this book, each element is presented individually. However, the verb element is especially important in governing the sense of a clause, so that will be described first (Chapter 8).

From elements to structures

Clause elements are of little use on their own. They need to be used in a structure so that we can see how they make sense. Young children do use isolated elements:

    Doggy.   Big bus.   Gone.   Push.

but they do not stay satisfied with this for long. *Push* is ambiguous. Who is pushing? Is someone being pushed? Has someone been pushed?

Around 18 months, two-element clauses begin to appear, and soon the order of elements is established. At that point the child can express the contrast between *Daddy push* and *Push daddy*. More refined observations about the world then follow, and by three the child has mastered all the clause types described in Chapter 4.

DESCRIPTIVE SUMMARY

Apart from a few exceptional cases, clause elements combine to make seven basic types of clause.

S + V:	David / laughed.
S + V + O:	David / shut / the door.
S + V + C:	David / is / tall.
S + V + A:	David / resides / in Wales.
S + V + O + O:	David / gave / me / a letter.
S + V + O + C:	David / reckoned / it / silly.
S + V + O + A:	David / put / salt / in the soup.

In each type, we need all the specified elements for the clause to feel complete. We cannot say:

~~Laughed.~~ ~~David is.~~ ~~David put.~~ ~~Gave me a letter.~~

But in each case, we could make the clause longer by adding extra adverbials:

David / laughed / loudly / in the garden / for ages.
David / resides / in Wales / now.

We can make other sentences by changing the order of these elements, as we shall see below. But we cannot put elements together randomly. English has no clauses like these:

S + S + V:	David / Hilary / laughed.
S + V + C + C:	David / is / my friend / tall.

If we want to talk about more than one thing at a time, we may do so, but we have to use a different grammatical technique – such as coordination (Chapter 64). Also, if we want to leave some elements out, we may do so, but only under strict conditions – see ellipsis (Chapter 62).

The combinations of elements that make up clause types express some of the most basic meanings that we would ever want to say. It is important to emphasize that there is **no single meaning** for any clause type. However, it is possible to illustrate some of their most commonly occurring semantic functions.

- **SV** – an event or experience happens to an entity:
  The bus appeared. They died. John went.
- **SVO** – an entity affects or experiences another entity:
  I kicked the ball. The cat saw a mouse.
- **SVC** – an entity is characterized or identified:
  Mary was helpful.   Music is the food of love.
  The sausages smell nice.
- **SVA** – an entity or event is put in a context, such as place or time:
  The bathroom is upstairs. I live in London.
  The meeting is on Monday.
- **SVOO** – an entity affects two other entities, making one of them a recipient or beneficiary:
  I offered Mary some tea. I gave some to her.
  We bought her a present. We bought one for her.
- **SVOC** – an entity affects another entity, at the same time characterizing or identifying it:
  The noise drove the neighbours mad.
  I named the wheelbarrow Fred.
- **SVOA** – an entity affects another entity in a context:
  We put the books under the bed.
  I set up the computer on my desk.

'Entity', in these examples, is simply a handy term for one or more persons, animals, objects, or abstract notions.

This account gives only a very general idea of what clause types do. Each type is in fact used to express a much more specific set of meanings, in which the verb plays a central role.

The role of the verb

The verb is the most important element in the clause because it governs the type of clause which is going to be used. Here are some examples. In each case, we begin with the verb, then ask: What is the *minimal* amount of information we need for the clause to make sense?

- If we choose *disappear*, it must be SV:
  The crowd disappeared.
  An entity must disappear, but we need say nothing more.
- If we choose *throw*, it must be SVO:
  She threw the ball.
  Here, two entities are needed: one to throw, and one to be thrown.
- If we choose *seem*, it must be SVC:
  The plan seems possible.
  Just one entity is needed, along with something to say about it.
- If we choose *steal* ('move stealthily') it must be SVA:
  The children stole into the kitchen.
  In this sense, an entity has to steal somewhere.
- If we choose *tell*, and want to give the whole story, it must be SVOO:
  Jules told Jim the answer.
  To say *Jules told Jim* is possible, but we are left guessing. The whole story requires three entities: a teller, someone to be told, and something to be told.
- If we choose *proclaim*, it must be SVOC:
  The people proclaimed Smith president.
  One entity must be doing the proclaiming, another must be being proclaimed, and a third must be the result of the proclamation.
- If we choose *put*, it must be SVOA:
  Mary put the book on the shelf.
  We need an entity to do the putting, a thing to put, and a place to put it.

Where are clause types used?

Virtually everywhere. Apart from those situations which demand minor sentences (Chapter 3), every variety of English will display a range of clause types, because the meanings they express are so central to the kinds of things we want to say. An important index of mature language use is the ability to select and arrange these structures to maintain interest and create dramatic effects.

Usually a stylistic effect arises not so much from the frequent use of a particular clause type, but from a contrast between them. For example, a short SV can stand out among a series of longer structures, or after a long sentence. Here are the space travellers in Douglas Adams' *The Restaurant at the End of the Universe* (Chapter 3):

Round the central console four figures hunched in tight concentration trying to blot from their minds the terrifying shuddering of the ship and the fearful roar that echoed through it. They concentrated. (SV)

Another example is the way we can achieve an effect by moving from SV into longer structures, adding adverbials and other optional elements to amplify the basic structure. This is what Adams does as he continues his story:

Still they concentrated. (ASV)
And still they concentrated. (conjunction + ASV)
The seconds ticked by. (SVA)
On Zaphod's brows stood beads of sweat … (AVS…)

The last sentence shows a further way in which we can manipulate clause types stylistically: we change the order of elements. This option is discussed in Chapter 71. Yet another stylistic possibility is available in certain circumstances: we can leave out some of the clause elements. This is discussed in Chapter 62. Several clause-type effects are illustrated in the following pages.

Using clause types: SV

The SV structure is ideal for situations where we want to say the bare minimum – to express an event or state of affairs involving a single entity:

> She's swimming.   Her dress tore.   Dinner is cooking.
> The door opened.   A leaf fell.   The wind blew.

Sometimes the entity can be taken for granted, though we then need an *it* subject to make the clause feel complete.

> It's raining.
>
> [stage direction] It darkens.

The minimalist structure of SV makes it appeal to anyone wanting to make a series of succinct points:

> I came. I saw. I conquered.

The SV structure focuses attention on the verb, and many writers have created atmosphere by using sentences in which the verb is left 'hanging in the air'. It is a favourite stylistic feature of Dylan Thomas, as illustrated by these sentences from *Under Milk Wood*:

> A farmer's lantern glimmers.   Time passes.
> The thin night darkens.

Variation can be introduced by adding adverbials or by joining clauses together. Here is Thomas's 'First Voice' using a series of SV clauses to describe a sunny afternoon in Llaregyb. The short clauses help to keep the pace of the narrative slow, and reinforce the relaxed mood of random observation.

> The dumb duck-ponds snooze. Clouds sag and billow on Llaregyb Hill. Pigs grunt in a wet wall-bath, and smile as they snort and dream.

SVs are also well suited to convey a succinct and snappy parallelism, as seen in the series of coordinated SVs used by Rosalind, in Shakespeare's *As You Like It* (V.ii.31), when she tells Orlando how Oliver and Celia fell in love:

> For your brother and my sister no sooner met but they looked; no sooner looked but they loved; no sooner loved but they sighed ...

And here is Margaret Drabble in the closing lines of *The Radiant Way*, inserting SVs to slow the narrative pace of the novel and bring it to a peaceful close:

The leaves glitter and dance. The spirit passes. The sun is dull with a red radiance. It sinks. Esther, Liz and Alix are silent with attention. The sun hangs in the sky, burning. The earth deepens to a more profound red. The sun bleeds, the earth bleeds. The sun stands still.

More generally, without the use of SVs to direct and comment on the discourse (p.334), conversational narrative in most novels would grind completely to a halt.

Mike laughed.   She chortled.   His mouth grimaced.

Using clause types: SVO

The SVO clause type expresses several meanings. The commonest is the first one below, and this is often used as the standard example of what an SVO structure does, using such terms as 'actor–action–goal' or 'agent–event–patient'. But SVO is much more useful than that.

- An entity causes an event to take place:
  Jane kicked the ball.
- An entity experiences an event:
  Jane heard the music.
- An entity maintains a state of affairs:
  Jane is holding a knife.
- Two entities are mutually affected:
  Jane married Jim. = Jim married Jane.
- Two entities share the same perspective:
  My writing resembles your writing.
  = Your writing resembles my writing.
- An entity expresses the location of another:
  The bus seats twenty.
- An entity expresses the time of an event:
  Yesterday saw three disasters.

The first SVO sense has attracted special attention because it is the staple unit of narrative action, where the primary concern is the relationship between an agent or causer of an event and the person or thing affected. 'A did B', 'C killed D', 'E solved F', 'G loves H', 'I hates J'. It would be perfectly possible to write a thriller consisting only of SVOs, though without something else happening linguistically this would soon get boringly repetitive.

> Adam saw Hanson. A flash of metal caught his eye. The man was holding a gun. Adam shouted a warning. Hanson dropped his gun and raised his arms. ...

What else has to happen to make this kind of writing effective? Real writers add atmosphere to the story through the use of optional adverbials, and vary the pace of the narrative by inserting SVs and SVCs into the sequence. Here is the basic text with some adverbials added:

> Adam saw Hanson in a doorway. Suddenly, a flash of metal caught his eye. The man was holding a gun. Adam shouted a warning. Hanson reluctantly dropped his gun and slowly raised his arms. ...

And here is the basic text with SVs and SVCs inserted at appropriate points:

> Adam saw the foreign agent, and froze. A flash of metal caught his eye. The man was holding a gun. Adam grimaced. This was no game. He shouted a warning. Hanson wasn't a fool. He raised his arms. ...

Of course, in a real story, writers would do both things at once, and wouldn't restrict themselves to short sentences.

The important point to note is that the core of an action narrative is SVO. Dramatic context is usually provided by the frequent use of SVA (p.55) and optional adverbials. Atmospheric scene-setting, the interpretation of events, and character notes are much more likely to use SV (p.50) or SVC (p.54).

This is how a real writer does it. It is the opening paragraph of Chapter 34 of John Grisham's thriller, *The Firm*.

Wednesday morning. Tarry Ross climbed the stairs to the fourth floor of the Phoenix Inn. He paused on the landing outside the hall door and caught his breath. Sweat beaded across his eyebrows. He removed the dark sunglasses and wiped his face with the sleeve of his overcoat. Nausea hit below the belt, and he leaned on the stair rail. He dropped the empty briefcase on the concrete and sat on the bottom step. His hands shook like severe palsy, and he wanted to cry. He clutched his stomach and tried not to vomit.

The skeleton of the narrative is conveyed by action-packed SVOs separated by clauses that describe the protagonist or the scene. We can see the pattern if we highlight the SVOs, ignoring the accompanying optional adverbials.

Wednesday morning. **Tarry Ross climbed the stairs** to the fourth floor of the Phoenix Inn. **He** paused on the landing outside the hall door and **caught his breath**. Sweat beaded across his eyebrows. **He removed the dark sunglasses** and **wiped his face** with the sleeve of his overcoat. Nausea hit below the belt, and he leaned on the stair rail. **He dropped the empty briefcase** on the concrete and sat on the bottom step. His hands shook like severe palsy, and he wanted to cry. **He clutched his stomach** and tried not to vomit.

It is a counterpoint of 'something happening' then 'something not happening', both between and within sentences. Indeed, sentences containing two clauses, one SVO and the other SV or SVA, in either order, the second with the subject omitted, are common in action stories:

He grimaced but drank the whisky. (SV + [S]VO)
He saw the train and stopped. (SVO + [S]V)

Using clause types: SVC

This clause type is used when we are wanting to answer such questions as 'What is X?', 'What is X like?', 'Which one is X?', or 'How did X change?'. It is therefore a very important clause type in describing things, such as scene-setting or character description, or discussing the significance of an action. The opening lines of a chapter in a novel commonly use an SVC construction. Here are some from the chapter-openings in John Le Carré's *Tinker Tailor Soldier Spy*:

Peter Guillam was a chivalrous fellow.

She was much more animated now.

'Perhaps she **was** ill,' said Smiley stolidly.

And here is a famous sequence from the opening page of Dickens' *A Tale of Two Cities*:

It was the best of times, it was the worst of times, it was the age of wisdom, it was the age of foolishness, it was the epoch of belief, it was the epoch of incredulity, it was the season of Light ...

A dictionary or encyclopedia, with its need to define, is reliant on SVC clauses to open its entries:

A cowrie is a kind of marine snail

though often the clause type is abbreviated

cowrie a kind of marine snail

And in science, SVCs are an important way of describing a current state of affairs or the results of a process:

Three nutrients are necessary.

The mixture turns green ...

$x + y = z$

Any exposition which makes general claims will use SVC a great deal, capitalizing on the 'universal' meaning of the verb *be*. We will find it frequently in such domains as advertising, religion, and academic prose:

Moggle is good for you.

Blessed are the meek. (with inverted order, CVS)

The causative factors are obscure.

Using clause types: SVA and SVOA

Only a few dozen verbs require an obligatory adverbial.

- For example, *put* and *place* always have to have one.
  I put the picture **on the shelf**.
  The picture has to be put somewhere.
- Sometimes it depends on the meaning of the verb. *Steal* needs
  one when we use it in its 'stealthy' meaning (p.48):
  We stole **into the house**.
  We have to steal somewhere. Similarly, adverbials are needed
  for certain uses of such verbs as *remain* (in town), *lie* (on the
  ground), *begin* (with a joke), and *last* (for hours). They give us
  the answers to such questions as 'Where?', 'When?', 'How?', and
  'How long?'.

Situations where it is important to know the place, time, and
manner of events will naturally prompt a high use of SVA and
SVOA clause types, because the primary purpose of the adverbial
is to express such meanings (see Chapter 12). Along with the
optional adverbials, which can be used with any verbs, they
therefore play an important role in such domains as journalism,
news broadcasting, and sports commentary:

  The fire lasted for several hours. (SVA)
  The storm drove the ship onto the beach. (SVOA)
  Beckham stays on the far side of the field. (SVA)

In real-life reporting, of course, extra adverbials would be drafted
in to add detail, drama, and atmosphere:

  After several hours, the storm drove the ship onto the beach
  near Brighton Pier.

And it is precisely this combination of obligatory and optional
adverbials which can add detail and movement to an account (see
also the thriller example on p.53):

  The King lived secretly upstairs in the castle for several weeks.

We need only one adverbial to make this clause feel complete, but
having four pushes the narrative along.

Using clause types: SVOO

The two types of object, direct and indirect, are discussed in Chapter 10. Here we need simply note that the SVOO structure is used to convey three main meanings:

- One of the objects receives the other object. The underlying meaning is 'to'. In this example, Ben is the recipient of the paper:

  I sent Ben the paper. = I sent the paper to Ben.

- One of the objects benefits from the action that produced the other object. The underlying meaning is 'for'. In this example, Di is the beneficiary of the knitting.

  I knitted Di a hat. = I knitted a hat for Di.

- One of the objects directly receives the effect of an action expressed by the other object.

  I gave my car a wash. = I washed my car.

  (We cannot say I gave a wash to/for my car.)

In each case, one of the objects is more central to the point than the other. It is the paper that was sent, not Ben; it is the hat that was knitted, not Di; it is the wash that was given, not the car. Ben, Di, and the car are the end-points of the whole process. So they can often be taken for granted in everyday conversation:

Lucy to Sue: I sent today's paper.

[they both know who the recipient is]

[on arriving at a party] Steve's brought a bottle.

[the beneficiaries are obvious from the context]

But in many situations, omitting the recipient or beneficiary would be at best tantalising and at worst infuriating. It could hardly be done in sports commentary.

Owen passes the ball. [we need to know to whom]

And it would be inept for a news report to leave out the crucial information, if it were known:

Sir Arthur Kettle has left ten million pounds.

Omitting the identity of a recipient or beneficiary when it is needed is a noticeable fault in immature writing.

Using clause types: SVOC

This clause type gives extra information about the object, but the exact meaning depends on the choice of verb.

- Expressing a general state, e.g. *hold, keep, leave*
  He kept us captives. They left us penniless.
- Stating facts, e.g. *call, profess, report, pronounce*
  I called John hopeless. I called him a fool.
- Expressing volition, e.g. *wish, like, prefer, want*
  I prefer coffee white. I want you ready.
- Expressing a mental state, e.g. *think, find, imagine*
  I found her clever. They thought me an athlete.
- Expressing a result, e.g. *send, turn, make, appoint*
  The cost sent us crazy. It made me a new man.
- Declaring, e.g. *declare, proclaim, certify, crown*
  I declare him innocent. They crowned him king.

With most verbs, either an adjective or a noun phrase can be used as the complement – but not in cases like *crown* or *appoint*, where only noun phrases are possible. We cannot say ~~They crowned him happy~~.

The wide semantic range of the verbs means that SVOC structures are widespread. We will find some of them clustering in certain styles, such as expressing a result in scientific English (*The acid turns the mixture green*), but their main use is as a succinct stylistic alternative to other ways of saying the same thing:

The disaster left the family penniless. (SVOC)
The family were left penniless by the disaster. (SVCA)

There is a joke which relies on an SVOO/SVOC contrast:
Hotel guest (to doorman): Will you call me a taxi.
Doorman: Sir, you are a taxi.
The guest intended an SVOO: 'call a taxi for me'. The doorman took it as SVOC – as if it patterned like this:
He called me a friend.   He called me a taxi.

THE LEARNING CENTRE
TOWER HAMLETS COLLEGE
POPLAR CENTRE
POPLAR HIGH STREET
LONDON E14 0AF

5 | Statements and questions

All the clauses in Chapter 4 express **statements**. It is usual to begin with statements in a grammar because they are much more frequent than other clause functions, and because other functions have a more distinctive range of uses. It is also easier to discuss the meaning and purpose of other functions by comparing them with statements.

Statements contrast with questions, commands, and exclamations. A clause can belong to one, and only one, of these types. In this chapter we examine the contrast between statements and questions.

To count as a statement, the clause usually needs to have a subject, and that subject usually goes before the verb. This is traditionally called a **declarative** structure.

We have travelled a long way.

Questions are sentences with an **interrogative** structure, in which the subject appears after a verb. In writing they end with a question mark. There are different ways of asking a question, depending on the kind of reply we want.

Have we travelled a long way?
Why have we travelled a long way?
We've travelled a long way, haven't we?

EXPLANATION

The chief semantic purpose of a statement can be simply stated: it is to convey information. The chief semantic purpose of a question is to seek information. But these two observations hide many subtleties of expression.

Why use questions?

To establish the truth

This is the main purpose of the **yes–no** or **polar** question – a question which offers the listener the choice of affirming or denying what is being proposed.

Is the train on time? Yes / No.

Of course, we can avoid the clear-cut nature of this reply:

By acknowledging our inadequacy: I don't know.

By evading the point: Good question!

By returning the question: What do you think?

By challenging the responsibility: Why ask me?

By challenging the assumption: Why would it not be?

Or we can add extra force to our response:

Certainly.   Of course.   No way.   Impossible.

Or we can find a midway position between *yes* and *no*:

Maybe.   It appears so.   Very likely.

To supply missing information

This is the main purpose of the **wh- question** – a question opening with a specific question word (usually beginning with *wh-*). One set of *wh-* words focuses on information expressed by adverbials: *when, where, why, how.*

When will they arrive? [They will arrive] Tomorrow.

Where was the car? [It was] In the garage.

The other set focuses on information expressed by the other clause elements: *what, which, who / whom / whose.*

What was the answer? [It was] A robin.

Who did she see? [She saw] John.

What were they doing? [They were] Swimming.

Whose was the car? [It was] Mary's.

We can also modify the meaning of *wh-* words by adding elements: *How long? What for? To whom? Why not?* (Usage problems are discussed on p.296.)

To select an option

This is the main purpose of the **alternative** question – a question
which presents the listener with a set of choices, shown by the use
of one or more *or*s.

Are you leaving on Monday or Tuesday?
Would you like tea or coffee or milk?
Would you like tea, coffee, or milk?

These are mutually exclusive choices: we choose one. We couldn't
answer *yes*! But where the choice involves different semantic
domains, a 'yes' response is possible:

Would you like tea or a sandwich or a book to read?
'Yes, all three, please.'

The most restricting use of alternative questions is in
interrogations, where a single answer is required – as in witness
examinations, quiz questions, and examination answers:

Did you leave the knife in the kitchen or the bathroom?
For two points, has a spider got six, eight or ten legs?

The *or* may be implicit, as in a multiple-choice test:

Tick the box which correctly answers the question.

To bias a response

This is the main purpose of the **tag** question – a question which
turns a statement into a question by adding a short VS question at
the end. Usually, if the first clause is positive, the tag is negative, and
vice versa. The tag predisposes the listener to give a particular reply.

John has left, hasn't he? (we expect the answer 'yes')
John hasn't left, has he? (we expect the answer 'no')

If a positive tag follows a positive statement, the effect can simply
be one of asking for affirmation, but it more often conveys a
negative implication, such as disbelief, sarcasm, or threat:

John has left, has he? [said Inspector James darkly]

Other kinds of tag include *am I right?*, *don't you think?*, or, very
informally, *right*? and *eh*?.

Special uses of questions

Knowing the answer

If the primary purpose of a question is to seek information, we normally assume that the questioner does not know the answer. There are however cases where questioners do know the answer, or think they do. Their questions then perform a different function.

- Examination or exercise questions, where the questioner knows the answer and wants to find out whether the reader does.
- Interview questions, where the interviewer wants to establish whether the interviewee knows certain facts or is capable of responding in a particular way.
- Witness-stand interrogations, where a barrister wants a witness to reply in a certain way. (An example of cross-examination is given on p.291.)

Gaining rapport

There are situations where people ask questions *not* to obtain any real information. These are mainly social utterances, used as formulae in conversations to build rapport between speakers, and are therefore classed as minor sentences (p.37). We do not expect an informative response after *How are you?*, and we can say *How do you do?* without obtaining any verbal response at all.

Expressing strong feeling

Many questions have the force of an exclamation, expressing a strong positive or negative attitude. **Exclamatory questions** always anticipate some kind of sympathetic reaction from the listener, but they do not need a reply.

Am I hungry!   [seeing a friend's child] Hasn't she grown!
[leaving a theatre] Wasn't that fantastic!

They are often printed with an exclamation mark.

Making a point

There are questions which seem to be making a genuine request for information, but the speaker is not expecting an answer. These **rhetorical questions** use the question-form to increase the strength of an assertion. A politician might say, in a speech:

You might well be wondering why the government is acting in this way. The answer is obvious.

But the effect is stronger if the second sentence is turned into a question:

Isn't the answer obvious?

Notice that if the rhetorical question is positive, it expects the answer 'no', and vice versa:

Is that a good reason for calling an election? ['no']
Isn't that a good reason for calling an election? ['yes']

Advertisements which ask rhetorical questions are well aware of this effect:

Do you want your washing to come out like this?
Wouldn't you rather have it come out like this?

Providing feedback

This is another situation where people use questions without requiring a response. When we participate in a conversation, we can interpolate the occasional question into the feedback remarks we use to let the speaker know that everything is proceeding smoothly. There is one in this extract, where listener comments are shown in square brackets.

anyway about a week later Jamey decided to have a go [mhm]
– so he wrote in to the firm – he'd tried once before you know
[had he?] but hadn't got anywhere ...

The listener is not expecting a reply to *had he*, for the obvious reason that the information has already been given. Surprising indeed, to have the question following the answer!

Eliciting a general reaction

Many questions are not asked to seek information or obtain an answer, but to make people do things. This happens when we use the interrogative structure to request, invite, offer, suggest, recommend, advise, and so on.

Will you stop talking? [*please* is often used to make the command more polite]
Would you like a sweet?
Why don't you go by bus?

There may well be a verbal response, but the test of the efficacy of the question is what the people actually do.

Checking on comprehension

Statements can be uttered with a rising pitch as a succinct way of inviting the hearer to verify what the speaker is saying. They are called **declarative questions**. Here, a positive question anticipates the answer 'yes' and a negative one the answer 'no'.

You've got the drinks? ['yes']
You didn't bring your raincoat? ['no']

Declarative questions have been around for centuries. Falstaff says to Prince Hal (Shakespeare, *Henry IV Part 2*, III.iii.166):

You confess, then, you picked my pocket?

But they have emerged as one of the most noticeable developments in English usage in recent years, especially among young people:

I bought the car in Merlin's?

This has a twofold function. It is first of all a succinct way of checking that the listeners do know about Merlin's. But – as in most cases the listeners do – it also generates rapport: the speaker knows the listener knows, so the question-form acts as a kind of mental hand-shake. There is no other way of explaining the usage in utterances where the answer could not possibly be unknown, such as *I live in London?*

Expressing a hidden threat

If you are walking down the street and you meet someone you do not know, and they ask you a sensible, answerable question, you have no particular cause for alarm:

Where's the bus station?   What time is it?

But if someone were to ask you a question that you could not possibly answer, you might well look round for help:

Has my aunty had her medicine?

Is it raining in Moscow?

People who ask questions that cannot be answered – we deduce – must be doing so for some other reason, and that suggests a possible threat to our well-being.

The opposite situation is just as threatening – questions whose answer is so obvious that they do not need to be asked:

Who are you looking at?

In the real world of muggings and confrontations, such interactions are not easy to document, but are doubtless common. In the literary world, we regularly find characters using questions to dominate, threaten, confuse, distract, or add menace.

If a lion & a shark had a fight – who would win?

A cool hero, of course, can address villains with any kind of question and get away with it. Here is Simon Templar, 'the Saint', being cheekily confrontational in Leslie Charteris's short story, *The Man Who Was Lucky*. He rings a doorbell, and a gangster answers it:

Presently the door opened to exhibit a blue chin and flat, fish-like stare which Simon easily identified as being more deserving of the neighbourhood's disapproval than himself. The door stayed open just far enough for that; and the stare absorbed him with the expressionlessness of a dead cod.

'Hello, body,' murmured the Saint affably. 'When did they dig you up?'

And here is an extract from the interrogation scene in Harold Pinter's *The Birthday Party*, where the menacing visitors Goldberg and McCann verbally hammer Stanley Webber into silence by asking him impossible questions:

McCANN: What about the Albigensenist heresy?
GOLDBERG: Who watered the wicket at Melbourne?
McCANN: What about the blessed Oliver Plunkett?
GOLDBERG: Speak up, Webber. Why did the chicken cross the road?
STANLEY: He wanted to – he wanted to – he wanted to ...
McCANN: He doesn't know!
GOLDBERG: Why did the chicken cross the road?
STANLEY: He wanted to — he wanted to ...
GOLDBERG: Why did the chicken cross the road?
STANLEY: He wanted ...
McCANN: He doesn't know. He doesn't know which came first!
GOLDBERG: Which came first?
McCANN: Chicken? Egg? Which came first?
GOLDBERG and McCANN: Which came first? Which came first? Which came first?

Speech and writing

Most of the examples in this chapter have been from real-life conversation or fictional dialogue. That is the natural home for questions. But the two varieties do not handle questions in exactly the same way. In particular, fiction makes much more use of *wh*-questions.

The chief function of *wh*- questions is to seek information, and they are therefore invaluable as a device to keep a plot moving. An author makes every question count, when trying to stay in tight control of the story. Sooner or later, in a crime or spy novel, there will be a dialogue like this one (from John Le Carré's *The Russia House*, Chapter 12):

'I bought a hat.'
'What kind of hat?'
'A fur hat. A woman's hat.'
'Who for?'
'Miss Coad.'
'That a girlfriend?'
'She's the housekeeper at the safe house in Knightsbridge,' Ned cut in before Barley could reply.
'Where'd you buy it?'
'On the way between the tram stop and the hotel. I don't know where. A shop.'
'That all?'
'Just a hat. One hat.'
'How long did that take you?'
'I had to queue.'
'How long did it take?'
'I don't know.'
'What else did you do?'
'Nothing. I bought a hat.'
'You're lying, Barley.'

Only more *wh*- questions will establish the truth.

The high-density use of *wh-* questions is unusual in real-world dialogues, which are more concerned with maintaining conversational dynamics and rapport. We tend to shy away from interrogating each other. In most other respects, though, conversation and fiction are similar. Declarative and polar questions are common in both. And nearly half the questions in both varieties are abbreviated, often with a tag (e.g. *Nice day, isn't it?*).

By contrast, it is rare to find questions in non-conversational speech, nor are they common in writing. But they do turn up in some spoken monologues, as 'rhetorical questions', and they feature in any writing which tries to 'involve' readers in its subject-matter.

- In news broadcasting
  A news broadcast might include a question quote:
  Will Britain recover? This was the question put by industry leaders today at their meeting in Blackpool ...
  And a news correspondent might introduce questions into a report, in an attempt to engage the listener or viewer:
  So does it matter whether rates go up? Probably not.
- In gaining attention
  Certain kinds of direct-address writing use questions to grab the attention of the reader. They include advertising slogans and tabloidy newspaper headlines:
  Why is *The Guardian* so special?   Do you use Twink?
  WHERE TO NOW?   WHAT'S THE ANSWER?
- In teaching
  Some academic textbooks and educational materials rely on questions as part of a didactic style:
  Are there any important differences between the two rates of growth? Table 3.4 shows that there are.
  The technique needs to be used sparingly. It is a common technique in children's readers: *Can you see the red car*? The use of many questions would make readers feel they were being treated as children.

6 Directives

DESCRIPTIVE SUMMARY

Directives are clauses which lack a subject and have the verb in
its basic form (without any endings, p.116). They are said to have
an **imperative** structure. Apart from the missing subject, we can
use all the elements of the clause types described in Chapter 4:

　Look! (V)　　Pass the key. (VO)　　Be quiet. (VC)
　Get downstairs. (VA)　　Give the book to me. (VOO)
　Keep it straight. (VOC)　　Put it on the table. (VOA)

In certain circumstances, we can add a subject:

　You stay there!　　Nobody move!

And we can begin certain uses with a *do* or *let* form:

　Do come in!　　Don't you dare!　　Let's go to town!

But we cannot change the tense (Chapter 23) or mood (Chapter
21) of the imperative verb. We cannot say:

　~~Did come in!~~　　~~Might give the book to me!~~

The use of the progressive (Chapter 24) is somewhat unusual:

　Be trying your hardest!

And the passive (Chapter 22) is usual only in the negative:

　Don't be deceived!　(compare: ~~Be deceived!~~)

EXPLANATION

The core meaning of a directive is to tell or urge someone to do
or not do something. Directives were usually called 'commands' in
traditional grammar, but commanding is only one of the many
functions that this structure can perform (see p.72). All directives
do, however, share certain properties.

What all directives do

- They all have at least one addressee, who is apparent from the context. That is why a subject is not needed. If we say *Look out!* we must have someone in mind. Anyone who went down the street using directives to nobody in particular would not, one imagines, remain a free agent for very long.

- They all elicit an action, and we judge the success of a directive in terms of whether or not it is complied with. This makes directives very different from statements, which are judged in terms of whether they are true or false.
  The cat is drinking the milk. [true or false?]
  Drink the milk. [will you or won't you?]

- They all require the action to be done straight away or in the future. We cannot use a directive to refer to past time, nor can we use one to express a habitual activity which extends into the past. That is why we cannot say:
  ~~Do it yesterday.~~   ~~Pass the key usually.~~
  (Time travellers are an honourable exception.)

- The same reason explains why we do not use imperatives with modal verbs, such as *may*, *should*, or *can*. These express meanings, such as possibility or permission, which are incompatible with the notion of something being done directly:
  ~~May do it!~~   ~~Can find the key!~~

- They are all to do with 'doing', so they are unlikely to be used with **stative** verbs, which express states of being in which no obvious action takes place (p.163). That is why we do not usually say ~~Need a car~~ or ~~Know the answer~~. However, it is always possible to read a dynamic meaning into a stative verb.
  Be early. ['Take some action to ensure you are early']
  Know the answer by Monday. ['Take steps to learn it']

What directives sometimes do

Add a subject

If the subject of a directive is obvious from the context, why should we ever need to add one?

- We want to give extra force to the directive, usually by making it more admonitory or insistent, but often by introducing a strong attitude, such as irritation or frustration:

  You sit down now!   You have this seat.   You shut up!

  The tone may be one of gentle persuasion:

  You run along now.   You show me what you can do.

- We want to single someone out. The utterance would need to be accompanied by eye-contact or a gesture to be sure of success. A vocative helps (Chapter 13).

  You come over here, John.

  These directives are rather peremptory and not very polite. We would hardly be likely to say:

  You come over here, officer.

- We want to avoid ambiguity. This is where directives in the third person (Chapter 45), such as *everyone* or *nobody*, are very useful:

  Everyone stand up.   Nobody move.

  Passengers on flight AB322 proceed now to Gate 4.

In all the *you* cases, the pronoun is spoken with emphasis. If we don't stress it enough, our utterance might be mistaken for a statement. Imagine a situation where an instructor is addressing three students. 'What should we do next?' asks Fred. The instructor could say one of two things:

  YOU send out the tickets.

  You send out the TICKETS. [= someone sends them out]

In the first case, Fred does the job; in the second case, they all do.

Add *do*

When the imperative is preceded by *do*, the meaning is extra insistence, urgency, or persuasion.

(Do) Come in.   (Do) Have a coffee.

This usage is especially common in British English, characteristic of elegant, polite speech, and more used by women than men. It is often found in older novels:

- Harriet, in Jane Austen's *Emma* (Chapter 7):
  Dear Miss Woodhouse, do advise me.
- An exchange between Joseph Sedley and Becky Sharp in William Thackeray's *Vanity Fair* (Chapter 4):
  'O you droll creature! Do let me hear you sing it.'
  'Me? No, you, Miss Sharp; my dear Miss Sharp, do sing it.'

Add *let*

To use *let* or *let's* before the verb allows the speakers to tell themselves to do something.

Let me see.   Let's all go to town.

In more formal or literary English, we find *let us*:

Let us pray.   Let us go then, you and I ...

In very informal English, *let's* can refer to a single speaker.

Let's see. [= 'Let me see']

Note also the related *Let's you and me go*.

Add a tag

A tag question, with a commanding tone, adds further insistence:

Behave yourself, will you!   Stop, will you!

Tags such as *would you* soften the force, as does a questioning or pleading tone, or the use of *just*:

Behave yourself, will you? / would you?

Just behave yourself.   You just stop that.

This usage is especially common in conversation.

Why use directives

Directives have a very wide range of uses:
- To command, demand, order: *Do this at once.   Stop!*
- To prohibit: *Don't walk on the grass.   Do not enter.*
- To request, make a plea: *Open the window.   Help me!*
- To advise, warn: *Wear your seat-belt.   Be careful!*
- To suggest: *Let's go to the beach.   Let's walk.*
- To instruct: *Take the first left.   Use 3-mm screws.*
- To invite: *Make yourself at home.*
- To offer: *Take a leaflet.   Let me try.*
- To give permission: *Go ahead.   Come in.*
- To reflect: *Let me see.   Give me a moment.*
- To express incredulity: *Come on!   Get on with you!*
- To swear at someone: *Go to hell!   Bugger off!*
- To wish politely: *Enjoy your meal.   Have a nice day.*
- To accept reluctantly – the weakest type of command:
  Do what you like.   Take it or leave it.

The politeness marker, *please*, is available to soften the force of many of these uses – more likely with some (e.g. requests and invitations) than others (e.g. prohibitions and swearing). However, to obtain maximum politeness, we need to do more than just add a *please* to an imperative: *Open the window, please* is still quite abrupt. Other structures are more effective, such as *Could you open the window?* or *I'd be most grateful if …*

Directives also have an important role in controlling the pace and direction of a conversation.
- They can make a fairly forceful interruption:
  Wait a minute.   Hang on!   Excuse my butting in …
- They can introduce a new idea or theme:
  Look, why don't we …   Say we left now …
- They can make a parenthetical comment or reminder:
  We were back well in time. Take it from me, it wasn't easy …

Where to use directives

In spoken dialogue

Directives arise from the interactive nature of a situation, where someone is being told to perform an activity, so they fit naturally into conversational speech or its dialogue representation in fiction. Abbreviated directives, omitting the verb, are common:

Two teas, please.   Scalpel, nurse.

In real-world conversation, only about 20 per cent of directives have 'extra' features, such as the use of *you* or a vocative. They are more common in fiction, where they help to avoid ambiguity over who is being addressed in a multi-party conversation. In this example from *The Big Sleep* (Chapter 15), Raymond Chandler adds a vocative to his detective Philip Marlowe's directive, to avoid giving the impression that Marlowe was talking to Brody:

Carmen said: 'You shot Arthur Geiger. I saw you. I want my pictures.' Brody turned green.
'Hey, wait a minute, Carmen,' I called.

In spoken monologue

So is there any scope at all for directives in a spoken monologue? Yes, in situations where the speaker enters into a pseudo-dialogue with imagined listeners:

• Where a radio or television news reporter is summing up a report:

So the chances of another fall in interest rates are slim. Let's face it, we're in for a tough few months.

Or: Be sure of this, we're in for another rise ...
Never doubt the Bank means what it says ...

• Where a broadcaster is telling listeners what to do:

If you want more details, write to this address ...

• Where people are addressing a deity in a prayer, using such verbs as *grant, give, forgive*, and *help*:

Give us this day our daily bread ...

Using directives in writing

Apart from deliberate attempts to represent conversation in creative settings, writing is essentially a monologic activity. We might therefore not expect to find directives in written texts. In fact, we find them in several varieties, and in some cases they are the norm.

INSTRUCTIONAL WRITING

Directives are unavoidable in texts giving instructions, such as repair manuals, travel guides, gardening books, behaviour guides, self-help leaflets, application forms, exam rubrics, medical directions, DIY guides, or cookery books. Directives are also common in notices, when we interpret these as having the function of minor sentences (Chapter 2):

- Answer three questions.
- ENTER
- Turn left into the square. Notice the clock ...
- Take two tablets twice a day after meals.
- If the answer is No, go to question 7.
- Stand when the Queen enters the Abbey.
- Cut the pork into thin strips. Heat the oil in a frying pan, and cook quickly to brown and seal the surface. Remove from pan ...

ADVERTISEMENTS

The forcefulness of an advertisement relies on the use of directives. Indeed, there is always an implicit directive in front of a product name: 'Buy ...'

Forget horrid stains. Wipe it off straight away.
Look in your local store now.

Slogans are often directive, such as in these drinks advertisements:

Don't be vague – ask for Haig.
Give me Gordon's.

And advertisements are one of the rare occasions where we will find passive directives:

Be driven around in style!

SERIOUS PROSE

The world of serious writing is not immune from the interactive appeal of a directive. Unusual in older style, the directive is common today, especially in writers who want to reflect the rhythms of speech. However, because the addressee is the general reader, there is no real scope for introducing such modifications as *you* or *do*.

> Remember that the King's precedessor on the throne had been executed. [Never: *Do remember* ...]
> Note that this conclusion has several implications. [Never: *You note* ...]

An example of a serious informal style is Alastair Cooke, who wrote his *America* very much in the manner of his weekly broadcast 'Letter from America':

> Let us glance at some of the other revolutionaries who signed then or later.

Another example is the present book. An example can be found in the middle of p.71.

In a more formal style, direct instructions to the reader tend to be avoided. But even the most formal of styles uses such instructions as *See p.345*, and directives are common in footnotes:

> Note that Smith (1945) makes a different point ...

Formulaic expressions are also often directive:

> Let $x =$ time and $y =$ place.

E-SITUATIONS

The interactive electronic world motivates directives:

> Insert   Edit   Shut down
> Log off   Contact us   Search

Even if a noun is used, there is an implicit directive behind it, such as 'Use' or 'Select':

> Tools   Help

The conventions of screen usage allow the verb to be regularly omitted. A hyperlink which says *NEWS* is automatically taken to mean 'Click here to go to News'.

DESCRIPTIVE SUMMARY: EXCLAMATIONS

Clauses with an **exclamative** structure are of two kinds.
- The full form begins with a *what* or *how* phrase, and is followed by a statement order – subject + verb:
  What a mess that is!   How lovely they look!
- The reduced form uses only the opening element:
  What a mess!   How lovely!

In speech, the exclamatory force is typically signalled by the use of high or wide pitch range, and also by increased loudness. In formal writing, we use a single exclamation mark; in informal writing, such as intimate letters or e-mails, depending on the strength of feeling, we may use more than one:
  I saw him!!!!!!

Any type of clause can be used in an exclamatory way – statements, questions, and directives, and minor sentences are also often exclamatory:
  He's a fool!   Isn't that sad!   Look at that!   Hey!
But exclamative clauses are the only clause type whose function is solely to express an exclamation.

Any clause element can be the exclamatory focus:
- In *What a journey we've had!*, the focus is on the object (compare: *We've had a journey*, SVO).
- In *How lovely it is!*, the focus is on the complement (compare: *It is lovely*, SVC).
- In *How smoothly it runs!*, the focus is on the adverbial (compare: *It runs smoothly*, SVA).
- In the less-used *What a lot of people came!*, the focus is on the subject (compare: *A lot of people came*, SV).

The purpose of exclamatives, as of any exclamation, is to express the strength of feeling behind an utterance. A huge range of emotions is involved – surprise, shock, astonishment, horror, excitement ... They are chiefly used in conversation and fictional dialogue, especially in older literary writing.

This is Alice reacting to what the Queen of Hearts thought about the March Hare (in Lewis Carroll's *Alice's Adventures in Wonderland*, Chapter 7):

'He's murdering the time! Off with his head!'
'How dreadfully savage!' exclaimed Alice.

Imaginative monologue uses them too. Here is Emily Brontë's Mr Lockwood recalling his feelings (in *Wuthering Heights*, Chapter 3):

Oh, how weary I grew. How I writhed, and yawned, and nodded, and revived! How I pinched and pricked myself ...

And in at least one case, a literary character's exclamative has become a catch-phrase. As Joe Gargery repeatedly says to Pip (in Charles Dickens' *Great Expectations*, Chapter 27):

What larks!

Especially in their abbreviated form, exclamatives have a succinct immediacy which makes them useful as titles and in headlines and advertisements:

What a great idea!   What A Wonderful World
How Late It Was, How Late
What a farce!   Wot a lot I got [advertising Smarties]

And they are a favourite device in hymns – three together in the opening verse of Frederick Faber's 1849 text:

My God, how wonderful thou art, / Thy majesty how bright /
How beautiful thy mercy seat, / In depths of burning light!

The subject and verb can invert in this style. This hymn continues: *How dread are thine eternal years ...* The inversion is often seen in older literary style:

How often did I think about Mary!

DESCRIPTION: ECHOES

Statements, questions, commands (here called directives), and exclamations are the four functions of the major sentence recognized by traditional grammar. A fifth function cuts across this classification: the echo utterance. Any type of sentence can be echoed, with changes sometimes needed in the pronouns:

- A: Have you got my key?   B: Have I got your key?
- A: They said they'd arrive by three.
  B: They said they'd arrive by three?
- Or, in reduced forms: They said what?   By three?

Any clause element, or a whole clause (as long as it is not too long), can be echoed in this way.

EXPLANATION: ECHOES

Although echoes resemble questions, they lack the properties of real questions. Genuine questions typically ask for information; echo questions ask about the character of the preceding utterance. Why echo? There are two main reasons.

- To recapitulate: we need to confirm what was said. Sometimes this is because we did not hear the speaker clearly. More often it is because we are surprised by what was said, or find it difficult to believe.
      A: They're leaving town.   B: Leaving town?
  The confirmatory role is often emphasized by a tag:
        B: Leaving town, did you say?
  The range of attitudes expressed is quite wide – from mild irony to total incredulity.

- To explain: we need to clarify what was said. This meaning is conveyed only by *wh-* questions:
        A: She's left a key.   B: Who's left a key?
        A: Look at this.   B: Look at what?
  This usage is often abbreviated:
        A: Look at this.   B: What?

Using echoes

Echoes ask for an immediate response from the speaker. This has to be verbal in the case of explanatory echoes, but it can be nonverbal (such as a nod) in the case of recapitulations.

By their nature, we will find echoes only in informal interaction or fictional dialogue. They are a feature of a familiar interactive style, and outside of an intimate setting they can appear abrupt and impolite:

A: She's left a key.   B: What key?
                            B: What did you say?
                            B: What?

There is some regional variation in the shortest response: British English finds *What?* rude, and prefers *Pardon?* or *Sorry?*, as in *Sorry, what key?*. American English is more likely to use *Excuse me?* or *Pardon me?*.

We can see the informality of the usage in utterances where speakers use *who* and *what* in unusual ways. In this example, a personal noun (Chapter 33) is being referred to by an impersonal question word:

A: My brother's an etymologist.   B: He's a what?

Here, it is being used as an adjective:

A: Todd has a very authoritarian manner.
B: A what manner?

In these sentences, we find *what* being used as a countable noun (Chapter 30):

A: I've bought some new clip-ons.
B: Some new whats?

and as a verb:

A: I've just harangued him about it.
B: You've just whatted?

The sense of general incomprehension or incredulity can be reduced to a single word:

A: I've decided to resign. B: What?

A social function

Echoes can have a social function, to fill an awkward gap in a conversation or to provide feedback to the speaker.

> Mary *(sadly)*: So John never got the job. *(Pause)*
> Jean: Never got the job? *(shaking head)*

Here, Jean has had no problem hearing the sentence or understanding what it means. She could have said *Well, well* ... to convey the same effect. Mary would not feel she had to reply.

When such exchanges are written down, we may be uncertain whether to end the echo with a question mark, an exclamation mark, or some other punctuation, such as dots. The choice depends on the kind of tone of voice we have in mind. Each of the following conveys a different nuance:

> Never got the job? [said in a puzzled way]
> Never got the job! [said in a shocked way]
> Never got the job. [said in an unemotional way]
> Never got the job ... [said in a reflective way]

This issue presents itself with all echo questions that are exclamatory in function.

Playing for time

Following a question, echoes can be a useful way of temporarily evading an issue or just playing for time while we decide what to say:

> A: Where is this line of argument taking us?
> B: Where is this line of argument taking us? That's a very good question.

It is a ploy much used by interviewees and examinees.

> A: What do you think about the 1745 revolution?
> B: What do I think about the 1745 revolution? Hmm ...

Of course, if we've never heard of the 1745 revolution, and don't want to own up, we can echo in a tone of voice which suggests that the answer is so obvious the question should never have been asked in the first place!

In e-conversations

The lag between sending and receiving makes them much less likely in e-mail exchanges, but they do occur in chatroom conversations. The only complication is that an echo may not appear next to the sentence it echoes, because interventions from other speakers can get in the way. Here is an example from a group discussing a James Bond film:

SPEEDY: it was great when he went over the cliff
FROGGER: yeah and the crash was brill
JO-JO: how they do that do you think?
FROGGER: I dunno – models I suppose
BONEHEAD: Fan - tastic!!
SPEEDY: they use stuntmen
SPEEDY: models? no way!!!

Speedy has already sent his reply to Jo-Jo's question, but Frogger's reply has managed to get to the screen first. Speedy then sends another message responding to Frogger – a dismissive echo question. By the time it gets to the screen, another message has arrived, so that the echo ends up being two sentences away from the stimulus. This doesn't seem to bother anyone, though.

Overdoing it

Some people echo out of habit. Other people usually find this very irritating.

What was that you said? - You'll throw me through the window if I repeat anything you say once more this evening?...

8 The verb element

DESCRIPTIVE SUMMARY

As already stated (p.47), the verb element is the most important component of clause structure because it controls the number and nature of the other clause elements. With just one minor type of exception (the 'verbless' clauses, p.125), all clauses must have a verb.

Only main verbs (p.114), auxiliary verbs, and certain particles can appear as the verb element:

Look!   We**'re** ready.   The cat **is eating**.
I **ought to go**.   We **haven't seen** John.

The most important grammatical distinction in the verb element is to distinguish main verbs in terms of their transitivity. **Transitive** verbs are those which need an object for the clause to make sense:

I want a book.   They liked the film.   I've found it.

Intransitive verbs do not need an object to make sense.

I digress.   We waited for hours.   Night fell.

EXPLANATION

In Chapter 4 we saw how the meaning of the verb used in a clause conditions the meaning of the clause as a whole, by selecting the entities needed for the clause to make sense. The examples suggest that verbs can be grouped into two very general types: those which express actions and those which express states of affairs (p.163). The old idea of the verb as a 'doing word' was only ever partly true, for it ignored the many verbs which do not 'do' anything, such as *seem*, *be*, and *know*.

The meaning of the verb element is so multi-faceted that it cannot be summarized in a single chapter (see Chapters 15 to 26). Here, we need to examine the basis of the notion of transitivity.

Why have transitivity?

The two terms **transitive** and **intransitive** are from the same root as *transition* or *transient*. The first term was introduced by grammarians to convey the idea that the action expressed by the verb 'passes over' to the object – in other words, the meaning is incomplete without an object. Conversely, the meaning of an intransitive verb does not need to 'pass over' in this way. The sense is complete without an object.

In actual fact, it is much clearer if we talk about transitive and intransitive **uses** of verbs. This is because a very large number of verbs in English can be used in both ways. An example is *eat*:

Mary was eating a cake.   Mary was eating.

In such cases we have a choice – and whenever grammar presents us with a choice, we need to know what factors govern that choice, so that we choose appropriately.

Sometimes the distinction in use has little effect on the verb meaning. In cases like *eat*, the transitive clause is obviously more specific or definite than the intransitive one, but it is patently the same verb action in each case. The same point applies to these examples:

She's reading a paper.   She's reading.
The train approached us.   The train approached.

However, with many other verbs the meaning changes markedly, as we move between transitive and intransitive. There are two main ways in which this happens. We can simply omit the object and not put anything in its place; or we can use a prepositional phrase to narrow the meaning down in some way.

Keeping the object unexpressed

RESTRICTING THE MEANING TO ONE

With some verbs, the intransitive use conveys the idea that a single kind of object is to be understood. Of all the possible things that might be drunk, expected, or written, just one stands out:

I drink herbal tea.   I drink. [alcohol]
Jo's expecting a letter.   Jo's expecting. [a baby]
John wrote a letter.   John writes. [literature]

Other such verbs include *bake* and *wash*.

EXPRESSING MUTUAL PARTICIPATION

With some verbs the intransitive use conveys the idea, without needing to spell it out, that two parties have been involved in a reciprocal relationship:

We've met. [each other, not someone else]
The two cars collided. [with each other, not with two other objects]
John and Mary are consulting. [each other]

Other examples include *embrace*, *kiss*, *touch*, and *fight*.

Although in theory *John and Mary are kissing* could mean that each of the two is kissing someone else, that is not how we normally take the usage. An important mutual involvement is implicit in the intransitive use. There is a big difference in meaning between the following sentences:

John kissed Mary.
John and Mary are kissing.

In the first case, Mary may or may not be responding; in the second, she definitely is.

TAKING FOR GRANTED

• If Lucy says *I need to wash* we assume she is talking about herself, not someone or something else. If she wants to avoid this meaning, she must specify the object: *I need to wash the children*. Other verbs with a 'reflexive' meaning include *pack*, *dress*, *shower*, and *shave*.

- If Steve says *I nodded*, we assume he is talking about his head. He does not need to say *I nodded my head*. Other similar verbs include *shrug, clap, blink*, and *wink*. Some people find expressions like *wink an eye* tautologous – as there is nothing else that could be winked.
- If Sue says *That dog bites*, we assume she is talking about people and not, say, a bone. With verbs like *bite*, the intransitive use takes a human object for granted, and to spell it out seems odd: *That dog bites people*. Other such verbs include *sting, offend, amuse*, and *please*.

NOT STATING THE OBVIOUS

With several verbs, we do not need the object because this is obvious from the verbal context.

> I was called for interview at six, so I attended.

It would usually be thought tautologous to repeat the object, and a sign of careless writing. Only if we were feeling very irritated would we say it a second time:

> I was called for interview at six, so I attended the interview. And what a waste of time *that* was!

Other such verbs include *follow, answer, obey*, and *watch*. Sometimes the situation is so obvious that we do not even need a verbal context. If someone says (a) *I failed* or (b) *We won*, we know that (a) is some sort of exam and (b) is some sort of game or contest.

NOT IDENTIFYING THE CAUSE

With some verbs the intransitive says that an event took place without having to say who or what caused it.

> The book is selling well.
> Tim doesn't frighten easily.
> That dress will iron nicely.

The subject is undergoing the process expressed by the verb. It is a generalization: we cannot really say:

> That dress will iron nicely on Mondays.

And we cannot tell who is doing the ironing, or what might be frightening Tim.

Replacing the object by a prepositional phrase

EXPRESSING ENDEAVOUR VS. SUCCESS

With some verbs the intransitive use conveys the idea that an effort is being made, whereas the transitive use conveys a successful outcome. In this transitive use of *kick*, my foot has made a definite contact with the ball:

I kicked the ball.

But when *kick* is intransitive, followed by an *at-* construction, the outcome is by no means so certain.

I kicked at the ball.

Here my foot may have missed it completely; or perhaps it touched the ball, but not very convincingly; or perhaps I wasn't really trying.

There are several verbs which allow this kind of definite vs. desultory contrast:

I poked the fire.	I poked at the fire.
I pushed the door.	I pushed at the door.
I sipped my wine.	I sipped at my wine.

EXPRESSING THE THOROUGHNESS OF A MOVEMENT

With some verbs the distinction is more to do with the thoroughness with which the direction of an activity is carried out. If Ben says

I climbed the mountain.

we assume he got to the top. But if he says

I climbed up the mountain.

he might only have got half way. There is a completeness of meaning implied by the transitive version; it suggests that the achievement is more significant. The same suggestion comes across if we read that highwayman Black Dirk *is roaming the countryside.* Here, he is reaching all parts, and everyone should be worried. By contrast, if we read that he *is roaming in the countryside*, we get the impression that he doesn't quite know what he's about. Other directional verbs include *cross, flee, jump,* and *swim.*

Creating effects with transitivity

Mature writing displays a balanced use of transitivity options. The unremitting use of transitive verbs in an action narrative can be very demanding:

> Smith heard a noise. He dialled the security code and entered the chamber. A masked man was holding the Manshur diamond. Smith shouted a warning.

Equally, an uninterrupted sequence of intransitive verbs in such a narrative lacks energy:

> Smith reflected. Time was passing, but nothing had changed. Mary waited. The plan was working.

Both styles would begin to bore, after a while.

Dramatic balance is well illustrated in this extract from the opening of Terry Pratchett's Discworld novel *The Truth*. The transitive verbs (in bold) chiefly mark the main action points; the intransitives (underlined) chiefly deal with the consequences. (Forms of *be* and related verbs are ignored.)

> William **opened** his eyes. I've <u>gone</u> blind, he **thought**.
> Then he **moved** the blanket.
> And then the pain **hit** him.
> It was a sharp and insistent sort of pain, <u>centred</u> right over the eyes. He <u>reached up</u> gingerly. There seemed to be some bruising and what felt like a dent in the flesh, if not the bone.
> He <u>sat up</u>. He was in a sloping-ceilinged room. A bit of grubby snow **crusted** the bottom of a small window. Apart from the bed, which was just a mattress and blanket, the room was unfurnished.
> A thump **shook** the building. Dust <u>drifted</u> down from the ceiling. He <u>got up</u>, <u>clutching</u> at his forehead, and <u>staggered</u> to the door. It <u>opened</u> into a much larger room or, more accurately, a workshop.
> Another thump **rattled** his teeth.

Giving instructions

In a set of instructions, such as a recipe book or a foodstuff label, the object is often omitted because it is obvious from the context what is being referred to. An elliptical style is the result. If we were to read this on a medicine bottle:

Take three times a day after meals.

we would know what is to be taken – the mixture in the bottle. It is natural to omit the object in such cases, especially when space is at a premium (such as on a label) or when the object would otherwise be repeated unnecessarily:

Select the section to be copied with F2 then **cut and paste** to your page. [cut and paste the section]

Include your remittance and send with a stamped addressed envelope to ... [send your remittance]

In some situations, if we did not use this strategy, the amount of repetition would soon reach intolerable proportions. A typical recipe reads like this:

Cook the spaghetti in fast-boiling water for about 10 minutes. Drain and serve on a heated dish with the sauce poured over.

not like this:

Cook the spaghetti in fast-boiling water for about 10 minutes. Drain the spaghetti and serve the spaghetti on a heated dish with the sauce poured over the spaghetti.

We read in the appropriate object after each verb. It is easy to repeat ourselves in this way when we are writing a first draft; re-reading is the way to eliminate it.

Omitting the object can sometimes suggest a potential ambiguity which can be exploited for comic purposes. When we are told *Stand for 30 mins*, we know the writer is talking about the food, not us. But not here:

A *(busy in kitchen)*: Why aren't you helping?

B: The book said I was to stand for 30 minutes.

Changing the role of the subject

With some verbs, the change in transitivity alters the connection between the subject and the verb. Compare:

Jo opened the door.　　The door opened.

In the transitive use, the subject Jo is the agent: she performs the action. In the intransitive use, we do not know the force which opened the door. It may have done so under its own steam. All we can say is that the subject has been 'affected' by the action. Several verbs work in this way:

I stopped the car.　　　　　　　　The car stopped.
The president united the country.　The country united.
The shop has increased prices.　　Prices have increased.

The unknown agent makes the intransitive a useful choice in cases where we do not want to assign any responsibility at all. In the transitive use, we have to opt for an agent. Even in the agentless passive (p.141: *Prices have been increased*) we are suggesting that somebody specific is the cause of the situation. But with *Prices have increased* there is no agent suggested at all. The situation just happened. (Government ministers love this usage.)

The usage is also common in narratives where the author wants to build up tension.

John heard a noise. A key was turning in the lock ...
I looked at the organ. The horrible music began again.

It is a favourite trick of ghost-story writers:

Suddenly the window broke. The gap slowly widened. The mirror cracked. His clothes tore.

A real example: in Larry Milne's *Ghostbusters* (Chapter 17), Dana is being attacked, but at this point she does not know by what. The intransitive helps to keep the action going while she waits for the identity to be revealed:

And the door is bending now, buckling under the onslaught of the tearing claws. ... The cushion rips ... The armchair swings round ... The Terror Dogs.

9 | The subject element

Virtually all clauses have a subject. It usually appears before the verb in statements and after the first verb in questions. It controls the form of the verb in the third person singular of the present tense, and also the form of certain pronouns and post-verb items.

That looks nice. **They** look nice. Do **they** look nice?
He asked **him**. **She** asked **her**. I cut **my**self.

Subjects can appear as noun phrases, including single nouns and combinations of nouns (Chapter 27); pronouns (Chapter 43); and some types of subordinate clause (Chapter 65):

A red car passed by. **Cars and bikes** passed by.
They passed by. **What she said** impressed me.

EXPLANATION

The subject occurs with all types of verbs. Its most general role is to introduce the **theme** or **topic** of the clause – what the clause is talking about.

Meteorological balloons are an unusual sight.

A smug cat was licking its paws.

To interpret the subject, we may need to look at the situation in which the clause is being used or refer to the linguistic context. This is especially the case when the subject is a pronoun or a definite noun phrase (p.205):

That's a 747. *[pointing]* **The knife** was in the kitchen.

The clarifying linguistic context is usually earlier; but sometimes it can be later. A novel might begin:

She was alone. or **The squire** was not amused.
and we have to wait a while to find out who it is.

The meanings of the subject

The subject expresses a wide range of functions. The role which first comes to mind is that of **agent** or **actor** – the animate being that initiates an action:

The boy kicked a ball.   **The dog** is chasing cats.

This is certainly the commonest use of the subject, but there are several others. The important point to note is that the exact nuance usually depends on the verb used.

- If the subject is an inanimate entity, we can hardly talk of it as an 'actor'; it is rather the **causer** of the action:
  The avalanche struck the small town at midnight.
- Some inanimate subjects have the more specific role of the **instrument** or **means** by which something happened:
  The stone broke the window.
- Some subjects don't initiate an action at all, but rather receive the effects of an action or state of being. These subjects are often called **affected**:
  The papers disappeared.   **Jane** was sad.
- In a similar way, animate subjects can experience or sense the action of the verb. **Experiencer** or **recipient** subjects don't initiate an action; it happens to them:
  I heard a noise.   **Mary** loves her car.   **He** found it odd.
- A **locative** subject expresses a notion of place:
  Wales is a mountainous region.
- A **temporal** subject expresses a notion of time:
  Tomorrow will be a lovely day.
- An **eventive** subject expresses a happening or occasion:
  The concert was in the park.   **The march** begins at five.
- Some verbs make us see the subject as occupying a stable position in space – **positioner** subjects:
  Mary was sitting in the garden.   **He** lay on the floor.
- And a subject can express no meaning, in talking about time, atmosphere, or distance: a **prop** or **empty** subject:
  It's raining.   **It**'s three o'clock.   **It**'s a long way.
  Another 'empty' subject (*there*) is described in Chapter 72.

Leaving out the subject

The fact that we have 'empty' subjects at all indicates just how important the subject position is in English. In theory, it would be perfectly possible to say:

Is raining.   Is three o'clock.   Is a long way.

Some languages (such as Spanish) do allow this kind of construction, and we therefore hear it as an error when people from these backgrounds are learning English. But the pressure in an English clause is always to express a subject, so 'empty *it*' is drafted in for the purpose. This is a very different use of the word *it* from its use as a pronoun (Chapter 45), where it does have a meaning. Given this pressure, the circumstances where we may omit the subject are therefore rather special.

In directives

When we are commanding, requesting, and doing all the other things that directives do (p.72), we do not need an explicit subject, because it is obvious from the interactive nature of the situation:

Sit down.   Have an ice-cream.   Take a break.

But, as we saw in Chapter 6, subjects are always available if we want to emphasize or clarify.

In some dependent clauses

There are a few types of dependent clause which leave open the question of who is doing something (Chapter 17). The issue can be resolved only by an adjacent clause or by our general understanding of the situation.

Walking down the street, Chas saw his old car.

Anxious for a decision, the chairman asked for a vote.

If wet, the party will be held indoors.

With this last example, we understand 'if the weather is wet', not the party! But this kind of construction can be ambiguous (p.125).

In coordinating

When we want to link two or more clauses using the same subject, we usually omit the second and subsequent subjects, especially in writing:

I went to town. I bought a coat. I had lunch.
I went to town and bought a coat and had lunch.
I went to town, bought a coat, and had lunch.

To keep them in writing is typical of an immature style (p.368):

I went to town and I bought a coat and I had lunch.

Special speech styles

In informal conversation, we may omit the subject when this is obvious from the context. The first-person pronoun often goes:

Told you.   Beg pardon.   Hope they'll come.

So do the second and third persons:

Want a drink?   Can't play for toffee!   Doesn't matter.

And empty *it* is often omitted:

Looks like rain.   Must be sweltering in London.

Special writing styles

Diaries and other personal notes usually omit the subject, even in a dependent clause:

Went to town.   Bought flowers 'cos wanted impress Mary.

And a literary development of this style is common. Here is Bridget Jones, beginning a diary entry for 6 January (Helen Fielding, *Bridget Jones's Diary*):

5.45 p.m. Could not be more joyous. Computer messaging re: presence or otherwise of skirt continued obsessively all afternoon. Cannot imagine respected boss did stroke of work.

And the day's entry ends as it began, subjectless:

Yesssss! Yesssss! Daniel Cleaver wants my phone no. Am marvellous. Am irresistible Sex Goddess. Hurrah!

DESCRIPTIVE SUMMARY

The object usually appears after the verb, though it can be placed earlier in the clause if we want to draw special attention to it (Chapter 71):

They serve **really nice food** at Brown's.

Really nice food they serve at Brown's.

Objects can appear as noun phrases, including single nouns and combinations of nouns (Chapter 27); pronouns (Chapter 43); and some types of subordinate clause (Chapter 65):

I drive **a red car**.   We bought **tea, cake, and cheese**.

They saw **them**.   I asked **what she said**.

These are examples of the use of a **direct object**, where an entity has been directly affected by the action expressed by the verb (p.51). Certain verbs permit an **indirect object**, which identifies the recipient or beneficiary of an action, or of the goods or services provided by an action:

I gave Jane a book.   I gave a book to Jane.

I made her a cocktail.   I made a cocktail for her.

I opened the door for the mayor.

When the two objects appear side by side, the indirect object precedes the direct object (we do not say *I gave a book Jane*). When the indirect object is introduced by a preposition (*to* or *for*) it usually follows (but cases like *I gave to Jane a book* are referred to below).

EXPLANATION

As the terms 'direct' and 'indirect' suggest, there is an important semantic difference between them.

Direct and indirect meanings

'Direct' and 'indirect' capture the notion that one object is more centrally involved than the other in the action of the verb. The main evidence is that it is usually not possible to omit the direct object (some exceptions are discussed in Chapter 8), whereas the indirect object can easily be omitted without affecting the semantic relationships in the rest of the clause:

I made you a drink. does not allow   ~~I made you.~~

I made you a drink. does allow   I made a drink.

In some cases, we can omit the direct object, but it radically alters the meaning of the clause:

I offered Mary £100 as a reward.

I offered Mary as a reward.

Direct objects are animate or inanimate. Indirect objects are either animate or personifications:

I gave the dog a bone.

I gave the mountain a fond farewell.

If an entity cannot be personified, it is unlikely to appear as an indirect object:

I gave consequence a fond farewell.

though in creative writing, anything can happen. If Dylan Thomas or James Joyce had used this last sentence, we could write an interesting essay on what it might mean.

An unusual order

We cannot usually say *I gave to Jane a book*. But if the direct object is lengthy, this order is perfectly possible:

I gave to Jane the book that had been on my shelf.

This follows the principle of end-weight (p.344): longer elements of structure tend to appear towards the end of a clause. The reverse order is much less easy to follow:

I gave the book that had been on my shelf to Jane.

Legal formulations often follow the unusual order, especially if there is a list of beneficiaries: *I bequeath to Jane ... .*

Meanings of the direct object

The role we most often associate with the direct object is to express the entity immediately **affected** by the verb — what is often called the **goal** or **patient**.

> I pushed **the door**.

But we can distinguish several other meanings.

- Although the **recipient** meaning is typically expressed by the indirect object; some verbs make the direct object the recipient:

    > I paid **the milkman**.   The deal benefits **everyone**.

- With some verbs, the direct object expresses the notion of a **result**:

    > I wrote **a letter**.   Steven painted **her picture**.

- Some direct objects are **instrumental**, because they express the means by which an action takes place:

    > Sue kicked **her feet** through the puddle.

    The meaning here is that Sue kicked *with* her feet, not that her feet were being kicked.

- A **locative** direct object expresses the notion of place:

    > We climbed **the hill**.

- A **temporal** direct object expresses a notion of time:

    > I hate **Monday mornings**.

- A **reaction** direct object expresses a response to some verbs of speaking or of nonverbal communication:

    > I nodded **agreement**. I smiled **my thanks**.
    > I mumbled **some appreciative words**.

- A **measure** direct object expresses a notion of quantity:

    > The load weighs **10 tons**. The theatre seats **300**.

- A **cognate** object repeats the meaning of the verb:

    > James grinned **a big grin**. She smiled **a secret smile**.

    The object is usually modified, to avoid the clause appearing to be tautologous. It is a usage much beloved of some writers of fiction.

- As with subjects (p.91), it is possible to have an 'empty *it*' direct object:

    > He legged it.   Beat it!   Spit it out!

Objects after light verbs

Consider the following pairs of sentences:

She looked at my work.   She had a look at my work.
She kissed me.   She gave me a kiss.
I calculated the cost.   I made a calculation of the cost.

In each case there is a choice between using a semantically specific verb or a 'light' verb – a verb which contributes relatively little meaning to the clause – chiefly *have, take, make, do,* and *give.*

Light constructions are often criticised in style books as being 'loose'. We might see an exercise of the following kind:

Replace the underlined words by a more specific verb:
The accountant <u>made a calculation of</u> the cost.

But this is to miss the point. There are important differences of meaning and use between the two versions.

• The light use makes it much easier to elaborate the meaning of the object.

Jo influenced me.
Jo had a fundamental and long-lasting influence on me.

It would be very awkward saying this the other way:

Jo influenced me fundamentally and long-lastingly.

• The object in a light-verb construction usually has an indefinite article. We cannot say: ~~She had the look at my work.~~ This introduces a restriction of quantity. If someone *gives you a kiss*, you get just one; if someone *kisses you*, you could get any number.

• Similarly, there is a difference in the duration of the event. If Mike *gave a shout*, it didn't last long. If Mike *shouted*, it could be for hours. We cannot say ~~Mike gave a shout for hours.~~

• There is also a difference of accomplishment. Compare:

John had a drink of my beer.   John drank my beer.

In the first case, he drank some of it; in the second, he drank the lot.

A complement adds meaning to that of another clause element. This grammar identifies two types.

- A **subject complement** refers back to the subject, and usually follows the subject and a linking (or **copular**) verb, such as *be* or *become*. It can be placed earlier in the clause if we want to draw special attention to it (Chapter 71):

  My name is **David**.   **David** my name is.

- An **object complement** refers back to the direct object (Chapter 10), and usually follows it.

  The judge declared Jane **the winner**.

Complements can appear as noun phrases (Chapter 27); adjective phrases (Chapter 49); pronouns (Chapter 43); and some types of subordinate clause (Chapter 65):

Mary is **a reporter**.   She became **a singer and dancer**.

It seems **ready**.   That's **him**.   That is **what I said**.

The verb *be* is by far the commonest way of linking a subject to a complement. A much wider range of verbs is available for linking an object to a complement (p.57).

The complement has one very general semantic function: it expresses an **attribute**, or property, of the clause element to which it refers. But the attribute has two roles:

- it can **characterize** the other element

  The house is hot.

- it can **identify** or **specify** the other element

  The house is No 6.

Characteristic or identity

The two roles are found both as subject complements and as object complements.

- Characterizing

  The house is hot. We thought the house hot.

- Identifying

  The house is No 6. We named the house No 6.

In the identifying role, when the verb is a form of *be*, we can reverse the order of the elements:

  No 6 is the house.

This provides a useful way of varying the emphasis, when identifying things. However, we cannot do this with the characterizing role without the sentence sounding somewhat unusual: *Hot is the house.* We would find such a construction only in poetry or poetic prose – or in the utterances of a character who speaks in a distinctive way, such as Yoda in the *Star Wars* films.

Current state or result

Another way of looking at the complement is in relation to the kind of verb which is present in the clause.

- Some verbs express a current state. Apart from *be*, we find *appear, feel, look, seem, remain, stay, keep,* and the sensory verbs *smell, taste,* and *sound*:

  That seems right.   The day stayed fine.

  The soup smelled spicy.

  Some of these verbs can be followed by noun phrases, as well as adjectives, and then we usually prefer to reinforce the meaning with *to be* or (more informally) *like*:

  He seemed a winner.   He seemed to be a winner.

  I felt a fool.   I felt like a fool.

- Some verbs express a result or development, notably *become, grow, turn, end up, prove, get,* and *do*:

  The wheel became rusty.   I got ready.

  She became an expert.   She ended up the winner.

Using complements

The usual position for the complement is at the end of the clause, where it tends to carry the main intonational emphasis (Chapter 70). This makes it very prominent, and thus an appropriate choice whenever the attribute is new information or we want to draw special attention to it.

He went mad.   The pressure drove him mad.
They were afraid.   The gun made them afraid.
The house was gloomy.   I found the house gloomy.
I name this ship Winnie.

The only other way of handling an attribute is to make it part of the subject or object (Chapter 48), but then it will be subordinated to the associated noun, and to the other information-bearing parts of the clause. Compare:

That wheel is rusty. [we focus directly on the rustiness]
That rusty wheel could be dangerous.
[the rustiness is part of the background]

If all we want to say in a clause is 'an entity has an attribute', the complement is the most direct and succinct way of doing it. But why would we want to focus attention directly on attributes?

Arousing curiosity

Writers of fiction love the usage because it provides an intriguing opening line in scene-setting and character-setting. Several of my examples would work very well as the opening line of a novel:

They were afraid.
The house was gloomy.

Who were? Why? Which house? Why? What's going on?
Here are some real opening lines:

The social worker was older than she had expected.
(P.D. James, *Innocent Blood*)
The book was thick and black and covered with dust.
(A.S. Byatt, *Possession*)
Some other examples are given on p.54.

Attention-grabbing

Commercial advertising is all about attributes – drawing a customer's attention to the way a product works, or how it is better than others. It therefore uses complements routinely, especially in questions, to remind us of our real or imagined needs, and to focus on the properties which will meet these needs:

Do you get tired?
Are you a jelly-addict?
You'll feel relaxed.
Is her skin really this beautiful?
Doggo is real value in a tin.

Defining and classifying

Expository texts rely greatly on the complement to focus on the critical attributes of an entity. Here is an extract from a biology textbook for schools (D.G. Mackean, *Introduction to Biology*). Chapter 7 begins:

A flower is a reproductive structure of a plant. ...

It goes on to define several parts of the flower:

An inflorescence is a group of flowers borne on the same main stalk. ...
The androecium is the male part of the flower and consists of stamens. ...
Nectaries are glandular swellings ...

Other constructions are also used, of course, such as 'X consists of Y' and 'X is called Y'. But the complement is the chief way of getting the essential information across.

DESCRIPTIVE SUMMARY

A clause can contain an indefinite number of adverbials in almost any position, though they are most commonly placed after the other elements.

> I ran quickly / to the station / at 6 o'clock.

This example shows three adverbials: the first is an adverb (Chapter 52), and the other two are prepositional phrases (Chapter 59). In addition, some nouns or noun phrases (Chapter 27) can function as adverbials, as can some types of subordinate clause (Chapter 65). 'When did I run?'

> ... yesterday – yesterday morning.
> ... when I went out.

Also, a single adverb can be expanded into an adverb phrase by the addition of one or more intensifying words:

> I ran quickly – very very quickly.

EXPLANATION

Apart from a few cases where an adverbial is obligatory (the SVA and SVOA clause types, p.55), adverbials are optional extras. But just because they are optional does not mean that they are rare. On the contrary, because a clause can contain several instances, the adverbial turns out to be the most widely encountered of all the clause elements, especially in conversation.

Adverbials have so many semantic and pragmatic functions that they cannot all be described in a single chapter. Their different meanings and uses are explained individually in Chapters 54 to 58.

Adverbials are common because we rely on them to add colour and detail to what we say. Here are two examples, with adverbials underlined, from opposite ends of the formality spectrum. Take them away and there is very little left.

Informal conversation

In this extract from a conversation between two friends, one is talking about where she lives. A dash represents a pause or the end of a rhythm-unit:

<u>so</u> the canal runs <u>at the end of our road</u> – it takes er – it's – <u>well</u> – a leisurely walk <u>in ten minutes</u> you're <u>down along by the canal</u> – and that <u>of course</u> is the nicest part – there's some lovely houses – but it's the trees – you can stand <u>on the bridge</u> – and look – look <u>along</u> – and the trees <u>at the moment</u> – oh it's beautiful – all gold <u>in the water</u> and everything

The adverbials perform several functions – linking the parts of the narrative, emphasizing elements of meaning, and adding crucial perspectives in space and time.

Imaginative literature

An even greater concentration of adverbials can often be found in imaginative writing. Here is Ophelia talking about her recent meeting with Hamlet (Shakespeare, *Hamlet*, II.i.87):

He took me <u>by the wrist</u> and held me <u>hard</u>.
<u>Then</u> goes he <u>to the length of all his arm,</u>
And <u>with his other</u> <u>hand</u> <u>thus</u> o'er his brow
He falls <u>to such perusal of my face</u>
As 'a would draw it. <u>Long</u> stayed he <u>so</u>.
<u>At last,</u> a little shaking of mine arm
And <u>thrice</u> his head <u>thus</u> waving <u>up and down,</u>
He raised a sigh <u>so</u> piteous and profound
<u>As it did seem to shatter all his bulk</u>
<u>And end his being.</u>

DESCRIPTIVE SUMMARY

A **vocative** is an element identifying the entity – usually a person or persons – to whom we are speaking or writing. It is an optional element, not part of clause structure. If we use a vocative, it usually goes at the beginning or end of a clause, separated by a comma in writing and by a distinctive intonation pattern in speech. Middle position adds special emphasis.

Mary, have you taken advice about this?
Have you taken advice about this, Mary?
Have you, Mary, taken advice about this?

We do not normally use more than one vocative per sentence, even if the sentence contains many clauses. A vocative may also be used alone: *Mary?*

Vocatives can be personal names or titles (Chapter 29), certain nouns, noun phrases, and noun clauses (Chapter 27), a few types of adjective (Chapter 48), or the pronoun *you*:

David   Prime Minister   Waiter   Young man
Whoever you are   Dearest   You, ...

EXPLANATION

We use vocatives only in a conversation when our addressee is present – physically or in our imagination. And this raises an interesting question: Why do we bother to identify the person(s) we are addressing? If we can see them, or imagine them, why do we need to name them? There must be more to the use of the vocative than a simple matter of identification.

Why use vocatives?

To identify

This is plainly an important function when taking part in a

conversation involving several people, and we want to point our remarks at an individual. We may even expand the vocative under such circumstances:

You with the red tie, move further back.

Tall Fred, stop talking! [said a teacher to a class containing two different-sized Freds]

But there are times when we have only one addressee in mind, and yet we still need to identify them. An obvious case is during the opening of a telephone conversation. And there may be other reasons why we cannot see our addressee, such as when we hear someone moving about in a dark room – a staple vocative of horror films.

Is that you, Michael? [It never is, of course.]

To call

If we want to catch someone's attention, a vocative is the most direct way of doing it:

Jane!   Mr Smith!   Waiter!   Madam!

We can add emphasis with an interjection (p.34):

Oh, waiter!   Hey, Jane!

Oy, Mike!   Ahoy, Mr Smith!

But we must be careful. *Oh* softens the force of a call, but some interjections reduce politeness: *Hey, waiter!* We do not use *hey* or *oy* with a polite vocative: ~~Oy, madam!~~

To express a relationship

The commonest use of the vocative is to define, maintain, or reinforce a social relationship. The speaker's choice of vocative to the addressee says something about their relationship to each other.

Darling, ...   Doctor, ...   M'lud, ...

Adjectives are especially likely in such circumstances:

Dear friends, ...   Young man, ...

Silly idiot! [addressing the driver of the other car]

Types of relationship

Our social relationships range from the most familiar and intimate to the most distant and deferential, and vocatives can signal points along this scale. They can also add strength of feeling.

INTIMACY
Vocatives can affirm a bond between people who are close:

   darling   dear   love   gorgeous   chuck

KINSHIP
Vocatives can show a family relationship:

   dad   son   gran   coz [= *cousin*, in earlier English]

GENERAL FAMILIARITY
Vocatives can express a friendly (maybe) attitude:

   bud   man   dude   bro   mate   folks

The qualification is needed because these vocatives may also be used to strangers. When someone we do not know addresses us as *bud* or *mate*, we may need to be on guard.

FIRST-NAME FAMILIARITY
Vocatives can use a person's first name, or a form of it, or a nickname based upon it, to express familiarity:

   Thomas   Tom   Tommy   Tommo   Tom-tit

This is the commonest use of a vocative, in informal conversation, accounting for 60 per cent of all cases. We might also include team-calls under this heading:

   Come on, Reading!   Come on, you royals!

SURNAME FAMILIARITY
Vocatives can use a person's surname, or a form of it, or a nickname based upon it, to express comradeship. This practice is uncommon today, though still heard in some schools, colleges, and professional situations. In earlier times, male adult acquaintances would routinely use surnames to each other – as would a wife to her husband:

   'My dear Micawber!' urged his wife.

   (Charles Dickens, *David Copperfield*, Chapter 12)

Surname distance

Vocatives can use a surname as an expression of different status – the addressee being lower than the speaker. This is the norm in hierarchies such as the armed forces, the prison service, or any job operating a strict naming code, where it may be used to males and females alike, as any James Bond enthusiast knows:

Come here, Smith!   What do you think, Moneypenny?

Title and surname

This is the default polite vocative for people who are acquainted with each other, and who do not have – or do not wish to have – any degree of intimacy.

A pound of bacon, please, Mr Smith.

Good morning, Mrs Williams.

Dr Brown, can I see you for a moment?

This usage was formerly standard throughout society, but is increasingly being replaced by a 'first-name' practice which highlights the individual nature of the relationship. The address system is currently in transition: some people welcome the development (much commoner in the US than in Britain); some hate it – especially when used in situations where the familiarity is unwarranted, such as in a 'cold' phone-call trying to sell them insurance.

Role alone

Vocatives which use the name of a person's occupational role, with no further name, always imply a social status difference between the speaker and the addressee. In such cases as these, the relationship is from low to high:

Mr President   Prime Minister   Doctor   Professor

But here the relationship is from high to low:

waiter   driver   nurse   guard [of a train]

In the former cases, the title is a long-lasting part of the person's identity; in the latter, the identity lasts only as long as the person performs the role. If we recognize a waiter at a hairdresser's, we do not call him *waiter*.

HONORIFICS

Vocatives like *sir* and *madam* convey a level of politness towards an addressee whose name is unknown.

Do sit down, madam.   Good morning, sir.

English has very few honorifics (compared with, say, Japanese), but some variants do exist, such as *ma'am, siree,* and *mum* (meaning 'employer' not 'mother') – all a little old-fashioned. Dylan Thomas's character, the butcher's home-help Lily Smalls, routinely addresses her mistress in this way (in *Under Milk Wood*):

MRS BEYNON: Oh, d'you hear that, Lily?

LILY: Yes, mum.

MRS BEYNON: We're eating pusscat.

LILY: Yes, mum.

If the addressee's name *is* known, of course, the usage is likely to be jocular, ironic, scolding, or rude:

[parent to child] You little madam, how dare you!

[son to father] Good day to you, sir!

This use of *sir*, today, is probably jocular. But in previous centuries it was the expected address between people being formally or coolly polite to each other. Dr Johnson, Boswell, and their companions 'sir' each other all the time, and we encounter *sir* and *madam* regularly in the exchanges of the characters of the nineteenth-century novelists.

INSULTS

Vocatives are a convenient way of insulting someone, whether the addressee's name is known or not:

nitwit   idiot   lazy   silly cow   stupid bastard

You by itself is always loaded – usually rude, sometimes cajoling (with different intonation, of course):

You, where's my car?   Come on, you!

Adding a second element can reduce the impact:

Where's my car, you guys?   Come on, y'all.

Insults provide a rare occasion when we can use more than one vocative at the same time:

John, you old devil!

All addressees

Vocatives can be all-inclusive in their reference:

Leave the building, everyone.
Ladies and gentlemen, I'd like to begin ...

Unknown addressee

Vocatives can even be used to identify a person or group whom the speaker does *not* know or is unable to specify:

Those of you who want to smoke, please use room 3.
Whoever said that, stand up!
Come out, come out, whoever you are!
What's-your-name, can you pass me the paper?

This category also covers cases where identifying the addressee is unimportant:

Get me a chair, someone.
One of you, make sure the door's shut.

Caution

The vocative system is complex and takes a long time to learn – though we acquire most of the conventions unselfconsciously when young. There are nonetheless some curious anomalies in usage. For example, the three titles *Mr, Mrs* and *Miss* are parallel in politeness, when used in front of a surname; but when they are used alone, only the last of them is polite.

Come in, Miss.

but not: ~~Come in, Missis.~~ [*Mrs* – also spelled *Missus*]
Comedians can get away with it (*So I said, 'Listen, Missis!'*) as can young children (*Hey, Mister!*). But if Clint Eastwood uses *Mister* to someone, there is usually trouble brewing. With strangers, it can be safer to use an alternative attention-phrase (such as *Excuse me!*).
The form *Ms* has evolved as a useful alternative to *Mrs/Miss* in writing, avoiding a decision about marital status. It has no standard spoken form as a vocative. We do not say, ~~Come here, Ms.~~

Where to use vocatives – in a sentence

In a conversation, 70 per cent of all vocatives occur at the end of a clause, where it is chiefly used to define or affirm a relationship.

Of course I love you, darling.   Hello, handsome!

It's raining outside, Tommy.

American English uses final vocatives with this function much more often than British English does.

Using a vocative at the beginning of a clause is likely only in three circumstances:
- To grab someone's attention, or to identify the addressee, which is not something we do very often:

    Mr Jones, there's a call for you.
- To begin a speech or other monologue:

    Ladies and gentlemen, I am here today to ask ...
- To precede a sentence which we know is going to be lengthy. The vocative fails to have much point at the end of a long utterance:

    I really do want to know what happened when you all went out to the restaurant and the wine got spilt and there was a dispute over the bill, John.

By contrast, in a short utterance, the most natural position for the vocative is at the end. If we put it at the beginning we introduce a note of seriousness or urgency:

What happened the other night, John?

John, what happened the other night?

Using repeated vocatives

It is unusual to repeat the vocative in a clause, unless you are making a special point, such as trying to add emphasis or keep someone's attention. Teachers use it:

The point, Smith, which is on page 3, Smith ...

And nervousness or anxiety to conform can increase the vocative rate, as in this soldier-to-officer utterance:

Yes, sir, I'll do that, sir, right away, sir!

Using no vocatives

We do not have to use vocatives. Indeed, if we are sure of our
social relationship, they cease to be of value. Husbands and wives,
or parents and children, do not use vocatives to each other very
often in a conversation. Indeed, when they do, especially with a
questioning intonation, there is often a 'special' agenda in mind:

Mum ...?   Darling ...?   [I want something]

And a supposedly close relationship which overuses endearments
is unlikely to stay close for much longer.

Where to use vocatives – outside of conversation

Vocatives can also be used in a few spoken or written settings
which have similarities with conversation:

- In letter-writing

  Letters conventionally begin with a vocative formula:

  Dear Jo   Dear Sir   To whom it may concern

- In advertising

  Advertisements, especially on radio and television, and tabloidy
  newspaper headlines, often summon their audience with a vocative:

  Men, ...   Hey girls, ...

- In broadcasting

  Informal presenters often address their audience directly:

  Listeners, ...   Viewers, ...   That's all, folks!

- In praying

  There is routine use of the archaic vocative marker, *O*:

  O God, who ...   O Lord, help us to ...

- In literature

  This is where we are most likely to encounter the extension of
  the vocative to inanimate or abstract entities, as in Charles
  Lamb's 'A Farewell to Tobacco':

  For thy sake, Tobacco, I / Would do anything but die.

  Poetry regularly personifies in this way, often using *O*. It is one
  of the oldest rhetorical techniques.

Concord, or **agreement**, is a way of showing that two grammatical units have a certain feature in common. It is chiefly seen in the 'third person' rule for verbs in the present tense: a singular subject requires a singular verb form, ending in -s (for singular vs. plural, see Chapter 31):

he / she / it say**s** vs. they say

the curtain close**s** vs. the curtains close

Other examples of concord are seen in the use of complements (Chapter 11), in some pronouns (Chapter 44), and also in the verb *to be*, where *I* has its own form in the present tense, and there is an additional distinction in the past tense:

This is a book. vs. Those are books.

I called him a fool. vs. I called them fools.

I asked myself ... vs. They asked themselves ...

I am / he/she/it was vs. they were

Some languages (such as Latin) rely heavily on concord as the main means of showing which words go with which – which adjective belongs to which noun, for example. However, in English, meaning does not rely on concord very much. Indeed, it would be perfectly possible to do without the third-person rule, and rely on the subject to make the distinction. This is exactly what happens in many regional dialects all over the world:

she / they goes   he / they go   she / they was   it / they be

Standard English, however, insists on the distinction.

Variations in usage

In formal English, the third-person rule is the norm, and great effort is expended by publishers to ensure that it is maintained in cases where usage varies. But in informal speech, people tend to express themselves according to the meaning of what they are saying, and this can often result in the rule being disregarded.

When a word like *none* occurs as a subject, the singular meaning of 'not one' conflicts with the plural meaning of the following noun:

None of the eggs is / are broken.

Which do we use? It is true that 'not one' of the eggs 'is' broken; it is equally true that 'all' of them 'are' unbroken.

Informal speech and writing tend to follow the meaning of the phrase as a whole, and thus use a plural. The plural noun is also right next to the verb, so this predisposes us to think in a plural way. The plural usage may even be heard in formal speech, as a consequence.

But this will not do for formal writing, where a failure to maintain concord irritates people used to the grammatical tradition, and can often be confusing. Although this next example was used in speech, it would disturb us in writing:

None of the girls have got bronchitis.

Accepted exceptions

There are some exceptions to the concord rule. Some plural subjects are conventionally given singular concord, when the entity is thought of as a unit:

• Measure expressions, such as:

Four miles is no distance **or** Six years is a long time.

• Plural names, such as:

The Times is ... **or** The US agrees.

Some nonstandard expressions break the rule on purpose:

Times is hard. I says 'no'! We was robbed!

Collective nouns such as *committee* are also a special case (Chapter 33) as are nouns after *there* (Chapter 72).

Verb phrase structure

The verb element in clause structure, symbolised by a capital **V** (Chapter 8), consists of one or more verbs comprising a **verb phrase**. In its simplest form, the verb phrase consists of a single verb, but this always has the potential for expanding into something more complex, by adding other verbs before it. When this happens, we can distinguish the **main** verb (in italics below) from the preceding **auxiliary** verbs.

I *asked*.
I have *asked*.   I haven't *asked*.   I might have *asked*.

Up to four auxiliaries can be present, though to use all four at once is very unusual:

I must have been being *asked* for months.

EXPLANATION

We need verb phrases of some complexity because there are so many nuances of meaning we want to express. After all, a verb by itself does no more than express an action or a state of affairs (Chapter 24). That is how children before age two use verbs:

Gone.   See.   Jump.   Catch.

But they soon learn that bare verbs are ambiguous. If they say *jump*, it could mean someone is currently jumping, has just jumped, or needs to jump. And it is not long before they draw attention to their abilities and intentions using auxiliary verbs like *can't* and *won't*. Basic verb-phrase structure is in place by age three.

What the elements of the verb phrase do

Main verbs

The main verb gives a verb phrase its content – a specific action or state. It tells us what the verb phrase is 'about'. Verbs which

114

have a clearly stateable meaning are called **full** or **lexical** verbs:

come ask send accompany develop

Auxiliary verbs

Auxiliary verbs allow us to see the meaning of the main verb within several perspectives.

- We use *be* and *have* as auxiliaries to help us express contrasts in time and manner (see Chapter 18):

    I am going / have gone / have been going / had gone

- We use *do* as an auxiliary to help us add emphasis or express a question (see Chapters 5 and 6):

    Do come in.

    I did see the comet.

    Do you know?

- We use verbs like *will*, *may*, and *could* as modal auxiliaries to help us express a range of judgements about the likelihood of events taking place (see Chapter 26):

    They will go. I may leave. Could you sit down?

A few other kinds of verb can appear in a verb phrase: these are discussed in Chapter 19.

Doing without auxiliaries?

It is unusual to find uses of language which succeed without auxiliaries, but they do occur when there is a need to convey generality. Most proverbs, for example, because of their 'timeless' character (p.152), do not use auxiliaries, and advertising slogans often avoid them:

A rolling stone gathers no moss. Splatto kills germs!

The impact of a quotation is often due to the directness conveyed by an auxiliary-less verb:

I came. I saw. I conquered.

To be or not to be; that is the question.

DESCRIPTIVE SUMMARY

Most verbs are **regular**, in that the forms they adopt can be predicted by a small set of rules. About 300 verbs in English are **irregular**, in that some of their forms (the -ed forms below) are partly or wholly unpredictable.

There is no difference between regular and irregular verbs in the way they use the first three forms:

- the **base** or **infinitive** form of a verb has no ending:

  stop   jump   try   go   take   see

- the **-s form** adds an -s to the base (often with a spelling change):

  stops   jumps   tries   goes   takes   sees

- the **-ing form** adds an -ing to the base (often with a spelling change):

  stopping   jumping   trying   going   taking   seeing

- the regular **-ed form** simply adds an -ed to the base (often with a spelling change):

  I stopped / have stopped

Like this are *jumped, tried*, and thousands more. The irregular forms use a different ending, no ending, a vowel change, or even, with *go*, a whole new word:

  I took / have taken   I saw / have seen
  I cut / I have cut   I went / have gone

EXPLANATION

Verbs change their forms in order to express, or help to express, different perspectives for viewing an action or state, such as the time an event happened, how long it lasted, and the number of entities involved.

Using verb forms

The base form

The base form focuses on the meaning of a lexical verb without considering its grammatical nuances. It is semantically the most neutral form, which is why it is used as the headword in a dictionary or in a language-teaching vocabulary list. It is found in several types of construction (see further, Chapters 17 and 21).

The -*s* form

This form is chiefly used to show that the third person of the verb in the present tense has a singular and not a plural subject (Chapter 14).

He / she / it wants a drink.   They want a drink.

But the presence or absence of the -*s* can also convey a subtle contrast of mood:

I demand that he gives us the money.

I demand that he give us the money.

This contrast is discussed in Chapter 21.

The -*ing* form

This form is a major means of conveying continuity or duration – something dealt with under the heading of **aspect** (Chapter 24):

Ed told me a joke.   Ed was telling me a joke [for ages].

Ed was telling me a joke when he was rudely interrupted.

It is also one of the main ways of expressing an action without restricting it to a particular time or person. If a sentence begins

Walking down the street ...

it leaves open the question of when the event happened, or how many people were involved. This is dealt with under the heading of **nonfinite** meaning (Chapter 17).

In older grammars, the -*ing* form was called the **present participle**, but the designation 'present' is misleading, for the form is by no means restricted to the expression of present time.

The -*ed* form

This form is more complex in its uses. When the lexical verb is on its own, the -*ed* form has just one use: to express the **past tense** (Chapter 23). But when it is accompanied by an auxiliary verb, it acts as a **participle** form, and then it has three different uses.

- It helps to express a particular perspective on past time: *I have asked John* [just now] is different from *I asked John* [some time ago]. See Chapter 24.
- It helps to express a passive meaning: *I was asked* [by someone] is very different from *I asked* [someone]. See Chapter 22.
- Like the -*ing* form, it is a main way of expressing an action without restricting it to a particular time or person. If a sentence begins *Asked to go out* ... it leaves open when the event happened, or how many were involved. See Chapter 17.

In older grammars, the -*ed* form was called the **past participle**, but the designation 'past' is misleading, for the form is by no means restricted to the expression of past time. But there is nothing misleading about the term **participle**, as such. It has long been used to refer to a word that 'participates' in two grammatical functions – as verb or as adjective:

the car was broken [verb]   the broken car [adjective]

We shall find this distinction useful in Chapter 50.

The point of irregular forms

Irregular forms – as everyone knows who has had to learn a foreign language – are a nuisance, because they have to be learned by heart. They are usually very old, evolving long before written records began. The distinction between regular and irregular forms is the one big exception to the approach of the present book, for they seem to have little semantic or pragmatic point.

However, some irregular forms do have a pragmatic value, because they vary in time and place, and thus can mark identity.

The verb phrase

Showing time variation

There are about a hundred differences between the verb forms of Shakespeare's time and today, such as:

I catched   was awaked   have writ   drave ['drove']

Such forms can therefore be used to add an archaic flavour in literary, religious, or jocular contexts: *I spake the truth*.

Showing regional variation

Dialects always have some nonstandard irregular verbs:

Lancashire: I was stood there (standard: *standing*)

Scotland: She was feart (standard: *frightened*)

Tyneside: They've etten it (standard: *eaten*)

Ireland: He could have went (standard: *gone*)

Such forms may of course turn up in other parts of the world, too, but they are always an index of local identity.

An interesting case is the common American use in speech (it is less common in writing) of *got* vs. *gotten*:

I've gotten a car ('I've acquired a car')

I've got a car ('I own a car')

British English uses *got* for both meanings.

Showing a different meaning or use

Some verbs have *both* irregular and regular *-ed* forms. They include:

knit/knitted   dreamt/dreamed   broadcast/broadcasted

hung/hanged   wed/wedded   lit/lighted   snuck/sneaked

Sometimes they are genuine variants: we could use either without intending any contrast in meaning. But we must always look out for stylistic or even semantic differences:

- *snuck* is more informal than *sneaked, dove* than *dived*
- people are *hanged*; pictures are *hung*
- We sped along the motorway. [probably legal]
  We speeded along the motorway. [probably illegal]

DESCRIPTIVE SUMMARY

We can classify verb phrases, and their associated clauses, into two very general types: **finite** and **nonfinite**.

- The finite forms of a verb allow us to make a contrast in tense (Chapter 23), aspect (Chapter 24), number (Chapter 31), person (Chapter 45), and mood (Chapter 21):

  you **see** / you **saw**   I **asked** / I was **asking**
  she **sees** / they **see**   I **am** / you **are**
  I insist that the house **be** / **is** sold.

- The nonfinite forms of a verb do not express these contrasts. They stay the same, regardless of whatever else is being expressed in other parts of the sentence.

  There are three nonfinite forms (p.116):
  - The *-ing* form
    I am **leaving** / He is **leaving**. **Leaving** the house, ...
  - The *-ed* participle
    I have **left** / you have **left**. **Left** alone, ...
  - The base form
    I will **leave** / They will **leave**.   To **leave** the house, ...

EXPLANATION

This distinction has evolved to allow us to make a fundamental choice about how we talk about actions and states of affairs. Sometimes we want to be specific about the time and manner of an event, or who was involved in it, or our attitude towards it, and sometimes we do not. Finite verbs let us do the former; nonfinite verbs let us do the latter.

Being explicit

A nonfinite clause is always less explicit than a finite clause, and needs clues from the accompanying finite clause, or from the context, to be interpreted.

- With finite clauses, we can easily answer such questions as:
  1: 'When did the event take place?'
  2: 'Who performed the event?'
  3: 'How many were involved – one or more than one?'
  We can try this out on a sample sentence:

  I was entering the shop ...

  Answers:

  1: When? Some time ago; not now or in the future.

  2: Who? Me.

  3: How many? One person.

- Now we can take a nonfinite clause, but without finishing the sentence, and try to answer the same questions:

  Entering the shop, ...

  1: When? We don't know. The sentence could continue in several time-frames:

  Entering the shop, I saw Jo. [last week]
  Entering the shop, I can see Jo. [now]
  Entering the shop, I will see Jo. [next week]

  2: Who? We don't know. Here are some possibilities:

  Entering the shop, I saw Jo.
  Entering the shop, you saw Jo.
  Entering the shop, Mike saw Jo.

  3: How many? We don't know. There are various options:

  Entering the shop, I saw Jo. [one]
  Entering the shop, Mike and I saw Jo. [two]
  Entering the shop, they saw Jo. [more than one]

  Only by adding a finite clause do we really know what is going on. The finite clause makes explicit the information taken for granted in the nonfinite clause.

Why be inexplicit?

We usually try to be explicit about the subject-matter of our discourse; but we sometimes find it necessary or useful to be inexplicit.

Avoiding repetition

In conversation, we do not need to repeat all the details.
> A: What are Sue and Lucy doing?
> B: Deciding which clothes to wear.

All we need to make the point is the nonfinite verb. It is obvious from the context who is doing the deciding, so we do not usually spell it out. If we did so, it would add an ironic note:
> B: Sue and Lucy are deciding which clothes to wear.

Introducing compression

Wordiness is not something most people want, in written English. Most of us aim for some sort of compactness of expression, and nonfinite clauses are one of the ways of achieving it.
> When I was entering the shop, I saw Jo.
> Entering the shop, I saw Jo.

With a lengthy subject, it would be absurd to duplicate:
> When the mayor and councillors entered the shop, the mayor and councillors saw Jo.

At the same time, we must always be on guard against potential ambiguity (see also p.125):
> Di saw Jim leaving the house.

Who was leaving the house? Probably Jim. And if there were a comma after *Jim*, it would probably be Di. But there are no commas in speech, and even in writing it is not always clear. To avoid doubt, replacement by a finite clause will clarify:
> Di saw Jim, who was leaving the house.
> Di saw Jim, when she was leaving the house.

The verb phrase

Making the audience wait

Nonfinite clauses at the beginning of a sentence are a useful way of building up tension, because their inexplicitness makes it uncertain what is going to happen. In Chapter 17 of Larry Milne's *Ghostbusters*, the Terror Dogs arrive (see p.89). The next sentence continues the moment:

Lifting their huge black snouts, ...

Go on, go on!

... the hanging flesh round their slavering jaws crinkles in what seems to be almost a smiling snarl of welcome.

Only when we get to the finite clause, do we know.

If clauses of this kind are placed at the beginning of a sentence, authors can keep adding to the drama as long as they want:

Crawling towards the house, slavering with greed, heart pounding with anticipation ...

Who? What? Depending on the effect we want to convey, the subject of the following finite clause might be *the alien from Mars* or *Grandma*.

Piling on the detail

The *Ghostbusters* story continues like this:

Their paws are raised, their viciously pointed claws, glinting redly, outstretched towards her.

The last two clauses are nonfinite, adding vivid detail in a succinct way. The value of the construction is that we can use it to add an indefinite number of descriptive points, with each point receiving separate focus because of its status as a clause. If we were to express the same meaning using adjectives, the impact of the individual points would be lost by becoming part of a list.

They raised their viciously pointed, red-glinting, outstretched claws.

(For adjective sequences, see Chapter 39.)

Adding the subject

There is a 'half-way house' between finite and nonfinite clauses:
we can add a subject – as happened in one of the examples on
p.123. We know what is pounding here:

Crawling towards the house, slavering with greed, heart
pounding with anticipation ...

This is a useful option when we want to avoid an ambiguity. If the
sentence had been

Crawling towards the house, slavering with greed, pounding with
anticipation ...

there is potential ambiguity over the verb *pounding*. Other things
can pound – such as the feet. Specifying the heart adds a welcome
clarity.

In principle, any nonfinite verb could be clarified in this way, but
we need to do so only when there is a genuine gain in meaning.
There would be little point in saying *mouth slavering with greed*.
As the mouth is the only part of the body which can slaver, we
hardly need to spell it out. We might do so only if we wanted to
add some extra information, such as an adjective:

the thick-lipped mouth slavering with greed

Novelists like the nonfinite clause with subject expressed, because
it allows a leisurely, impressionistic description to build up. Here is
Graham Greene, in *The Quiet American* (Chapter 3):

When my cup was empty they refilled it and continued their own
occupations: <u>a woman ironing</u>, <u>a girl sewing</u>, the two boys at
their lessons, <u>the old lady looking at her feet</u>, the tiny crippled
feet of old China – and <u>the dog watching the cat</u> ...

But it is not just a literary device. The need to clarify a nonfinite
clause prompts us quite often to specify the subject.

The best thing is to tell the truth.

The best thing is for me / you / John to tell the truth.

Verbless constructions

Verbless clauses are often discussed along with nonfinite clauses because they can make a sentence even more compressed.

When ready, Jane left the office.   She waved, **happy**

There are several types, but usually such clauses are adverbial (Chapter 65), the omitted verb is a form of *be*, and the omitted subject is the same as that of the finite clause.

A combined example

The three types of clause combine to generate a mood of understated menace in the opening of Mervyn Peake's *Gormenghast*. A single finite clause provides an identity. Nonfinite and verbless clauses then outline the character in a series of notelike observations.

Titus is seven. His confines, ⋏ Gormenghast. Sucked on shadows; weaned, as it were, on webs of ritual: for his ears, ⋏ echoes, for his eyes, ⋏ a labyrinth of stone: and yet within his body ⋏ something other – other than this umbrageous legacy. For first and ever foremost he is *child*.

The omitted elements (⋏) suggest a grudging, reluctant story-teller, and anticipate the hidden evil within the castle.

Caution

Beware nonfinite clauses where the subject cannot be identified in the accompanying finite clause, or where the relationship between the two clauses is ambiguous:

Reading the paper, the dog started howling.

Because we know that dogs cannot read, this sentence is not ambiguous, but we can be disturbed by the missing subject, and the potential absurdity is distracting. Usage books condemn such 'dangling participles'. They are especially misleading when there is real ambiguity:

Watching the television, the dog started howling.

There are two types of auxiliary verb:

- **Primary** auxiliaries *be, have*, and *do* have *-s* forms (*is, has, does*) and nonfinite forms (e.g. *to do, doing, done*: Chapter 17); they can also be used as main verbs.
- **Modal** auxiliaries have no *-s* or nonfinite forms, and cannot be used as main verbs:

  can/could   may/might   will/would   shall/should   must

Some auxiliaries have shortened (**contracted**) forms, as seen in *I am going* vs. *I'm going*:

  am > 'm   are > 're   is > 's   have > 've   has > 's
  had > 'd   will > 'll   would > 'd

All auxiliaries can be made negative, by adding a full or contracted form of *not* (*n't*):

  She could not go.   She couldn't go.

EXPLANATION

Auxiliary verbs specify the way their associated lexical verbs are to be interpreted, helping them convey several basic grammatical contrasts of meaning, such as time and number. English is (unlike Latin) not a language where the main verb can do this alone.

The only main-verb inflections (Chapter 16) are *-s* (marking the third person in the present tense), *-ed* (marking past tense and participle forms), and *-ing* (marking progressive aspect). For everything else, auxiliaries express, or help express, the meaning.

Auxiliary meanings

Person

Only two auxiliaries, *am* and *is*, are uniquely associated with

The verb phrase

person: first and third, respectively (Chapter 45):

ʌ am interested [omitted item must be *I*]

ʌ is in the garden [omitted item must be *he*, *she*, or *it*]

By contrast, *are*, *did*, and *have* could be any person – *we*, *you*, or *they*.

Number

If we use *am*, *is*, *was*, *has*, or *does*, we must have a single entity in mind – *I*, *he*, *she*, *it*. If we use *are*, *were*, *have*, *do*, we usually have more than one entity in mind – *we*, *they* (Chapter 43). The second person pronoun is ambiguous: in *you are going* it is impossible to say whether one or more persons is involved. English has largely lost the *thou* form which once distinguished singular and plural.

Time

Time contrasts are conveyed by the choice of *am*, *are*, *is*, and *does* for present tense and of *was*, *were*, and *did* for past tense (Chapter 23):

I am going / I was going   Do you see? / Did you see?

Aspect

Aspectual contrasts are conveyed by the use of *am*, *are*, *is*, *was*, and *were* for progressive meaning, and of *has*, *have*, and *had* for perfective meaning (Chapter 24):

I am going (vs. *I go*)   I have gone / I had gone

Judgement

Judgements about whether what we are saying is true are conveyed by the modals or similar verbs (Chapter 19):

I might / could / had rather / ought to see.

For the meanings of individual modals, see Chapter 26.

Auxiliaries are also used in the expression of questions, negation, emphasis, and voice (Chapters 5, 6 and 22).

Exploiting the expressiveness of auxiliaries

Using contractions

Contracted forms are a major feature of informal speech and writing, widely used in conversation, letter-writing, e-dialogues, fiction, advertising, and many genres of broadcasting. They are characteristic because they are so frequent. Virtually every time we use a finite verb, we open the door to the use of a contraction.

IN CONVERSATION

Their conversational frequency is chiefly due to the use of many short clauses (most of which contain a verb), and of many pronouns, which attract contracted forms much more than nouns do. The longer a noun phrase, indeed, the less likely a contraction:

He's eating. [extremely common]
The wolf's eating. [common]
The big bad wolf's eating. [less common]
The big bad wolf in the forest's eating. [most unlikely]

The nature of the genre is also a factor. In conversation, people argue and disagree a lot, and speed of speech generates contractions, as can be seen in any fast-moving play-script. Here are the protagonists having a meal in Alan Ayckbourn's *Table Manners* (Act 2):

ANNIE: Everyone finished. <u>I'll</u> get the rest.
SARAH: Tom <u>hasn't</u> quite finished.
TOM: All right, all right. <u>Don't</u> worry about me.
RUTH: Do you mean to say <u>there's</u> more?
ANNIE: Just some stew so called.
RUTH: Well, <u>I'll</u> try and squeeze it in.
ANNIE: Look, if you want to take over and try and do any better ...
RUTH: All right, sorry.
ANNIE: Sitting there on your backside complaining.
RUTH: <u>Who's</u> complaining? <u>It's</u> a feast.
SARAH [shrilly]: <u>Don't</u> <u>let's</u> quarrel, please.

When people report their thoughts, they usually do so in an informal style, often compressed or elliptical, which well suits the use of contracted forms. Here is Ralph Messenger recording his stream of consciousness into his tape-recorder, in David Lodge's *Thinks...* (Chapter 19):

> <u>It's</u> 5.30 on Friday 21st March and <u>I'm</u> in my office killing time till I meet Carrie at six for a quick bite in the Arts Centre Café before a concert <u>we're</u> going to ... Haydn and Mozart, I think ... Carrie booked the tickets ... a waste of time, really ... I like listening to music as background, while <u>I'm</u> doing something else, but not sitting in a concert hall ... After a few bars, <u>I'm</u> away, daydreaming, free-associating ...

Avoiding contractions

By contrast, we rarely find contractions in formal writing, especially when the subjects use long noun phrases. They are never used in institutional writing, such as the texts of law, religion, and parliament. Here is an item from *Butterworth's Insolvency Law Handbook* (§17, 1990):

> The administrator shall summon a meeting of the company's creditors if – (a) <u>he is</u> requested, in accordance with the rules, to do so by one-tenth, in value, of the company's creditors, or (b) <u>he is</u> directed to do so by the court.

The high level of formality of the discourse precludes the use of *he's*, in such circumstances.

And contractions are rare in academic prose, though authors do introduce them when they want to strike an informal note. You'll find a few in the present book. But there would be a noticeable shift in style if I were to start using them routinely. I'd not want to do that, I don't think, if it's to stay a serious book about grammar. A casual style too readily suggests a casual treatment.

Mixed styles

Many varieties contain a mixture of contracted and uncontracted forms, reflecting varying formality levels, a different subject-matter or attitude, or a concern to make a point in a contrastive way. A change of emphasis, for example, can produce sequences such as the following:

'Jill <u>wasn't</u> there.' Mike saw the disbelief in their faces. 'I tell you, she <u>was not</u> there!'

There is no single rule which covers all the articles in a newspaper, for example. We would not expect to find contractions in an article reporting past events, because most contracted forms relate to the present tense. However, the accompanying headline may well use a contraction, because it adds a colloquial impact (and also saves space):

HE'S NOT GOING   IT'S GOING TO BE HOT

A contraction is especially likely if the headline is a (real or supposed) quotation:

I'VE MESSED UP MY LIFE

On the whole, journalism – including tabloid journalism – avoids contractions, other than in reported conversations and quotations. Even in genres which do use the present tense, such as interviews, reviews, and editorials, they are little used – as in these extracts, where a contraction might easily have occurred at the underlined point:

Hello–I am Polly. I am a very clever but rather formal parrot. I do hope I am not getting on your nerves. Who is a pretty boy then? I expect you will be putting the cover on my cage soon....

Her career <u>has</u> gone from strength to strength.
She <u>is</u> currently filming in Monaco.
Beckham <u>is</u> likely to miss two matches.

The verb phrase

When we note a varying use of contractions, especially in writing, we should always look carefully at the context for factors which might explain the variation. If we can find none, we may have to conclude that the writer has been inconsistent. In some genres – such as writing an essay or a report – there is usually no reason to vary. Inconsistency then is a sign of a careless style.

Other kinds of variation

Reflecting region

Auxiliary usage varies to some extent between regional dialects, and thus acts as a marker of local identity. *Amn't I*, for example, is a usage in Ireland and Scotland. And several dialects in British and American English allow modals to co-occur, as in *they might could go*.

Reflecting period

Auxiliary usage changes over time. *Mayn't* is found only in older British fiction. *Shall* and *shan't* are uncommon today, especially in American English. Old inversions of *not* will be found in archaic styles (such as law and religion), in literature, and in modern jocular contexts. Here is a biblical and a Shakespearian example.

they know not what they do (Luke 23.34)
I know thee not, old man (*Henry V*, V.v.50)

Reflecting intention

Auxiliaries do not appear with equal frequency in all varieties. Academic prose, for example, is often tentative in its conclusions, so modals like *may*, *could*, and *should* are common. By contrast, in a political speech, we are more likely to hear *will*, *shall*, and *must*. No politician will rouse supporters with the slogan: *We may lower taxation*. Promises have to be *will*.

19 | Other verbs

DESCRIPTIVE SUMMARY

The distinction between main verb and auxiliary verb (Chapter 18) is not clear-cut. Several verbs fall between the two categories, not behaving exactly like either (**marginal auxiliaries**). For example, *dare* and *need* can act both as an auxiliary verb and as a main verb.

as auxiliary: She **needn't ask**.   We **daren't leave** now.
as main: She **won't dare**.   They **will need** tickets.

The other verbs which have intermediate auxiliary status are the following. Each can be used in the frame: *I ... go.*

used to, ought to, had better/best, had/would rather, have got to, have to, be to

There is also a series of *be ... to* constructions, such as:

be going to, be about to, be ready to

The *be* verb varies in the usual way: *am going to, is about to,* etc.

Somewhat different are the many lexical verbs which can act as **catenatives** – so called because they can appear in a 'chain' (catenated) – such as *try to, seem to,* and *happen to*. Grammars differ greatly about the best way of analysing them:

I avoided the issue.   I tried to avoid the issue.
I didn't want to appear to be trying to avoid the issue.

EXPLANATION

Each of the above verbs has individual grammatical properties; but from semantic and pragmatic points of view, their functions are similar to auxiliaries, expressing modal meanings or (as with *used to* and the *be to* constructions) aspect or time (Chapter 18).

Reflecting formality

Several of these verbs are markers of informality, and are thus common in conversation and rare in formal writing. Some have even developed special informal spellings:

got to → gotta   going to → gonna   have to → hafta

Had better/rather allow two stages of informality:

I had better go → I'd better go → I better go

On the other hand, some verbs can be rather formal:

The opening is to take place at three.

Used she to travel by bus? [increasingly uncommon]

Reflecting regional or social background

There are several variations in usage around the English-speaking world. For example, *had better* and *have got* are much more common in British English; *have to* and *going to* are more common in American English. *Ought we to go?* is British; *Ought we go?* is American, though increasing in the UK. *We didn't ought to go* is considered nonstandard.

The social constraints on these verbs are quite often alluded to in fiction. For example, in Charles Dickens' *Great Expectations* (Chapter 35), the newly genteel Pip visits his old home and picks Biddy up for calling him 'Mr Pip':

'Biddy,' said I, in a virtuously self-asserting manner, 'I must request to know what you mean by this?'

'By this?' said Biddy.

'No, don't echo,' I retorted. 'You **used not** to echo, Biddy.'

'**Used not**!' said Biddy. 'O Mr Pip! **Used**!'

Biddy is evidently shocked to hear such a refined usage coming out of the mouth of someone who, earlier, would have said *You did not use to echo*.

There has long been uncertainty over how to spell *used* in negative clauses: *usedn't* (vs. *usen't*) and in *I didn't use(d) to go*. The items in parentheses are often criticized.

Multi-word verbs are lexical verbs which consist of more than one word. The commonest kind consists of a verb plus one or more particles (prepositions or adverbs), and there are also some idiomatic constructions:

come on   shut up   go on   talk about   come up with
get rid of   make do with   get going   send packing

There are three types of verb + particle construction:

- **prepositional verbs** have a preposition as the particle, such as *at*, *for*, and *from*
- **phrasal verbs** have an adverb as the particle, such as *aside*, *away*, and *back*
- **phrasal-prepositional verbs** have one of each, such as *do away with* or *look forward to*

Sometimes the same word can be either a preposition or an adverb, distinguished only by their grammatical behaviour. For example, *call on* can mean either 'visit' or 'invite to be present'. The former is a prepositional use, requiring the particle to stay with the verb; the latter is an adverb use, allowing separation:

I called on my friends [I visited my friends]
I called my friends on [I invited them to be with me on stage]

EXPLANATION

These types do not behave in the same grammatical way, but their use reflects the same semantic and pragmatic factors.

Formality contrasts

Most multi-word verbs are informal in tone – often extremely so. They use some of the language's most frequent verbs (notably *take*, *get*, *come*, *put*, and *go*) and particles (notably *up*, *out*, *on*, *in, off,* and *down*). The colloquial tone is most noticeable with directives (Chapter 6):

come on   shut up   hold on   fuck off   go ahead

They are an important feature of conversation and fiction, therefore, and unusual in formal writing unless used with an appropriately 'intellectual' verb:

point out   apply to   depend on   refer to

Combinations of a multi-word verb and modal are very typical of academic style:

may be used as   can be derived from   should result in

The contrast in formality is most evident when a multi-word verb is replaced by a single-word synonym:

carry out ~ undertake   look at ~ observe
find out ~ discover   ask for ~ request

The two versions never convey *exactly* the same meaning, but the more formal variant is the one usually recommended for writing where an author wants to convey an impression of precision or to avoid a colloquial tone. And avoiding an end-placed particle in formal usage is a stylistic recommendation several hundred years old (p.296):

That's the film I was referring to.

That is the film to which I was referring.

Exploiting multi-word verbs

The multiple usage of these verbs makes them an ideal source of humour. Fritz Spiegl exploits their properties while reminiscing in *The Joy of Words* (Part 1):

We hoped that getting on with a girl might lead to getting off with her (i.e. from hitting it off to having it off) unless, of course, she told one where to get off. Though again, you might invite a bus-conductress to tell you where to get off.

DESCRIPTIVE SUMMARY

Finite verb phrases (Chapter 17) can be grouped into three broad types, called **moods**, identified by the verb forms used:

- The **indicative** is normal in statements and questions:
  I'm downstairs.   Mary was outside.   Where's Joe?

- The **imperative** is used only in directive utterances (Chapter 6):
  Ask me a question.   Don't forget your book.

- The **subjunctive** has a very limited use. It is found:
  - in the present: the base form of the verb (Chapter 16) replaces -s in the third-person singular:
    I suggest that John **write** to the mayor.
  - in the past: *were* replaces *was* in the first- and third-person singular of the past tense of *be*:
    If I **were** you ...   I wish she **were** here.
  - in some fixed expressions, with a formulaic tone:
    Heaven **forbid** you should leave.   **Be** it noted ...
    Adding an -s can change the meaning significantly:
    Heaven forbids you should leave.
    This is now something Heaven has actually done.

EXPLANATION

A mood is a state of mind. To know a person's mood is to know how that person is currently looking at the world. It is the same with language. To know the mood of a clause is to know something about how that clause is talking about the world.

The three moods convey different kinds of meaning, but only the first two are routinely used in Modern English.

- the indicative, for stating ('indicating') or questioning matters of a factual kind (Chapter 5)
- the imperative, for clauses which tell or urge (Chapter 6)
- the subjunctive, to express nonfactual situations, such as hypothetical events, wishes, and conditions.

Using the subjunctive

The name *subjunctive* reflects an old view in traditional grammar that nonfactual meanings occur in subordinate clauses (Chapter 65) – that is, in clauses 'subjoined' to a main clause. And indeed, most subjunctives do occur in such clauses, introduced by a conjunction expressing condition or purpose – such as *lest, if, whether, unless, so that,* or *in case.*

Money is like muck, not good **except** it **be** spread.
(Francis Bacon, 1625)
The committee does not mind **if** the request **go** today or next week.

Lest is the most formal of these conjunctions in British English (it is commoner in American English), and is almost always followed by a subjunctive:

Let us not write **lest** our letter **be** misunderstood.

Using the present subjunctive

IN MANDATING

This subjunctive is often called the **mandative**, because it is used to express various kinds of demand, with such verbs as *request, propose, vote, pledge,* and *insist.*

I request there be no delay in processing the form.

We have voted that the team manager resign.

Sentences of this kind are quite widely used in American English. However, they convey a very formal or legalistic tone in British English, which prefers a *should* construction or avoids the subjunctive altogether, replacing it by the indicative:

We have voted that the team manager should resign.

We have voted that the team manager resigns.

IN EMPHASIZING

Academic writing also makes use of this type of subjunctive when stressing the importance of an action, after adjectives, nouns, or verbs:

It is critical that the temperature be maintained.

The advice is that the temperature be maintained.

The manual insists that the temperature be maintained.

This usage is also heard in speech expressing urgency:

It's crucial that Bond get to the island by six o'clock.

And also in aphorisms:

The first requirement of a statesman is that he be dull.

(Dean Acheson, 1970)

Here too, British English prefers a *should* construction.

For some time, the British trend has been a steady reduction in subjunctive use. However, exposure to the American preference during the twentieth century has led to a noticeable increase in subjunctive usage in *that-* clauses, especially in contexts which suggest that the agent in the subordinate clause is willing to perform the action.

I recommend that she reapply for the job.

Using the past subjunctive

The past-tense subjunctive (or **were- subjunctive**) is used to express an unreal or hypothetical meaning:

I wish he were here.   If Jane were leader ...
Suppose he were lost ...   If only I weren't so hungry.

An equivalent use of *was* is heard in informal speech:

I wish he was here.   If Jane was leader ...

These forms routinely attract criticism when used in writing, unless the text is consciously informal.

Because of this criticism, some people are sensitive about the use of *was*, and avoid it even in contexts where it would be acceptable:

From where Mary was sitting, she couldn't see if John were for or against the motion.

It is a fact that John voted one way or the other, so the indicative mood would be appropriate here. However, an extra tentativeness can be introduced by the use of *were*:

John asked if the king was dead.
John asked if the king were dead.

The latter version suggests a greater uncertainty on John's part, or perhaps a more cautious politeness.

Using the formulaic subjunctive

Formulaic subjunctives are set expressions which tend to be used as minor sentences (Chapter 2). They are always formal, and usually ceremonial:

Long live the Queen!   God be praised!

Formulaic subjunctives may also be used as part of a longer discourse, expressing a will that something should happen, similar in force to *let* or *may*. The effect is always archaic:

Be it known to all here present ...

A few are heard in conversation as rather stiff idioms:

Come what may ...   Suffice it to say ...   So be it.
As it were.   If need be.   Far be it from me ...

22 Active and passive

The action expressed by the clause can be viewed in either of two ways:

The critics praised the film.

or: The film was praised by the critics.

Jane could hear a noise.

or: A noise could be heard by Jane.

This kind of contrast is referred to as **voice**. The first type of construction is called the **active** voice. The second is called the **passive** voice. The being that performs or experiences the action is usually called the **agent** – *the critics* and *Jane,* in these examples. Most transitive verbs (Chapter 8) can appear as either active or passive.

EXPLANATION

This is actually a rather unusual type of grammatical relationship, because it expresses no difference in meaning. So why do we have the distinction at all? What is the point of saying the same thing in two ways?

There are both semantic and pragmatic answers:

• We can do things to passive clauses that we can't do to active ones, and this allows us to express some important nuances of meaning. In particular, we can leave out the agent.

• We use the distinction between active and passive in order to convey important effects of tone and style.

The verb phrase

Leaving out the agent

The clauses illustrated above each contain an agent. And the biggest difference between active and passive is that we can omit the agent in the latter, but not in the former. We cannot say, as a self-contained unit:

~~Praised the film.~~   ~~Could hear a noise.~~

but we can say:

The film was praised.   A noise could be heard.

By omitting the agent phrase, we turn a 'long passive' into a 'short passive'.

Why would we ever want to omit the agent? There are a number of circumstances.

- We omit the agent if we do not want to identify the performer of the action (and especially if we don't want to draw attention to ourselves):

    Teacher: What was that noise?
    Pupil: The window's been smashed, sir.

  Or in such contexts as these:

    The catalogue has to be checked.
    The organist needs to be asked to stand down.

  Tactful suggestions that someone else might do the job?

- We omit the agent if there is no need to identify the performer of the action, because it is obvious from the context. We say:

    Bob played Jim today, and Jim was beaten.

  and not

    ~~Bob played Jim today, and Jim was beaten by Bob.~~

  Similarly, we say:

    We're getting the house painted.
    Smith was acquitted.
    Mary's had her hair done.

  We don't need to say 'by a painting firm', 'by a judge and jury', or 'by a hairdresser', and it can sound odd if we do:

    Mary's had her hair done by a hairdresser.

  Does she normally have it done by someone who isn't?

- We omit the agent if we have no choice in the matter, either because we do not know the performer of the action, or because it is impossible to say who or what it is:

  Order is being restored in the capital.
  No trace has been found of the runaways.
  Three killed in motorway pile-up.
  Our house was built in the 1930s.
  The pictures have been stolen.

  Who is restoring order? Who hasn't found the runaways? Who killed, built, and stole? We may never know.

  In such circumstances, it is actually quite difficult to find an active clause that corresponds to the passive. If we try answering the question 'Who or what did it?' we end up being uncertain or very vague:

  Who restored order in the capital? [The government? the president? the army? the police? all of them?]
  What killed the people in the motorway accident? [A lorry? Several vehicles? Fog? Fatigue? Carelessness?]

- We omit the agent if we want to generalize. Consider this example:

  Our car can't be driven by young Mary.

  Presumably she isn't old enough, or isn't insured. But if we omit the agent, the clause gives a general prohibition:

  Our car can't be driven.

  Now there must be something seriously wrong with it.

  There are many situations where we do not want to refer to the performer of the action, because it would particularize the meaning too much. If we were reading a science report, we might well expect to see this:

  Water was added to the powder and the resulting mixture poured into a test-tube.

  but not this:

  Water was added to the powder by Fred and the resulting mixture poured into a test-tube by Mary.

  Why not?

In a scientific experiment, who actually does the mixing and pouring is irrelevant. Science deals with methods and results which aim to be as general as possible, and any specifying of agents reduces this generality. The same chemical reaction would take place whoever added water to the powder or poured the mixture into the test-tube. That is why scientists make so much use of the passive: the construction enables them to focus attention on events without having to say who caused them.

It is not only scientific discourse. Passives are frequently used in all kinds of academic discourse – not all the time, of course, because many verbs do not allow the passive, and some writers try to avoid it (p.149). In fact, only about 25 per cent of the verbs in an academic account will be in the passive. But this is enough to provide the impression of detached objectivity which has long been fostered as a desirable feature of Western academic enquiry.

Caution

The agent phrase always refers to the entity that performs or experiences the action, and it always begins with *by*. Beware other phrases which also begin with *by*, but which express different meanings. For example, there are time phrases, answering the question 'When?':

Jean needs to finish this report by six o'clock.

Means phrases answer the question 'How?':

Jack can find the number by asking Mary.

If these are used in passive clauses, they look very like agents – but their meaning is quite different:

This report needs to be finished by six o'clock.

The number can be found by asking Mary.

What are the effects of using the passive?

Both in speech and writing, passives always convey a formal tone, compared with their active counterparts. But they often convey other effects as well.

Giving a scholarly impression

In academic discourse, short passives tend to occur in clusters, producing a uniformity of style which is often succinct and elegant in its rhythmical parallelism.

- When the jug is **emptied**, it should be **cleaned** and **disinfected**, so that it can be **used** again.
- During the next century, older monasteries were **refounded**, new abbots **appointed**, monastic rules revised, and fresh translations of the Bible **initiated**.

It is the cumulative effect of a series of passives which produces the impression of a consistent, impersonal style. It is incongruous when a personal tone is added to such a text, by switching to an active after several passives:

When the jug is emptied, it should be cleaned and disinfected, so that we can all use it again.

We probably wouldn't notice the switch in a spoken commentary, but it can be stylistically disturbing in a written text.

Of course, a balanced alternation between active and passive permits a variety of expression which many writers employ. Two-part sentences often do this:

We must disinfect the jug before it is stored away.

The jug must be disinfected before we store it away.

But if there is erratic switching between active and passive in a long sentence, the varying perspectives can cause a text to lose its flow and reduce its coherence:

During the next century, older monasteries were refounded, they appointed new abbots, monastic rules revised, and people initiated several new translations of the Bible.

Adding a tone of authority

The association of the passive with an impersonal, scientific style means that it can be used to convey a sense of authority in any setting. A television advertisement, for example, can be given extra gravitas by the use of the occasional passive:

You can remove stains more efficiently with Blotto.
Stains can be removed more efficiently with Blotto.

The latter, very likely, would be said in a much more assertive tone of voice. And in this recipe, the writer switched from active to passive to introduce a note of caution:

Use raw in salads or soften the leaves in butter or margarine.
Sorrel has a distinctive acidic flavour and should not be used alone in salad.

Avoiding a personal tone

The passive allows us to avoid being personal when we do not want to be. Officials who send letters to members of the public have a choice to make. In a letter explaining the failure of a cheque to arrive, the writer has various options, such as:

The delay is regretted.
The company regrets the delay.
We regret the delay.
I regret the delay.

Some organizations pride themselves on a personal style. At the same time, people have to be careful. The 'active' style could lay the writer open to a charge of admitting personal liability. You can't get sued for a passive.

Many official or instructional texts use passives to avoid a personal tone. Sentences can sound more professional, judicious, unemotional, routine:

The lid should be fixed to the frame with the three screws provided.
Tax allowances may be claimed as follows ...

Reporting an event succinctly

Short passives are very common in newspaper headlines, where their brevity suits the need for immediate impact. Often, the writer has no choice but to use a passive because the identity of the agent is not known. And even if the agent *is* known, the headline can still act as a 'teaser', tempting you to read on – or, in a news vendor's poster, to buy the paper.

£1M STOLEN	**300 KILLED**	**ENGLAND CAPTAIN STUNNED**

Short passives are also common in news articles and broadcasts, because they allow reporters to avoid repeating themselves or stating the obvious. They keep the focus on the information that listeners and readers really want to know about.

> The file on Michael Barnaj was finally closed today, when he was sent to prison for four years. He had been arrested in his flat following a surveillance operation planned over several weeks.

It is hardly important to spell out the agents in such a story. Everyone knows who it is that plans, arrests, and sends to prison. We are unlikely to encounter a wordy news report like the following:

> The file on Michael Barnaj was finally closed by the metropolitan police today, when he was sent to prison by a judge and jury for four years. He had been arrested by the metropolitan police in his apartment following a surveillance operation planned by the metropolitan police over several weeks.

Apart from the boredom factor, spelling out the agents makes the text 25 per cent longer.

Why use long passives?

This chapter has focused on short passives, because they are the common ones (comprising about 80 per cent of all passives). Long passives – those which express the agent – are sporadic. We don't find clusters of long passives.

Why use them at all? If we want to talk about an agent, the active voice seems the most natural way of doing it in English – first we report who the agent is, then the action, and then who or what is affected by the action. This is how it is in conversation, where only two per cent of the verbs are passives. That ought not to be surprising. Human curiosity rules, in daily chat, and the identity of who or what we are talking about is a major concern. So passives have little role to play.

The reasons for using long passives are different from those governing the use of short passives. We are no longer trying to be impersonal or succinct. Because long passives express the agent, they are just as personal and lengthy as their active counterparts.
- John Smith has given a prize to the raffle.
- A prize has been given to the raffle by John Smith.
The latter is simply more formal in tone.

So what are long passives for? The answer is all to do with the distribution of weight in a clause. The principle of **end-weight** is a 'natural' feature of English (p.344): a clause where most of the information occurs after the main verb is much easier to follow than one where most comes before:
- It was good that John managed to answer all the questions before the bell rang.
- That John managed to answer all the questions before the bell rang was good.
The latter feels cumbersome and rhythmically awkward. The passive follows this principle.

Long passives keep the weight right

If an agent gets very lengthy, or if several agents need to be mentioned at the same time, there can be an indigestible piling up of information at the front of the active clause, before the main verb (shown here in bold):

A combination of cheap imports, a strong pound, and a policy of extra investment in small businesses **has influenced** the price.

The passive version locates the lengthy agent after the verb, and is much more comfortable to assimilate.

The price **has been influenced** by a combination of cheap imports, a strong pound, and a policy of extra investment in small businesses.

A common writing weakness puts too much information before a main verb. The long passive avoids this problem.

However, if we use a long passive, we must make sure that we use the agent properly. That is the place where we express any 'new information' we have in mind. We can report an event using two active clauses, like this:

The prime minister and the foreign secretary are in town today. They will be giving speeches on Europe.

But if we want to make the second clause passive, we can't do it like this:

The prime minister and the foreign secretary are in town today. Speeches on Europe will be given by them.

That sounds very awkward. However, if we expand the agent, the sentence suddenly sounds much better.

The prime minister is in town today. Speeches on Europe will be given by him and by the local MP.

This is because we associate the agent with giving fresh information, and we do not like it when the agent is made to appear uninteresting, compared to the subject. 'Speeches on Europe' is fresh information; 'by them' is not. If we use a long passive, we need to keep the agent at least equal in interest to the subject, and full of extra interest if possible.

The verb phrase

Using the passive

Not everyone likes the passive. Some writers, such as George Orwell, have condemned it out of hand, saying that it should never be used when an active counterpart is possible. Such critics want to see writing in English take on a more personal and direct character. They have called passives bland, distant, boring, difficult – even dishonest (in that personal feelings are hidden). And certainly, there is a much greater personal engagement and sense of excitement in the first of these two clauses:

We discovered paintings on the walls of the cave.

Paintings were discovered on the walls of the cave.

But the whole point of the passive is that it allows us a choice. If we *want* to sound impersonal, academic, or authoritative, then English gives us a way of being so.

The passive must be avoided at all costs.

said someone once, using the passive to make the point as forcefully as possible. All the alternatives were weaker:

You must avoid ... (not the writer?)

We must avoid ... (who is 'we'?)

Writers must avoid ... (not speakers?)

I recommend avoiding ... (other people don't?)

The passive sidesteps all these unwanted implications.

The choice between personal and impersonal is always with us. Both contribute to a mature style. But we must be careful to make our choices in a consistent way. What is wrong with this sentence?

The play was found to be absolutely wonderful.

The emotive adjective jars alongside the impersonal verb phrase. And which of these two signs are we likely to see outside a military establishment?

Access is prohibited.   We prohibit access.

The inclusive warmth of *we* would be unusual, to say the least, in a situation of cold dismissal.

DESCRIPTIVE SUMMARY

The term **tense** traditionally refers to the way a verb changes its endings to express the time at which an action takes place. On this basis, English has only two tenses, present and past. Other temporal meanings are conveyed through auxiliary verbs, as part of the systems of aspect (Chapter 24) and mood (Chapter 21).

- The **present** tense occurs in two forms:
  - the *simple present* uses the base form of the verb, with an *-s* ending for the third-person singular:
    I/you/we/they run   he/she/it runs
  - the *progressive present* uses the present tense of *be* with the *-ing* form of the verb:
    I am ... you/we/they are ... he/she/it is running

- The **past** tense also occurs in two forms:
  - the regular *simple past* adds *-ed* to the base form; there are several irregular verbs (Chapter 16):
    I climbed   I asked   I ran   I went
  - the *progressive past* uses the past tense of *be* with the *-ing* form of the verb:
    I was ...   you/we/they were ...   he/she/it was going

EXPLANATION

The purpose of tense is to express the time at which an action or state occurs. The present tense, as its name suggests, often refers to present time; similarly, the past tense often refers to past time. But there are also many cases where this simple relationship does not obtain.

The meanings of the present tense

Referring to present time

EVENTS TAKING PLACE RIGHT NOW

The present tense can refer to an action or state of affairs which begins and ends roughly at the moment of speaking (the **instantaneous present**). It is the obvious choice if we want to say we have noticed something, or to convey the mood of the moment:

Here comes the bus.   There you go again.

[knocking on a door] I want to see Mary.

I think so.

This is the way we keep up with the activity taking place in demonstrations and commentaries:

I pour in some milk and add two eggs ...

Jones passes to Smith ... and he heads it high into the penalty area where Griggs is ready ....

The ship is slowly moving alongside the dock where a large crowd is waiting ...

With certain verbs ('performatives'), the utterance in the present tense actually carries out the action:

I apologize.   I resign.   I name this ship Rosie.

EVENTS TAKING PLACE ON EITHER SIDE OF NOW

The present tense can refer to an action or state of affairs which lasts on either side of the moment of speaking (the **state present**). The time-span might be quite short, or it could last for days or months – or a lifetime.

Fred is 42 years old.

Mary lives in France.

Mr Smith speaks French and German.

Many news headlines express this meaning:

Forest fires spread in France

Politicians fear backlash over taxes

Events which last for ever are sometimes distinguished as a separate 'timeless' category (see p.152).

Events taking place routinely

The present tense can also refer to an action which takes place regularly or routinely (the **habitual present**). This is similar to the state present, but here we intend the activity to be seen as a series of repeated events rather than as a single, on-going state.

    I eat eggs.
    John travels to work by bus.

I eat eggs might be a vegetarian's answer to the question, 'What can you eat?' It does not mean that the speaker eats eggs continuously – just at mealtimes. We often need to add an adverbial of frequency (p.278) to make the time reference clear, such as *every day* or *on Fridays*.

Events which are 'timeless'

The present tense can refer to actions or states which have no specific time reference (the **timeless present**). These situations include:

- The universal truths found in scientific statements:
    Water consists of hydrogen and oxygen.
    The planets move round the sun.
- Mathematical generalizations:
    Two and two are four. $x + y - z = 0$ [equals]
- Geographical descriptions:
    The Amazon rises in the Andes.
- Proverbial utterances:
    Honesty is the best policy.
- Expository statements:
    This example shows three things.
- Stage directions:
    Paul leaves the room.
- Synopses, reviews, blurbs, abstracts:
    The film is set in Vienna in the 1940s.
    'Living On' is a play about language death.
    This book offers the reader advice and support.
    We show that the flow of oxygen is the main factor.

The verb phrase

The man is expressing a timeless or state present; the woman interprets it as a habitual or instantaneous one (pp.151–2).

Referring to future time

The present tense can refer to future time in several situations. These include:

SCHEDULING
With a future time adverbial, we can use the present tense to refer to an action which has yet to begin:

We leave tomorrow.   I'm travelling next week.

We are suggesting that an event is as certain as it would be, were it taking place in the present.

MAKING CROSS-REFERENCES
Authors can use the present tense to make a reference to later parts of their book, when they want to stress the current relevance of the subject-matter:

In the next chapter we discuss the results of the war.

To say *will discuss* distances the topic somewhat.

NEWS REPORTING
News reports use the present tense to make an event seem as if it is taking place very soon:

A new era in computing begins on Monday ...

Next month sees the start of the Grand Prix season.

Referring to past time

We can use the present tense to describe an event in the past as if it were happening now (the **historic present**). These situations include:

STORY-TELLING
The present tense adds a dramatic 'eye-witness' effect to conversational narratives, such as joke- or story-telling:

This chap goes into a shop and asks for a chicken. ...
I'm standing outside Smith's last Thursday and I see ...

NEWSPAPER HEADLINES
Many headlines refer to an event which has happened in the very recent past – usually the day before the paper appears – and which does not carry on into the future (unlike the state present, p.151):

SPORTS STAR DIES   PARTY ELECTS SMITH

A similar usage is found in photographic captions:

Crowds queue before the opening of the sales.

HISTORICAL SUMMARIES
Chronologies of events regularly use the present tense:

1997 Tony Blair becomes prime minister

RECEIVING NEWS
Verbs like *hear*, *see*, *learn*, and *understand* are often used in the present tense to report the reception of news.

I hear that three cars were involved in the accident.
The weather forecast says that it's going to rain.

This does not mean that the speaker is in the process of hearing the news. The hearing has taken place some time before. The speaker could have used *heard* or *said*, but the present tense suggests that the impact of the news is still having an effect on the speaker.

This is an important use when we want to convey the impression that a past event is of real contemporary relevance:

The Bible tells us that we should ...
The 1944 Education Act reminds us that ...

The meanings of the past tense

Referring to past time

Most uses of the past tense refer to an action or state which has taken place in the past, with a gap between its completion and the present moment. The speaker has a definite time in mind, and this is often made explicit by an accompanying time adverbial.

This usage is the conventional point of reference for any narrative, whether a brief conversational exchange or an extended monologue.
* A: I met Steve at the theatre last night. B: Did you?
* I was walking down the high street yesterday, and I saw this chicken in the middle of the road. ...

It is the expected starting-point in fiction:
In the latter days of July in the year 185—, a most important question was for ten days hourly asked in the cathedral city of Barchester, and answered every hour in various ways — Who was to be the new Bishop? (Anthony Trollope, *Barchester Towers*)

As with the present tense, the events can refer to a single event, a period, or a habitual act:
The volcano erupted in 1600.
They practised a primitive form of medicine.
The Olympic Games were held in Ancient Greece.

Referring to present or future time

To express tentativeness
With verbs expressing a mental state, such as *wonder* and *want*, the past tense can convey a tentative state of mind currently held by the speaker (the **attitudinal past**). It is a usage which conveys a more polite tone than would be achieved by using the present tense. Compare these pairs of sentences:
Did you want to come in? Do you want to come in?
I was hoping you'd visit. I hope you'll visit.

To express something indirectly

A verb of 'saying' in the past tense allows the verb in the subordinate clause to be past tense as well, even though it refers to present time. This is an example of indirect speech (Chapter 69). If Mary asks Mike:

Did you say that you had a ticket?

she is politely checking whether Mike has the ticket now. If she had used direct speech, the underlying present time reference immediately appears:

Do you have a ticket?

To express a cancelled arrangement

The past progressive can be used to refer to an activity scheduled in the future but which is no longer happening. The sentence needs an appropriate future adverbial to make the time reference clear:

I was leaving tomorrow, but I'm not now.

This usage is regularly heard in news reporting:

The meeting was due to take place in Paris next week.

In speech, a doubtful intonation pattern (usually a falling–rising tone) on the verb conveys the same effect:

Well ... I **was** hoping to see you.

To express a hypothesis

The past tense can be used to express a view that is contrary to what the speaker believes or expects (the **hypothetical past**):

I wish I had a new car.

The use of the past tense does not mean that the speaker has got a new car; that would be *I had a new car*. On the contrary, the speaker does *not* have the car, but hopes to have one in the future. Similarly:

It's time we rested. [i.e. we haven't rested yet]

If we ran fast, we might catch the train. [i.e. we haven't run fast yet, and we might not bother]

The last example contrasts with the present tense, where the speaker *does* expect everyone to start running:

If we run fast, we might catch the train.

Contrasting present and past

Literary story-telling routinely uses the past tense, but sometimes a whole novel can be given a present-tense time frame. Here is an extract from Chapter 1 of Peter Cheyney's *Dames Don't Care*. The narrator is the detective, Lemmy Caution:

> I go in the front door. The place is built Mexican fashion, an' there is a sorta passage with a curtain at the end. The guitar playin' is comin' from the other side of the curtain. I string along the passage an' pull the curtain an' lamp in.
>
> I am surprised. The place is sweller than I thought. It is a big adobe walled room with a wooden floor. Dead opposite me is a bar and by the side of the bar is a flight of stone steps leadin' up the wall ...

It is as if we are looking over the writer's shoulder, or watching a film of the events unfolding.

The only time the author regularly uses the past tense is when his characters need to talk about past events. This produces sequences such as the following:

> 'An' what did you say?' he asks me.
> 'I asked you how you was, sissy,' I tell him.

Otherwise Lemmy Caution uses a past tense only when he is thinking back to something that happened earlier in the novel, in the manner of a film flashback. But such moments pass quickly, and the present tense resumes:

> I told you that I sent a wire to the New York 'G' Office before I went inta Mexico. ... Well, here is the reply.

The unusual use of the past tense in the closing lines of the novel provides an effective closure, as if a line is being drawn at the end of the story.

> I look at her again an' I start thinkin' of my old mother. Ma Caution usta tell me when I was a kid that I always put food before everything.
> An' for once Ma Caution was wrong.

DESCRIPTIVE SUMMARY

Aspect refers to how the time of an action or state is regarded or experienced with respect to time. English has two aspectual contrasts: perfective and progressive:

- the present and past **perfective** aspects use forms of auxiliary *have*, and contrast with past tense (p.150):

    I **have been living** in Paris for a year [and still do]

    I **was living** in Paris for a year [but now I don't]

    I didn't know that Jane **had been living** in Paris while I was there

- the present and past **progressive** (or **continuous**) aspects use forms of auxiliary *be* along with the -*ing* form of the main verb. Nonprogressive forms are known as **simple** forms.

    I **am living** vs. I live

    I **was living** vs. I lived

    I have **been living** vs. I have lived

    I had **been living** vs. I had lived

EXPLANATION

Aspect allows us to see the time of an action or state from within two perspectives:

- With the perfective we see a period leading up to a known time in the present or past.
- With the progressive we see an on-going event at a known time, present or past.

Neither of these forms is very common (they occur in less than 10 per cent of clauses), but when they do occur, they make available some important differences of meaning.

The verb phrase

The meanings of the perfective

Present perfective

This form relates a past action or state to an orientation in present time.

John's broken his arm. [so he can't take part]

I've closed the door. [so now we can talk privately]

The distinction between this form and the past tense can be seen in these sentences:

Have you seen *Hamlet* at the Globe? [it's still on]

Did you see *Hamlet* at the Globe? [it's no longer on]

Sometimes the contrast is quite subtle, but there is always a difference of perspective:

Where have I put that book?

Where did I put that book?

The first version is more urgent and relevant to present concerns; the second is somewhat more distant and casual. We might follow up the first sentence with 'I need it right now' – the second with a more tentative 'Do you happen to remember?'

Past perfective

This form relates an earlier past action or state to a later-occurring past time – a meaning sometimes described as 'past within the past'. It often appears in a subordinate adverbial clause (Chapter 65):

Jo didn't go out, because she **had hurt** her foot.

When everyone **had eaten**, the speeches began.

The hurting and the eating took place before the going and the speaking.

A time adverbial can also be used to specify the previous time orientation:

We got to the restaurant just after twelve. I'**d already booked** a table, so we went straight in.

Several words and phrases are available for this purpose, such as *previously*, *earlier*, and *some time before*.

Using the perfective

Because the perfective enables us to draw a fairly subtle distinction between the time and duration of events, it is likely to be common only in those situations where time factors play a central role.

News reporting

The primary thrust of news reporting is to tell us about recent happenings. We might therefore expect the present perfective to be widely used, and so it is:

The Bank of England has announced a cut in interest rates.
Eight people have won this week's lottery.

Even the past perfective has its place, when two time perspectives are being reported:

At three o'clock the judge **began** his summing up. He **had earlier told** the jury to pay no attention to reports in the press ...

Academic discussion

In intellectual writing, the continuing validity of an earlier finding or conclusion is regularly affirmed using the perfective:

As we **have seen**, three factors were involved.
We **have shown** that formula A cannot be correct.
Smith *et al* (1996) **had claimed** to find oxygen, but later findings by Brown showed serious errors in their methodology.

Conversational remoteness

A 'double' use of the perfective seems to be on the increase in informal speech, emphasizing the perceived remoteness of an event:

If it had've fallen on the floor, I would've found it.
I wish they hadn't've done it.

This is not acceptable in Standard English, which prefers *If it had fallen ...* and *... they hadn't done it.* The *'ve* is often spelled *of*, in informal writing.

The verb phrase

In fiction

Subtle changes of temporal perspective within a plot are the stuff of sophisticated fiction. For example, an alternation between present tense and present perfective is likely to be a dominant feature of any journal-narrative framed in the present tense. Here is the opening of Day 51 of William Golding's *Rites of Passage*:

> This is the fifty-first day of our voyage, I <u>think</u>, and then again perhaps it is not. I <u>have lost</u> interest in the calendar and almost lost it in the voyage too.

A four-way movement from perfect to past to present to future opens a later section:

> What a day this <u>has been</u>. I <u>commenced</u> it with some cheerfulness and I <u>end</u> it with – but you <u>will wish</u> to know all!

Such intricate time-shifts are difficult to manage successfully; they demonstrate a confident, mature style.

When a story is framed in the past tense, character description is often handled by alternating past tense and past perfective. At the start of Jane Austen's *Emma*, the past tense (in bold) gives Emma a core identity; the past perfective (underlined) adds biographical background.

> Emma Woodhouse, handsome, clever, and rich, with a comfortable home and happy disposition, **seemed** to unite some of the best blessings of existence; and <u>had lived</u> nearly twenty-one years in the world with very little to distress or vex her.
>
> She **was** the youngest of the two daughters of a most affectionate, indulgent father; and <u>had</u>, in consequence of her sister's marriage, <u>been</u> mistress of his house from a very early period. Her mother <u>had died</u> too long ago for her to have more than an indistinct remembrance of her caresses; and her place <u>had been supplied</u> by an excellent woman as governess, who <u>had fallen</u> little short of a mother in affection.

The meanings of the progressive

The progressive, present or past, has three main strands of meaning: it emphasizes the duration of an action, its temporary character, and the fact that it may still be going on at the time of speaking. All three are in Samuel Beckett's famous line:

We're waiting for Godot.

And this is how the form is most commonly used.

The policeman is waving us on.   It's raining.

I was travelling when I heard the news.

The chief contrast is between progressive and simple forms.

A COMPLETE VS. AN INCOMPLETE EVENT

The simple form can present an event as a completed whole; the progressive as an event which is still on-going:

I read *Hamlet* last night. [I read the whole play]

I was reading *Hamlet* last night. [I may not have finished it]

A GENERAL VS. A PARTICULAR EVENT

In the present tense, the simple form can express a generalization; the progressive shrinks the time-frame, so that it focuses on a particular time of action:

Eve plays the piano well. [she is a good player]

Eve is playing the piano well. [on a given occasion]

A WHOLE EVENT VS. A POINT WITHIN

In the past tense, the simple form suggests a whole event; the progressive focuses on its internal time-structure:

Eve played the piano well.

Eve was playing the piano well.

The simple past suggests that Eve played well throughout the concert; the progressive stretches the time-frame, and asks us to focus on what happened when the concert was taking place.

The verb phrase

Verbs which favour the progressive

When an agent (usually human) is actively controlling or experiencing an action or state, verbs readily take the progressive:

We're starving. I'm waiting. You're joking!
I've been looking at you. They were chatting.
The army was marching back to camp.

Verbs expressing a specific action (**dynamic** verbs), are commonly used in the progressive, as long as the action has potential duration. Examples are *write*, *eat*, *swim*, and *talk*. Inanimate forces also readily take the progressive.

It's raining.
The clouds were gathering.
The weather's improving.

Verbs which do not favour the progressive

When a verb is used with a **stative** meaning, it expresses a state of being in which no obvious action or change is taking place. These verbs are rare in the progressive. We are unlikely to hear:

He is having a scar on his arm. [cf. He has a scar ...]
She is being tall for her age. [cf. She is tall ...]
We are owning a car. [cf. We own ...]

To take this last example: 'owning' is not something which alters. I do not own my car more this morning than I do now. The meaning does not 'progress'. In such cases, we tend to use the simple present.

Dynamic verbs which express a very short time-span, such as *catch*, *exclaim*, and *shut*, do not often take a progressive. We do not usually say:

I've been exclaiming. I'm catching the ball.

But of course we can add a durational perspective if we need to:

I'm shutting the door now – are you satisfied?

And a sports commentator might excitedly say:

The ball's gone high in the air, and yes, Smith is catching it, he's catching it!

Using the progressive

To add a nuance

When we use a normally stative verb with the progressive, we add some special meaning. This is very clear with verbs which are obviously stative, such as *be* and *have*:

John is helpful. [that is his normal character]
John is being helpful. [that is not his normal character]
I have a car. [I am in possession of a car]
I'm having a car. [for a special occasion]

In science, where subjects are often inanimate, we are less likely to see the progressive:

X correlates with *Y* not *X* is correlating with *Y*

But even here, there are occasions when a dynamic interpretation is possible. A surprised scientist might well shout out in delight:

X is correlating with *Y*!

To alter formality

The choice between simple and progressive can have a marked effect on formality or politeness. In letter-writing, for example, there is a significant difference in tone between an official letter and a less formal one:

I write to let you know that ...
I'm writing to let you know that ...

The first is likely to be followed by some such conclusion as ... *your bank account is overdrawn* or ... *your appeal has been disallowed*. The second more like ... *we won't be needing the car after all.*

The same effect can be conveyed in speech, where we find a possible four-way contrast:

We hope you'll come. [rather formal or polite]
We are hoping you will come. [less formal]
We're hoping you'll come. [informal]
We were hoping you'd come. [informal with extra tentativeness: see p.155]

Not using the progressive

Some parts of the world use the progressive more than others. They are found more in American English than in British English, and even more in South Asian English, which regularly uses progressives with verbs expressing states of mind or perception, such as *understand*, *know*, *want*, *feel*, and *smell*.

I am understanding what you are saying.

Progressives are more likely in conversation than in any other domain; but we are still dealing with very small numbers. Less than five per cent of clauses use a progressive. We can listen to a long stretch of talk and never hear a single one. In this extract, the speaker is comparing the quality of football grounds in Europe and Britain. He has already spoken 25 clauses using only simple forms of the verb, and he carries on in the same way. (/ marks a rhythm unit; – a pause)

cos they're all purpose built for modern conditions and ours aren't / – and every time a disaster like this happens / or somebody gets killed or trampled in a crush / – a stand breaks / – this highlights it and they sort of patch it up / and it's botched / you know / because – I suppose it's alright / easy to talk / but if you've got so many thousand quid's worth of stand there / you're not going to sort of knock it all down / and build it up from scratch / – you just patch it up / don't you / – of course the continentals / I suppose they came in late / and they build them – you know / this Milan ground / there's a famous one there isn't there / – you know / they <u>were saying</u> how superb they were / but the one in Spain was the best ...

At last an example! Interestingly, it is a past progressive, which is unusual in conversation apart from with the verbs *say* and *think*:

I was thinking ...   I was saying only the other day

When conversation does use a progressive, it tends to be the present rather than the past – notwithstanding the example on p.165. It also tends to be found in nonfinite clauses (Chapter 17) as part of a general description. For example, a little later in the football chat, we find the speaker talking about a television programme:

> it showed the photographs of them / – people sitting there in the hot sun / you know / smoking cigars / and it showed the crowds emptying ...

The progressive in literature

In prose

The following nonfinite use is widely employed in fiction as part of scene-setting, as the narrator's eye moves about a scene. It occurs in the 'fog everywhere' sequence in the opening page of Charles Dickens' *Bleak House*:

> Fog creeping into the cabooses of collier-brigs, fog lying out on the yards, and hovering in the rigging of great ships; fog drooping on the gunwales of barges and small boats.

Fiction, with its tendency to narrate past events, also makes regular use of the past progressive in finite clauses. Many literary passages rely heavily on the progressive. But while they sound natural enough, we must not forget the creative skill involved in using an effect which is largely missing from daily conversation.

Here is Holden describing his school-leaving day, in J.D. Salinger's *The Catcher in the Rye* (Chapter 1):

> I kept standing near to that crazy cannon, looking down at the game and freezing my ass off. Only, I wasn't watching the game too much. What I was really hanging around for, I was trying to feel some kind of a good-bye. I mean I've left schools and places I didn't even know I was leaving them. I hate that.

The effect of the succinct simple form following the series of progressives is notable.

In poetry

Poets like the progressive. Poetry is a medium which privileges personal reflection – something well-suited to the durational meaning of the form:

> I have been studying how I may compare
> This prison where I live unto the world
> (Shakespeare, *Richard II*, V.v.1)

Poetry also privileges succinctness of expression, and the nonfinite use of the progressive allows a lot to be said in a short space (see below). For poets who rhyme, it is an easy option.

Pairs of progressives are sometimes primitively simple, such as the threefold iteration in Wordsworth's extempore twenty-line poem, 'Written in March':

> The Cock is crowing,
> The stream is flowing ...
> The cattle are grazing,
> Their heads never raising ...
> Small clouds are sailing,
> Blue sky prevailing ...

A much more subtle use of the form is seen in the opening lines of T.S. Eliot's 'The Waste Land', where the nonfinite -*ing* form, prominent in its end-of-line position, focuses our attention on the states being described, with a powerful recurring resonance:

> April is the cruellest month, breeding
> Lilacs out of the dead land, mixing
> Memory and desire, stirring
> Dull roots with spring rain.
> Winter kept us warm, covering
> Earth in forgetful snow, feeding
> A little life with dried tubers.
> Summer surprised us, ...

The simple past tense effectively changes the mood and introduces the narrative. As always with the progressive, it is the contrast with the simple form which counts.

English has no verb ending to express future time, so it has no future tense as such. However, it has a variety of ways to talk about the future:
- modal auxiliaries (Chapter 18), especially *will* (*'ll*) or *shall* followed by the base form of the verb or the progressive:

  I will leave.   I'll leave.   I shall leave.   I may leave.
  I'll be leaving.   I may be leaving.
- present-tense forms (Chapters 23 and 24):

  I'm leaving tonight.   I leave tonight.
- the imperative form (Chapter 6):

  Do give Joan a hug.
- marginal auxiliaries (Chapter 19), especially *be going to*, *be about to*, and *be to*:

  I'm going to leave.   I'm about to leave.
  I'm to leave by six o'clock.

EXPLANATION

The future is a rather long period of time, hence it is useful to have a range of alternatives to focus attention on points within it. Most of us are more concerned about what is going to happen in the near future, leaving the more distant future to look after itself. And it is this contrast which provides the main grouping:
- *will* / *shall* / *'ll*: a nonspecific future reference
- everything else: dividing up the near future

The latter group allows several semantic possibilities.

Happening soon

Several forms suggest that an event will happen very soon:
- The present progressive suggests that an event is imminent, carrying out an arranged plan:

  I'm leaving you.

- The marginal auxiliaries emphasize immediacy:
    I'm on the point of leaving.   I'm about to leave.
- *Be going to* is slightly less immediate, but the event still takes place very much sooner than it would with *will*:
    I'm going to leave. [cf. I will leave]
This form no longer has any sense of motion or progression. It is especially useful because the *be* allows it to be used in a much wider range of contexts than is possible with *will*.
    She**'s going to** leave. They **were going to** leave.
    I **may be going to** leave.
It also tends to be informal, as the nonstandard spelling *gonna* suggests. It is very common in conversation.

Happening sometime

- Imperative forms are nonspecific:
    Leave!
- Modals other than *will* and *shall* are vague:
    I may / might / could leave.
- *Be to* suggests a future plan or obligation:
    You are to leave by six.
- The progressive form suggests a lack of definiteness or forward planning, or an event which is a matter of course:
    I'll be leaving, then.   I'll be seeing you.

Happening never

When *be going to* is used in the past tense, it refers to a projected future time dating from some point in the past. The event may therefore never have taken place:
    I was going to leave last Friday.

For the pragmatics of these forms, see Chapter 26.

The **modal** range of verbs includes the central class of modal auxiliaries, with their contracted forms (Chapter 18), and a number of other verbs and idioms (Chapter 19).

- Central modals:
  can/could   may/might   must/will/would   shall/should

- Other verbs with modal meaning include:
  used to   ought to   be going to   have got to
  had better/best   had/would rather   be supposed to

EXPLANATION

Modals express a wide range of meanings which blur into each other, so that it is not always possible to be precise about the sense of a usage. Three semantic factors obtain:
- the stance of the subject towards the main verb:
  I forget. [the speaker is asserting a fact]
  I might forget. [the speaker is making a judgement]
- whether or not the subject can influence the action or state expressed by the main verb:
  John must be careful. [it is up to John]
  The dam must burst. [it is not up to the dam]
- the time-frame in which the subject is locating the action or state expressed by the main verb:
  I will go. [future]   I used to go. [past]

Because time is only one of the factors involved in modal meaning, modals are not called tense forms.

Adopting a stance

The modals allow us to make three kinds of judgement about the action or state expressed by the main verb.

PROVIDING AN OPTION

Four modals express permission, possibility, or ability –
judgements which involve a choice of alternative outcomes: *can,
could, may, might*:

  May I borrow your book? [permission: yes or no]
  Kath may be right. [possibility: or she may not]
  Can you recall? [ability: yes or no]

MAKING A REQUIREMENT

Several modals express an obligation or necessity: *must, should,
need to, ought to, had better, have got to, be supposed to*:

  I ought to take these pills twice a day. [obligation]
  It must be a mistake. [necessity]
  You've got to be at work by six. [obligation]
  You've got to be joking. [necessity]

ANTICIPATING THE FUTURE

Four modals anticipate the way the future will appear, either by
expressing an intention (often called **volition**) or by making a
prediction: *will, would, shall, be going to*:

  We're going to stay for a week. [volition]
  The weather will be good tomorrow. [prediction]

Suggesting a time

Modals always operate within a time-frame, as indicated by these
examples:
- future: *will, shall, be going to*
- present or future: *can, may, must*
- habitual past: *used to*
- past or tentative non-past: *could, might, should, would*

However, other factors are usually present which reduce the
importance of the time element. The tentativeness in the last
example is discussed on p.174.

Influencing the action

All modals express two semantic perspectives about the relationship between the subject and the main verb.

Subject in control

In one perspective, the subject acts as an agent directly controlling the action expressed by the main verb. The typical meanings are permission, ability, obligation, and volition. In most cases, the subject is animate, usually human, and the verb is dynamic (p.163).

You can buy the tickets if you want. [permission]
I must get the tickets before they close. [obligation]
I'll buy the tickets when I've a moment. [volition]

Here, the modals have an **intrinsic** (or **deontic**) meaning.

Subject not in control

In the other perspective, the subject has no influence, because the clause is expressing the logical status of some event. The typical meanings are possibility, necessity, and prediction. In most cases, the subject is inanimate or abstract, and the verb expresses a state (p.163).

The effects of the fire could be awful. [possibility]
The cabinet must have discussed it. [necessity]
The weather will not change all week. [prediction]

Here, the modals have an **extrinsic** (or **epistemic**) meaning.

Modal adverbs

Modal meanings can be reinforced by a number of adverbs and adverb phrases, such as *perhaps*, *possibly*, *probably*, *definitely*, *certainly*, *maybe*, *surely*, *very likely*, and *necessarily*. Choosing the right one is important as these sentences show:

I must definitely get the tickets before they close.
I must perhaps get the tickets before they close.

The verb phrase

Using modals in conversation

The informality of some modals makes them common in conversation – (in informal spellings) *gonna*, *gotta*, *useta*, and *(had) better*. *Shall* and *may* are more formal. *Must* has an interesting 'over-the-top' polite usage:

> You *must* have some cake!

The effect arises because no real obligation is involved.

Who's who

The choice of a modal often depends on 'who's who' in the social situation.

- In an organization, a senior person might ask a junior, *Can I borrow your pen?*, but hardly *Might I borrow your pen?*, unless perhaps he was being sarcastic.

- On the other hand, juniors would very likely say *could* or *might* to their seniors.
- A use of *may* from a senior to a junior is likely to be interpreted not as permission but as obligation: *You may leave the room.* Failure to comply would probably result in a straight directive: *Leave the room!*

Being tentative

Tentativeness is an important factor in conversation, expressed chiefly by *could, might, should,* and *would.* Although once called the 'past tenses' of *can, may, shall,* and *will,* these forms do not usually refer to past time:

I could go to town on Thursday.
I should ask Mary, if I were you.

The time reference is plainly future – but these forms also convey diffidence, thus making the sentences more polite. We can see this by contrasting an assertive clause with clauses expressing increased tentativeness:

* You are wrong. → You may be wrong. → You could be wrong. → You might be wrong.
* Can I help? → Could I help? → Might I help?

Using modals in other varieties

There is no pragmatic restriction on the range of modals which can appear in a variety of English, but some varieties do rely on certain modals.

Consumer advertising

Underneath all advertisements there is a 'will' and a 'can'. The 'will' conveys the promise of the product: if you buy X, Y will happen. The 'can' assumes that everyone who sees the ad is able to purchase the product.

Your cat will love Moggo.
Blatch will make your floors squeaky clean.
You can do everything you want with Blatch.
It's the best you can buy!

Academic writing

Academic – and especially scientific – discourse routinely deals with logical possibility, the making and testing of predictions, and the arriving at tentative conclusions, so modals with these meanings are common:

These effects could be the result of a magnetic field ...
We shall show in this chapter ...

The modals contribute to the impersonal effect conveyed by the passive (p.144):

It can be seen that ...   This can be illustrated by ...

Instructions

Instructional language not only directs (p.74), it directs with caution. Advisory modals are very much in evidence:

Care must be taken.   It should be noted that ...
Two washers need to be inserted.

Regional variation

As with all auxiliaries, modal use varies regionally (p.131), sometimes even reflecting other languages, as in the Yiddish-influenced use of *should*:

I should be so lucky. [= I'm unlucky]

Caution

We need to be careful when using modals. It is all too easy to convey a different meaning from what we intend. These sentences have two meanings:

You can't see the room. ['I'm not letting you' or 'It isn't possible from where you're standing'?]
You must be very understanding. ['You always have been' or 'You're going to have to be'?]

Context usually helps to clarify matters; but the risk of ambiguity is always there.

DESCRIPTIVE SUMMARY

The **noun phrase (NP)** is the main construction which can appear as the subject, object, or complement of a clause (Chapter 3). It consists of up to four components:

- an obligatory **noun** or noun-like word which acts as the centre, or **head**, of the phrase (Chapter 28):

    bus   interest   contestant   music   essence

- a **determiner**, along with any associated words, which appears before the noun (Chapter 35):

    the   my   some   all   all the   the many

- the **premodification**, which comprises everything appearing between the determiner and the noun – adjectives and adjective-like words, along with any associated words (Chapter 39):

    green   difficult   wooden   very tall

- the **postmodification**, which comprises everything appearing after the head, such as prepositional phrases and certain types of clause (Chapter 40):

    in the garden   which I borrowed

Four-element noun phrases can be quite complex:

    The / interesting / books / which I borrowed were lost.

The whole noun phrase may be replaced by a pronoun:

    They were lost.

EXPLANATION

Noun phrases are the most frequently occurring item in all varieties of English, usually making up between half and three-quarters of the 'bulk' of a text. They are therefore the main information-carrying items.

What noun phrases do

Noun phrases tell us what a text is about. The point can be easily demonstrated by taking a text and displaying it in two forms: first with its noun phrases omitted, then with only its noun phrases present. It is not difficult to see which version conveys more information.

• The full text (from a news article about Mars)

Mars can be seen in the night sky from anywhere on Earth with the naked eye, but stargazers at lower latitudes will have the best chance of a spectacular sighting. The mysterious planet is visible in the night sky as a bright orange object. Right now, Mars outshines any other celestial body except the Moon and Venus.

• No NPs

— can be seen in — from — with — but – will have —. — is visible in — as —. Right now, — outshines — except —.

• Only NPs

Mars — the night sky — anywhere on Earth — the naked eye, — stargazers at lower latitudes — the best chance of a spectacular sighting. The mysterious planet — the night sky — a bright orange object. — Mars — any other celestial body — the Moon and Venus.

In this example, the NPs, measured by number of words, comprise 70 per cent of the text.

The critical components

The head and the determiner are the two essential components of the noun phrase:

• The head tells us what entity is being referred to.
• The determiner specifies the kind of instance of the entity we are talking about.

It is therefore logical to begin the study of noun-phrase structure by considering the nature of nouns (Chapter 28).

Using noun phrases

Apart from a few situations which use only minor sentences
(Chapter 2), all uses of English employ noun phrases with great
frequency. However, varieties differ greatly in the complexity of the
NPs they use, and in their use of pronouns as substitute forms.
The chief contrast is between speech and writing, and – within this
– between informal speech and formal writing.

Informal speech

Conversation relies heavily on pronouns. In this extract, A needs a
screwdriver, and B goes looking for it. (Pronouns are in bold;
noun-based NPs are underlined.)

> A: **It**'s in <u>the drawer</u>, **I** think. (Pause)
> B: Can't find **it**.
> A: Well **I**'m sure **it** was there before.
> B: **I**'ve looked.
> A: Let **me** have <u>a go</u>. (Pause)
> B: **Anything**?
> A: **You**'re right. ... **It**'s <u>a puzzle</u>. **It** was there yesterday.
> B: Well **it** didn't walk by **itself**.
> A: (Laughs)
> B: Or maybe **it** did, if **it**'s one of those automatic **ones**.

More complex NPs only start to build up when a speaker launches
into a monologue, or an argument of some complexity develops.
Even then, the pronouns are the constant factor, as seen in this
extract from a discussion between two teachers.

> it's very awkward / – **it**'s difficult mind **you** / with <u>a class of</u>
> <u>thirty odd</u> / – occasionally / **you** know / **we**'ll have <u>a debate</u> /
> **what** do **you** want to talk about / and **this** is **something I**
> usually spend <u>one lesson</u> arranging / **what they** want to talk
> about / and then tell **them** to go and think about **it** / and we
> have <u>the discussion</u> in <u>a later lesson</u> /

Conversation in fiction

Some writers are good at capturing the laconic nature of conversational exchanges. Here are the opening lines of Harold Pinter's *The Birthday Party*:

> MEG: Is **that you**, <u>Petey</u>?
>   *Pause.*
>   Petey, is **that you**?
>   *Pause.*
>   Petey?
> PETEY: **What**?
> MEG: Is **that you**?
> PETEY: Yes, **it**'s **me**.
> MEG: **What**? (*Her face appears at the hatch.*) Are **you** back?
> PETEY: Yes.
> MEG: **I**'ve got <u>your cornflakes</u> ready.

Three out of four NPs are pronouns, in this kind of dialogue, which depends heavily on the situation for its meaning.

Formal writing

By contrast, formal writing is highly explicit and autonomous. Pronouns are rare other than for purposes of abbreviation, to refer back to a previous noun phrase (Chapter 62). Indeed, we can encounter long stretches of text with hardly any pronouns at all, as in this entry from *The New Penguin Encyclopedia*:

> **atom trap** <u>A device for trapping atoms whose velocity has been greatly slowed using laser cooling</u>. <u>The trapping</u> is performed either by <u>magnetic fields</u> or by <u>an intense laser beam focused to a spot</u>. <u>Magneto-optical atom traps, using combined magnetic fields and lasers,</u> first appeared in <u>1987</u> and quickly became <u>the most widely used optical trap</u>. <u>The trapped atoms</u> allow <u>a detailed study of their properties,</u> and can be used in <u>atomic optics experiments</u>.

Note that, in such entries, the whole of the opening definition is a single (complex) noun phrase.

DESCRIPTIVE SUMMARY

A noun can be recognized by a combination of up to five factors:
- it acts as the head of a noun phrase (Chapter 27):
    a tall **soldier** in a coat
- it is preceded by one of the class of determiners (Chapter 35):
    the soldier   a soldier   some soldiers
- it changes its form to express singular and plural (Chapter 31):
    soldier / soldiers   mouse / mice
- it changes its form to express the genitive case (Chapter 34):
    the soldier's weapons   the soldiers' weapons
- it uses a special ending which can be attached to verbs, adjectives, or other nouns (Chapter 74):
    refuse → refusal   rapid → rapidity   book → booklet

These factors combine in different ways to produce different classes of nouns:
- common vs. proper (see Chapter 29)
- count vs. noncount (Chapter 30)
- concrete vs. abstract (Chapter 30)

EXPLANATION

As we saw in the introductory section (p.17), to say what we mean we need both content words and grammatical words. And of all the content words, nouns are the main means of giving what we say a point of reference in the real world.

Defining nouns?

Traditional grammars used to spend a lot of time trying to give a semantic definition to a noun. The most famous is: 'the name of a person, place or thing'. The main problem with this definition is that it excluded thousands of nouns, notably abstract nouns (e.g. *desire, music*), action nouns (e.g. *flight, visit*), and quantity nouns (e.g. *zero, lot*). 'Naming' is not enough. Nouns do name entities, but so do verbs name actions and adjectives name attributes. This is not a very illuminating way to study nouns. It is far better to examine what nouns actually do.

What nouns do

Our reliance on nouns for self-expression is remarkable. The nouns alone are enough to convey the gist of an utterance. Here are all the content words in the first seven lines of a famous Shakespearian speech:

- nouns: *dagger, handle, hand, vision, feeling, sight, dagger, mind, creation, brain*
- verbs: *see, come, clutch, have, see, proceed*
- adjectives: *fatal, sensible, false, heat-oppressed*
- adverbs: *yet, still*

For comparison, here is the full text:

Is this a dagger which I see before me,
The handle toward my hand? Come, let me clutch thee –
I have thee not and yet I see thee still!
Art thou not, fatal vision, sensible
To feeling as to sight? Or art thou but
A dagger of the mind, a false creation,
Proceeding from the heat-oppressed brain?
(*Macbeth*, II.i.33)

The nouns convey a specificity of reference which enables us to focus on the subject-matter of a text. When people ask, 'What is that text about?', nouns capture the topic more readily than other content words do. As Hamlet might have said: 'The noun's the thing.'

29 | Common and proper nouns

Common and proper nouns differ grammatically:

* Proper nouns can be used on their own, whereas only some common nouns can:

  Oslo is sunny.   See you in May.   Simon is in.
  Justice is needed. **but not:** ~~Table is needed.~~
* Proper nouns do not usually allow a plural, whereas most common nouns do (Chapter 30):

  not: ~~Oslos~~   ~~Mays~~   ~~Simons~~
  cats   dogs   communities **but not:**   ~~musics~~
* Proper nouns do not usually show a contrast of determiners (Chapter 35), whereas common nouns do:

  not: ~~an Oslo~~   ~~the May~~   ~~some Simons~~
  a / the / some books   the / my music

The function of proper nouns is to identity a unique, definite, point of reference in the real world. There is only one May, one Oslo, one Rolling Stones.

Having said that, we must allow for cases where:
* proper nouns are treated as if they were common:

  I love Fridays.   I remember the May I left home.
  He's acting like a little Hitler.
* common nouns are treated as if they were proper:

  I'm off to seek Fame and Fortune.

The distinction is not clear-cut – as we sense whenever we are unsure whether to begin a noun with a capital letter: *earth* or *Earth*? Publishers vary in their practice.

The noun phrase

Knowledge of the world

Proper nouns give us knowledge that is encyclopedic, not linguistic. We may know a lot of places in Greece, but still not be able to speak any Greek. Proper nouns have no lexical content – with just one exception.

We need to make a distinction between **proper nouns**, which are individual words, and **proper names**, which are sequences of words. In such cases, common nouns may be used as part of the name, which therefore acquires a modicum of lexical content: at least we know that *Oxford Street* is 'a street'.

In a proper name, all the nouns can be proper (underlined below), or some of them, or none of them:
- all: <u>Butch</u> <u>Cassidy</u> and the <u>Sundance</u> <u>Kid</u>, <u>Jo</u> <u>Smith</u>
- one: <u>Tate</u> Gallery, Colonel <u>Sanders</u>, <u>Oxford</u> Street
- none: Channel Islands, Spice Girls, Lord of the Rings

In each case, though, the whole name functions as if it were a single proper noun, and often requires an obligatory definite article:

I'm going to the Channel Islands.
Do you remember the Spice Girls?

We learn such names as single units.

Why use proper nouns?

Proper nouns are important in situations where uniqueness is important. We will therefore expect to find them prominent in such domains as geographical and historical writing, consumer advertising, gazetteers and event guides, and any context which focuses on entities as specific individuals – such as the names of persons, places, products, institutions, political parties, religions, festivals, buildings, languages, and nationalities. In speech, they provide an important means of using the vocative construction (Chapter 13) – singling out our addressee.

DESCRIPTIVE SUMMARY

Common nouns (p.182) can be classified into two types:

- **Count** (or **countable**) nouns refer to individual entities that can be counted. They can be used with *a* or with numerals; they need some sort of premodification in the singular (Chapter 39); and they vary between singular and plural (Chapter 31):

  I see a dog / dogs / three dogs. but not: I see dog.

- **Noncount** (also called **uncountable** or **mass**) nouns refer to an undifferentiated mass or notion. They can be used without any premodification; they occur with *some* in the singular; and they do not vary between singular and plural:

  I'll give you advice / some advice. but not: advices

Some nouns have both noncount and count uses:

  I want cake. **vs.** I want a cake.
  It needs discussion. **vs.** We had two discussions.

EXPLANATION

The distinction between count and noncount is part of the grammatical character of a language, and cannot simply be explained by referring to the nature of the entities as they appear in the real world. Whatever 'information' is, in the world, it is the same in Britain and France; but *information* is uncountable in English whereas *les informations* is countable in French. When we talk about countability we are really talking about the way nouns can be *used* in a language. Many nouns can be used in either a countable or an uncountable way.

Exploiting countability

When a noun is used in a countable way, we view it as an entity which can exist as many separate instances. When noncountable, we see it as a general phenomenon – as a quality or substance. There are thus two possibilities:

- We can treat count nouns as uncountable:
    I like eggs.   I cooked myself egg and chips.
- We can treat noncount nouns as countable:
    I like wine.   I like German wines.

There are many cases where the same noun is used in both ways:
    football vs. a football   paper vs. a paper
    education vs. an education

But quite often, we need different words to express the two perspectives:
    I like pigs / pork.   I read a poem / poetry.
    I have a permit / permission.

Some stylistic effects

- We can create an effect by treating as uncountable an entity which is normally countable:
    There was dog all over the carpet.
    'I love shelf,' said the woodworm.
- There is a further way of turning a noncount noun into a count noun: by using a **partitive** expression, such as *bit of* or *piece of* – or one of many specific terms:
    a piece of cake / advice   a bit / loaf of bread
    Immature writing tends to overuse *bit / piece*, instead of using more focused expressions (e.g. *round of applause, blade of grass, item of equipment*).
- In large stores, the various departments are often named with an uncountable noun, referring to the aggregates of entities they contain: *furniture, footwear, tableware*. This then allows us to use apparently anomalous sentences:
    [approaching an assistant] Are you furniture?

Abstract and concrete

Both count and noncount nouns can be divided into two semantic types, which have major stylistic implications.

- Concrete nouns are entities which can be visually observed and measured:

    count: bicycle, egg, table, computer
    noncount: butter, machinery, crockery, clothing

- Abstract nouns refer to unobservable notions:

    count: difficulty, refusal, likelihood, instance
    noncount: farming, officialdom, fear, grief

As with count / noncount, the distinction is not absolute:

- We can take an abstract noun and make it concrete by particularizing it:

    That's an example of fortitude for you.
    A grief ago [title of a poem by Dylan Thomas]

- We can take a concrete noun and make it abstract by generalizing it. An example is in the description of Titus in the extract from *Gormenghast* on p.125:

    For first and ever foremost he is *child*.

Some nouns are of uncertain status. Although we cannot visually observe *music*, usually taken as an abstract noun, we can certainly hear it, which makes it rather less abstract than, say, *basis*.

There are a number of suffixes (p.374) whose role is primarily to turn a concrete noun into an abstract one. They include *-age*, *-dom*, *-ship*, *-hood*, and *-ism*:

    mileage   friendship   brotherhood

Using the distinction

The use of concrete and abstract nouns is bound up with subject-matter and genre. The former will come to the fore when we want to draw attention to physical objects and properties, as in consumer advertising, guide-books, and passages of natural description. The latter will predominate in reflective and discursive treatments.

The noun phrase

Concrete exposition

Here is a description of a field on a hot May day, taken from the final chapter of A.S. Byatt's novel *Possession*. Only one noun is abstract (*abundance*):

> There was a meadow full of young hay, and all the summer flowers in great abundance. Blue cornflowers, scarlet poppies, gold buttercups, a veil of speedwells, an intricate carpet of daisies where the grass was shorter, scabious, yellow snapdragons, bacon and egg plant, pale milkmaids, purple heartsease, scarlet pimpernel and white shepherd's purse, and round this field a high bordering hedge of Queen Anne's lace and foxgloves, and above that dogroses, palely shining in a thorny hedge, honeysuckle all creamy and sweet-smelling, rambling threads of bryony and the dark stars of deadly nightshade.

And the paragraph continues thus for several more lines – *a tour de force* of concrete linguistic expressionism.

Abstract exposition

We are most likely to encounter heavily abstract passages in intellectual exposition, as practised by academics and essayists. Here is an extract from Ralph Waldo Emerson's essay on *Nature* (1836), in which only two nouns (*food, animals*) move us in a concrete direction:

> Space, time, society, labour, climate, food, locomotion, the animals, the mechanical forces, give us sincerest lessons, day by day, whose meaning is unlimited. They educate both the Understanding and the Reason. Every property of matter is a school for the understanding – its solidity or resistance, its inertia, its extension, its figure, its divisibility.

This is difficult subject-matter, undoubtedly, but it is by no means unclear. It is a corresponding *tour de force* in abstract linguistic expressionism.

Exploiting the difference

Some varieties have a definite preference for concrete nouns, some for abstract; but it is the way in which we exploit the contrast between the two which produces some of the most effective uses of language.

IN FICTION

A widely used device in satire is to begin a sentence with abstract nouns then switch to concrete. We can see it operating in Laurence Sterne's *Tristram Shandy* (1761):

> It was not an easy matter in any king's reign, (unless you were as lean a subject as myself) to have forced your hand diagonally, quite across your whole body, so as to gain the bottom of your opposite coat-pocket. (Book 3, Chapter 3)

An even more marked contrast occurs in Chapter 34:

> It is a singular blessing, that nature has form'd the mind of man with the same happy backwardness and renitency against conviction, which is observed in old dogs, – of not learning new tricks.'

IN ADVERTISING

Advertising copywriting manuals usually recommend writers to use concrete rather than abstract words, but this is mainly achieved through the use of adjectives, not nouns (Chapter 48). In fact, ads could not survive without abstract nouns, as this short selection illustrates:

> freshness   simplicity   luxury   reliability   performance

Even the basic language of selling uses them:

> offer   chance   opportunity   cost

Here too, the abstract / concrete contrast can be exploited:

> Happiness is a cigar called Hamlet.

IN EVERYDAY EXPRESSIONS

The contrast is often exploited in everyday expressions:

> Curiosity killed the cat.   Fine words butter no parsnips.
> Time and tide wait for no man.

The anti-abstract movement

The use of abstract words has sometimes had a bad press, because they readily lead to vagueness, and it is true that they can be overused. But no-one can do without them. A famous antagonist was George Orwell, who parodies the fashion of using abstract words where concrete ones will do, in his essay, 'Politics and the English language' (1946). He takes a biblical verse (*Ecclesiastes*):

> I returned, and saw under the sun, that the race is not to the swift, not the battle to the strong, neither yet bread to the wise, nor yet riches to men of understanding, nor yet favour to men of skill; but time and chance happeneth to them all.

and rewrites it thus:

> Objective consideration of contemporary phenomena compels the conclusion that success or failure in competitive activities exhibits no tendency to be commensurate with innate capacity, but that a considerable element of the unpredictable must invariably be taken into account.

The parody makes its point, but it is actually a criticism of long words, not abstract ones. One of Orwell's stylistic axioms was 'Never use a long word where a short one will do'. The biblical quotation actually uses several abstract words, notably *understanding*, *skill*, *time*, and *chance*, and we might argue that usages such as *the wise* add a degree of abstractness too.

It is not possible to do without abstract words, and literary writing generally aims for a balance between the abstract and concrete, especially in its figures of speech. Some lines from a famous speech illustrate:

> The slings and arrows of outrageous fortune ...
> For who would bear the whips and scorns of time ...
> Thus conscience does make cowards of us all.
> (Shakespeare, *Hamlet*, III.i)

DESCRIPTIVE SUMMARY

Most nouns are **variable**: they have both a **singular** and a **plural** form. A small group of nouns is **invariable**, allowing no number contrast (Chapter 32).

- **Regular** plurals add an *-s* ending to the singular, often with an associated spelling change:

  horses   books   languages   nouns   plurals

- **Irregular** plurals are formed in some other way:
  - adding a different ending: *oxen, algae, crises, bureaux*
  - adding no ending: *sheep, p* (pence), *Chinese* (the people), *aircraft, cod*
  - changing the vowel: *man → men, mouse → mice*
  - changing a consonant + *-s*: *leaf → leaves, wife → wives*
  - in some compounds, changing the first element: *passers-by, coats-of-mail*

EXPLANATION

The singular/plural distinction has one of the simplest semantic explanations in the whole of grammar: *singular* refers to 'one' of an entity; *plural* to 'more than one'. But, as always, there are exceptions. We can name what grows on a tree as either *foliage* or *leaves*; the former is singular and the latter plural, but the number of leaves is the same in each case. Likewise, there is no difference between singular *wheat* and plural *oats* in the real world.

Irregular forms are an aberration in any semantic approach to grammar. It is a fact of linguistic history that at one point *man* became *men* and not *mans*. Such changes have minimal semantic/pragmatic consequences.

Exploiting the plural form

In a few cases, we find nouns with two plurals, regular and irregular, and this allows us to make a stylistic contrast. In each of the following cases, the second choice is more formal – often more 'professional' – than the first:

cactuses / cacti   formulas / formulae
bureaus / bureaux   court-martials / courts-martial

Most irregular foreign nouns have conformed to the regular pattern (*foetuses, apparatuses*), but it is still possible to hear a very formal and somewhat self-conscious use of the foreign plural in such words as *fora* (*forums*) and *stadia* (*stadiums*). In cases such as *foot* and *pound*, the regular plural is actually the more formal:

3 feet / foot of cloth   6 pounds / pound of sugar

We need to note the rare cases where plurals have developed different meanings: *indexes* (books), *indices* (numerals); *appendixes* (people), *appendices* (books).

Character types

A failure to cope with irregular plurals is a conventional feature of certain characters in literature:

- Child-like speech: Gollum, in J.R.R. Tolkien's *The Lord of the Rings*, speaks like a four-year-old:

    They won't hurt us will they, nice little hobbitses? We didn't mean no harm, but they jumps on us like cats on poor mices, they did.

    (Book 4, Chapter 1)

- Foreigner talk: Lubijova, the guide to Slaka, in Malcolm Bradbury's *Rates of Exchange* has problems with irregular plurals (Chapter 8):

    You know, everything is different, the people, the language, even the foods. ... Also there are many opportunities of leisures. ...

Invariable nouns do not change their form, and usually express no contrast of number. They are either singulars or plurals, as shown by their concord with a verb (*is/are*):

- Singular-only nouns include proper nouns (Chapter 29) and such items as *physics, music, measles, darts*:

    The music is very loud. not: ~~The music are ...~~

- Plural-only nouns include such items as *trousers, goggles, stairs*:

    Your trousers are ready. not: ~~Your trousers is ...~~

- A few invariable nouns have developed a number contrast, such as *headquarters, means, crossroads*.

    The headquarters is/are a mile away.

EXPLANATION

Singular-only nouns

These fall into three semantic types, ending in *-s* or *-ics*:
- Names of some diseases or ailments:

    measles   mumps   shingles

- Names of sports or fields of study:

    athletics   robotics   phonetics   physics

- Names of some games:

    billiards   ninepins   cards   darts

Plural-only nouns

There are rather more nouns within this category, and in a few cases they have developed variant usages, some of which have been exploited for stylistic purposes. Most end in *-s*, but there are some foreign plurals (e.g. *regalia*) and some which have no ending (e.g. *police*).

Examples of plural-only invariable nouns:
- Garments relating to the lower part of the body: *trousers, jeans, knickers, shorts, braces*
- Tools: *pliers, forceps, secateurs*
- Optical items: *glasses, goggles, binoculars*
- Collections: *contents, goods, remains, stairs, cattle, leftovers, livestock, dregs, regalia, minutiae*
- Landscape features, when seen as having no clear boundaries: *the mountains, the woods, the steppes*
- Rewards and compensations: *returns, wages, amends*
- Formal expression of feelings: *apologies, regards, condolences*
- -*ings* nouns: *savings, beginnings, goings-on*

A few invariable nouns do not fit neatly into semantic types, such as *brains, heads/tails, genitals, looks.* There are also some fixed phrases which are plural-only: *in cahoots with, for keeps, friends with.*

Number-contrast nouns

Nouns like *headquarters* offer a semantic choice. When we use it in the singular, we see the noun as a single entity; in the plural, as an aggregate of units.

The headquarters is at this point on the map.
The headquarters consist of thirty buildings.

The same point applies to collective nouns such as *committee* (p.199).

Different meanings

In a few cases, there is a semantic distinction between an invariable noun and another version of the noun with a regular singular and plural. An example is *savings*, which in its invariable form refers only to money; in its variable form, it has a much wider range of meaning:

We want a great saving of time / energy / resources.
We want savings of time and energy.

Likewise, the landscape nouns can be used in two ways.

I climbed a hill – two hills, actually – this morning.
There are bandits in the hills.

The variable character of the noun in the first example is illustrated by the fact that we can ask: 'How many hills did you climb?' It makes no real sense to ask a similar question of hills in the second example:

How many hills have bandits?

The invariable usage is telling us: 'the bandits could be *anywhere* in the hills'. No specific locations are being suggested.

Stylistic variation

• The first three categories on p.193 are sometimes called **bipartite** nouns: they can be preceded by *pair of*. In a commercial setting, or in a historical survey of product types, we may find them used in the singular:

That's a very elegant trouser, sir.
They developed a scissor with a special handle.

Animals which can be hunted or caught have developed a 'professional' invariable plural, alongside the regular singular/plural contrast. We normally say:

I can see a duck / three ducks.
          a rabbit / three rabbits.
          a fish / three fishes.

But those who engage in hunting talk differently:

I brought home three duck / rabbit / fish.

Divided usage

The invariable noun is one of the areas of English grammar where we find several points of divided usage.

- The countable use of bipartite nouns without *pair of* is often heard in informal speech, but many people find this unacceptable:

  a scissors   two pliers   a binoculars

  The singular use of these nouns is increasing, but remains nonstandard, and is avoided in formal writing.

  The pliers is on the table. [formal: *are*]

  Her jeans was torn. [formal: *were*]

- A few variable nouns have developed alternative usages, in recent years, so that they might now be considered as invariable. They include:

  criteria   data   bacteria   phenomena   insignia   graffiti

These are today often heard followed by both *is* and *are*.

In the context of computing, *data is/are* nowadays works just like *headquarters*, showing two perspectives:

  The data is backing up now.

  The data show several interesting patterns.

Outside computing, the usage is still divided, leading some writers to avoid the noun altogether, replacing it by an uncontentious plural such as *results* or *findings*.

Conservative users insist on maintaining the variable status of these nouns (*criterion/criteria*), though even they can have difficulty when the foreign singular is obscure, as in the case of *insignie* or *graffito*.

The changes are continuing, and one day we may find them all used as variable regular nouns (*datas, criterias*), as has already happened with *agendas* and *candelabras*. *Insignias* is already common in American English. For the present, formal writing and speaking tend to follow the conservative pattern, and this is wise when our writing is to be subject to scrutiny, as in an examination or a job application.

---

33 Gender

English makes a limited classification of nouns on the basis of **gender**. We can distinguish:

- animate beings from inanimate entities:
  girl / dog   table / problem

Animates are of two types:

- **personal** nouns are human – male, female, or either:
  man   actress   singer
- **nonpersonal** nouns are animals:
  cat   beetle   octopus

These distinctions are grammatically expressed through the agreement of nouns with pronouns (Chapter 43), chiefly *he*, *she*, *it*, *who*, and *which*:

The man, who ...   He ...
The woman, who ...   She ...
The problem, which ...   It ...

EXPLANATION

In modern usage, the word 'gender' is closely related to sex; but sex is only one of the factors involved in the above set of distinctions. The *he/she* distinction is based on sex, but the *who/which* one is not – it is based on animateness – and the pronoun *it* can be used for both sexes, in certain circumstances:

The cow is eating **its** food. [a female animal]
The bull is eating **its** food. [a male animal]

The gender of a noun depends on the type of pronoun with which it can be used. On this basis, we can recognize three categories:

- **Single-gender** nouns pattern either with *he* (*man, husband, policeman, king*) or with *she* (*girl, queen, nun, princess*) or with *it* (*door, arrival, issue, bath*). The *it* group is by far the largest, including both concrete and abstract nouns.

- **Dual-gender** nouns are of three kinds:
  - those (mainly human) which pattern with *he/she*:
    actor   friend   poet   parent   person   angel
  - those which pattern with *she/it*:
    lioness   hen [animal]   mother   car, ship   France
  - those (mainly animals) which pattern with *he/it*:
    bull   cock   stallion   [animal]   father   spanner

- **Triple-gender** nouns, which allow *he/she/it*, are fewer in number:
    baby   child   cat   dog   horse

Using *it*

It is normally used with inanimate nouns. Its use with animate nouns is largely in relation to animals whose sex we do not know or (with lower-order animals, such as *ants* and *cod*) whose sex is unknowable to lay observers. Its use with humans is restricted to contexts where the speaker is unable to distinguish the sex of a person or wishes to express disparagement:

[identifying which of a group of babies is crying] It's the one in the blue pram.
[father to enquirer, of a teenage son] It's in bed.

We cannot use *it* when referring back to a personal proper noun (Chapter 29). We can say:

That baby is waving its arms.
but not: ~~Mary is waving its arms~~

It has to be: *Mary is waving her arms* (unless, of course, she is waving some object's arms). Similarly, we can say *The dog is eating its food*, but not ~~Patch is eating its food~~. This last example could only mean that Patch was eating some other animal's food.

Using *he/she*

He and *she* (or their other forms – *him, his,* etc.) usually refer to animate nouns. Their use with inanimate nouns suggests a high level of human interest in an entity, or a close working relationship – such as that which might exist between a vehicle-owner and a vehicle, a politician and a country (but only when seen as a political entity), or workers and features they routinely encounter in their environment.

The usual usage is *she*; it is rare to find an entity referred to as *he*.
    She's a fantastic car to drive.
    France has a marvellous future ahead of her.
    He's not going to move, is he! [said by a plumber trying to unscrew an especially stiff pipe]
In some dialects (such as in south-west England) count nouns are routinely referred to as *he* or *her*:
    Get the brush ... he's in the cupboard.
    [of a tractor] You can't start her easily on cold mornings.

Using *who/which*

The norm is for *who* to pattern with humans (*he/she*) and *which* to pattern with everything else (*it*). But there are some special cases.

The noun phrase

Collective nouns

Both *who* and *which* can be used with human collective nouns, depending on whether they are being seen as a group of individuals or as a single organization:

class   crew   cast   crowd   enemy   gang   family
jury   team   government   the UN

The individuating sense has a plural verb (p.193):

Illness has affected several members of the team who are playing on Saturday. [we are talking about particular individuals]
I've chosen the team which is playing on Saturday. [we are talking about the team as a whole]

Animals

Both *who* and *which* are used with animals that have a close relationship with humans, such as pets:

We've got a budgie who / which is always singing.

People who do not like certain animals are unlikely to use *who* in talking about them. We may well hear this:

Have you dealt with the spider which / that was in the bathroom?

but not this:

Have you dealt with the spider who was in the bathroom?

Inanimates

Inanimates that can pattern with *he* or *she* nonetheless do not pattern with *who*:

The Queen Elizabeth is a ship which made many fast transatlantic crossings.
She made many fast transtlantic crossings.

but we cannot say: The Queen Elizabeth is a ship who made many fast transatlantic crossings.

DESCRIPTIVE SUMMARY

A case is an ending added to a noun or pronoun to show its function within the clause. Nouns have only two cases: **common** (no ending) and **genitive** (shown by *'s* or *s'* in writing) – often called the **s- genitive**. Some pronouns have three cases (Chapter 43).

A few nouns have no ending in speech, and only an apostrophe in writing. These include some proper nouns ending in *-s* and some fixed phrases:

Xerxes' triumph   for goodness' sake

In the **group genitive**, the ending is attached to a noun which follows the head noun of the phrase:

the Duke of York's car (compare: *the Duke's car*)

We can use a genitive without a following noun if the context makes the meaning clear (the **independent genitive**) or in referring to a location (the **local genitive**):

Smith's vote was larger than Brown's.
I'm going to stay at Brown's.

There is a close relationship between nouns in the genitive case and nouns followed by *of* (the **of- genitive**):

the car's owner   the owner of the car

EXPLANATION

The genitive identifies the definite reference of the head noun in the noun phrase, in much the same way that a determiner does (Chapter 35):

the cake   some cake   Smith's cake

That is why we cannot use a determiner with a genitive:

~~the Smith's cake~~   ~~Smith's my cake~~

The noun phrase

The genitive is usually described as being the marker of possession, and called the **possessive case**. This is certainly its primary semantic function, but the form expresses a range of other meanings.

- Possession: this relationship is well illustrated by *John's car*: it answers the question 'Whose?'
- Measurement: used for time-periods and valuations:
    a week's holiday   a pound's worth of peas
  Here the apostrophe is often omitted:
    He was on a hundred pounds bail.
- Origination: my uncle's birthplace
- Expression of feelings: Jane's delight, Mike's dislike
- Description or classification: used mainly for humans and animals, and the occasional inanimate noun:
    a summer's day   women's college   ship's doctor
    a bird's nest   cow's milk

This usage answers the question 'What kind of?'. It is very close to a compound noun (as in *school-doctor, country-house*: p.376), and as a result the apostrophe is often omitted – a usage which can attract criticism:
    womens college   gents outfitters
The usage is not systematic: we do not say ~~a spring's day~~ or ~~a school's doctor~~.

Caution

Because of its many possible meanings, the genitive can be ambiguous if the context is unclear:
    Smith's murder will be revenged [is Smith the killer or the corpse?]
    David's picture was on the table [of him? or belonging to him?]
    Mary's team has won [the one she plays in? or the one she supports?]

To avoid the ambiguity, we need to rephrase, such as:
    The picture of David was on the table.
    The picture belonging to David was on the table.

's or *of* ?

Most nouns rarely or never occur with the *s*- genitive; the *of*-genitive is much more common. This construction also expresses a wider range of meanings than those found with the *s*- genitive.

- Collectivities: *I have a collection of old postcards.*
  not: ~~an old postcards' collection~~
- Kinds: *I'm growing two types of tomato.*
  not: ~~two tomatoes' types~~
- Quantities: *I have a bottle of red wine.*
  not: ~~a red wine's bottle~~
- Age: *I met a farmer of 80 years.*
  not: ~~an 80 years' farmer~~
- Size: *I've had a salary increase of 10 per cent.*
  not: ~~a 10 per cent's salary increase~~
- Composition: *I've got a coat of high-quality leather.*
  not: ~~a high-quality leather's coat~~

Influencing factors

Several factors condition our choice of *'s* or *of*:

- We generally use the *s*- genitive for humans, some animals, times (*July's storms*), and locations (*London's bridges*). Other inanimates usually use *of*.
- If we use an *s*- genitive, the information it contains is likely to be already known in the previous context (it is 'given': Chapter 70). If we use an *of*- genitive, the information is more likely to be 'new':

    David Mamet's plays [I assume you know of him]
    the plays of David Mamet [I make no such assumption]

- If the genitive element becomes lengthy (a **phrasal genitive**), we are more likely to use the *of*- genitive. We will say *the man's views*, but probably

    the views of the man from the Welfind Insurance Company
  Postmodification allows a more comfortable rhythm, and follows the principle of end-weight (p.344).

Using the genitive

The *s-* genitive is a concise way of presenting information. Indeed, the meaning can sometimes be so compressed that the result (as we saw on p.201) is ambiguity. It is therefore most often used in situations where conciseness of expression is a major consideration or where problems of ambiguity can be quickly resolved (as in conversation).

Broadcast news

The use of impersonal nouns with the *s-* genitive is a notable feature of news reporting:

last week's rise   Friday's announcement

Academic writing

Science, philosophy, and other intellectual domains express limited human involvement and have a concern for precision. Both factors motivate the frequent use of the *of-* genitive rather than the *s-* genitive in academic writing – as on the present page:

conciseness of expression   problems of ambiguity

There are four instances in the opening sentence of the definition of *hip* in *The New Penguin Encyclopedia*:

The outer rounded region at the side **of** the upper thigh – in anatomical terms, the joint between the head **of** the femur and the pelvis, and the point **of** articulation **of** the lower limb with the trunk.

Conversation

The only *s-* genitives which have any frequency in conversation are those expressing measure and the most abbreviated type – the **independent genitive**:

A month's supply of electricity.   I'm visiting a friend's.

DESCRIPTIVE SUMMARY

A determiner appears before a noun in order to specify its number and definiteness. The notion includes three types of word:

- **central determiners** comprise the definite and indefinite articles (*the/a*) and a few other words which can take their place, such as *this* and *some*.
- **predeterminers** are words which can be used before a central determiner, such as *all* and *double* (Chapter 37).
- **postdeterminers** are words which follow a central determiner but precede adjectives, such as *first* and *several* (Chapter 38).

This chapter deals only with the central class of determiners.

EXPLANATION

The central determiners have a clear semantic role. As the name suggests, their role is to 'determine' the reference of the nouns they precede – and thus, of the noun phrase as a whole. They enable us to answer such questions as: What sort of noun are we talking about? Is it a definite or an indefinite entity? Does it belong to anyone? How many entities are being referred to?

We can of course use many nouns without any determiner at all; but the choices offered by the central determiners allow us to characterize nouns in a number of very specific ways, chiefly with reference to various kinds of quantification.

Determiner meanings

- Definiteness: This contrast is primarily expressed by the articles *a* and *the*. Because this meaning is so basic to the noun phrase, and also because the articles are used so much more frequently than any other determiner, they have their own chapter (Chapter 36).

- Distance: the proximity of the noun to the speaker is expressed by the **demonstrative** determiners, *these* vs. *that/those*. The former are nearer (**proximal**); the latter further away (**distal**):

     this chair/moment   that chair/moment

- Possession: the ownership of the noun is expressed by the **possessive** determiners *my, your, his, her, its, our, their* (see also the genitive, Chapter 34):

     my car   your turn   their interests

- Personalizing: identity with a group of people can be expressed by *we, you*, and *them*:

     we followers of the party   you enemies of the state

  Them is nonstandard; standard English prefers *those*.

- Quantifying: a wide range of quantitative meanings can be expressed:
  - a universal meaning, using the indeterminate *all* and *both*:

       All soldiers are recalled.   Both cats ran.
  - an existential meaning, using the indefinitely positive *some* and negative *any*:

       Some shops are open.   I don't want any tea.
  - a distributive meaning, using *each* and *every*:

       Each stamp is valuable.   I've offered every chance.
  - a disjunctive meaning, using *either* and *neither*:

       Either hat will fit.   Neither horse won.
  - an alternative or additive meaning, using *another*:

       I've joined another party.   Have another banana.
  - a negative meaning, using *no*:

       No stone will be left unturned.

- a sufficiency meaning, using *enough,* expressing the lower bound required to satisfy some need:

    Enough money has been collected.
- an interrogative meaning, using *which, what, whichever,* or *whatever:*

    What answer have you got?

    Whatever result you get, I'll be happy.

The boundary between the central class of determiners and the other classes is not clear-cut. Some grammarians list as central determiners items that in this grammar are classed as postdeterminers (such as *many* and *several*).

Using determiners

We can sense the importance of determiners if we note the early age at which children begin to learn them. They appear before age two, as children explore their identity with reference to the objects, events, and other people around them. Here are some two-year-old examples:

   my teddy   want **that** car   see **them** doggies

Every variety, spoken or written, uses determiners with frequency. Only items in a telegraphic style and a few minor sentences (Chapter 2) tend to drop them:

   MOB ATTACKS EMBASSY   KEEP OFF GRASS

But even newspaper headlines cannot avoid determiners entirely, for they express some newsworthy distinctions:

   SOME HOSTAGES RELEASED

   ALL HOSTAGES RELEASED

   NO TAX CUTS

And minor sentences need them too:

   NO EXIT   NO WAITING

Determiner-less speech is also sometimes used as a marker of 'primitive' linguistic skill, as in the depiction of young children's speech, foreigner-talk, or the pidgins of supposedly primitive people (see also p.191).

Variety differences

An impression of the frequency with which determiners are used can be gained from this extract of conversation, where the determiners are underlined:

... he was telling me a lovely story about <u>this</u> chap who wanted to get <u>some</u> new tyres for <u>his</u> bike from <u>that</u> new shop in <u>the</u> High Street ...

Dialect uses of determiners are also sometimes found, such as the widespread nonstandard use of *them* or (in Scotland) *they*:

Have you got them books? (... they books?)

or southern US *y'all's* for *your*:

I passed y'all's house.

We can see trends of usage for individual determiners in different varieties. For example, academic discussion, and other domains with an interest in cautious generalization, make considerable use of indeterminate quantifiers such as *some* and *whichever*. Science writing, dealing with entities rather than people, avoids personal possessives – other than 'expository *our*':

Our aim in this study is to show ...

By contrast, we would expect the focus on human relationship which is at the heart of prose fiction to use possessives frequently – and so it does, especially in novels written in the first person. Here are the opening lines of Anne Brontë's *The Tenant of Wildfell Hall*:

You must go back with me to the autumn of 1827. <u>My</u> father, as you know, was a sort of gentleman farmer in —shire; and I, by <u>his</u> express desire, succeeded him in the same quiet occupation, not very willingly, for ambition urged me to higher aims, and self-conceit assured me that, in disregarding <u>its</u> voice, I was burying <u>my</u> talent in the earth, and hiding <u>my</u> light under a bushel.

And possessives are fundamental in prayers:

<u>Our</u> father, who art in heaven, hallowed be <u>thy</u> name ...

The article system comprises the **definite article** (*the*), the **indefinite article** (*a* or *an*), and the non-use of either in front of a noun, which is often called the **zero article**. This last concept is somewhat unusual, but it is plainly an option in several contexts – often, as here, the most natural or idiomatic option:

I'm going to have a lunch today. [I missed having one yesterday]

I'm going to have the lunch I missed yesterday.

I'm going to have lunch.

Semantic factors govern the choice of the articles. They relate to whether a noun is to be interpreted as specific or generic, or as definite or indefinite.

Specific vs. generic

The articles are the main way in which we can express a contrast between **specific** and **generic** meaning. If we want to refer to a specific, individual entity, we can use *a* or *the*:

I was dreaming about a lion.

I was dreaming about the lion.

If we want to refer to a class of entities, the generic meaning, we can use zero with the plural:

I was dreaming of lions. [lions in general]

Note the contrast with:

I was dreaming of the lions. [a specific group of lions]

Definite vs. indefinite

The

The is the basic marker of definiteness, capable of marking all common nouns. It asserts that a noun is identifiable from the previous or following linguistic context, the nonlinguistic situation surrounding the user, or the user's general knowledge or expectations:

> I found a pencil and a pen, but **the** pen was broken. [*the* refers backwards, to *pen*]
> I've just met **the** professor of linguistics. [*the* refers forwards, to *linguistics*]
> I was in **the** hall and I saw **the** cat. [*the* refers to a familiar situation]
> **The** sun's come out. [we know there is only one sun]
> We're going to **the** theatre. [we know the type of occasion this is]

Sometimes, a speaker assumes knowledge which the hearer doesn't possess:

> A: They've shot the president. B: Which president?

But as most conversations are on the basis of shared knowledge, this kind of ambiguity is uncommon.

Likewise, we do not find a written notice ambiguous:

> BEWARE OF THE DOG

We do not ask 'Which dog?'. That is beside the point.

The identifies a particular noun – but that does not necessarily mean that the noun is familiar to us. If someone says:

> the brother of our gardener is at the door

we may never have met this person, but he is certainly identifiable.

The with a singular noun usually identifies an entity uniquely: *the cat* = one cat. Occasionally, it refers to either of two entities:

> Jane grabbed me by the arm.

A or *an*

A(n) is the basic marker of indefiniteness, used with count nouns (Chapter 30) in two main ways:
- To express quantity:
  I bought a book.   We jog twice a day.
- To classify an entity:
  Fred Jones is a quantity surveyor.

A(n) does not assume that the noun has been previously mentioned nor that it can be identified from the user's situation or knowledge:

A coach is pulling up outside. [we know nothing further about it]

Zero

The article is commonly omitted with singular nouns in several varieties:
- Instructional writing, such as recipes and manuals:
  Beat egg lightly with fork.
  Disconnect cleaner from outlet before replacing belt.
- Notices, headlines, and other 'block' uses of language (Chapter 2):
  KEEP OFF GRASS
  FILM STAR MARRIES MODEL
- Informal writing, especially when space is short, as in postcards, diaries, and cables:
  Having marvellous time. Weather wonderful.
  Met Jim outside restaurant. Had great time.
  Send spare wheel urgently. Letter follows.

Using the articles: definiteness

Several varieties of language are characteristically definite, describing a situation which the listener or reader knows, or is assumed to know, or is in the process of getting to know. They are heavily reliant on the use of *the*, as well as other definite determiners (p.205).

The noun phrase

Instructions

Manuals, explanatory leaflets, and other instructional materials, expound states of affairs which are intrinsically definite, as in this extract from a manual supplied with a do-it-yourself heater-construction kit:

To remove the heater from the floor pedestal, turn the black locking screw anti-clockwise.

This is a clear use of the definite article reliant on the nonlinguistic situation (p.209), with a diagram supplied.

Guide books

Also very reliant on the use of *the* is the kind of language found in guide books:

Turn left outside the museum and you will see the Memorial Arch at the end of the street. The Arch was erected at the end of the Napoleonic Wars ...

The use of *the* in the first sentence is situational, relating to the accompanying map. The second sentence begins with *the* referring back to the previous sentence, and concludes with articles reflecting assumed knowledge.

Sports commentary

All forms of sports commentary describe on-going events about which the commentators can be definite, because they can assume listeners know such things as the lay-out of the playing area and the artefacts used in a game:

The referee is showing Smith the red card ...

He smashes the ball, and it's gone well over the sight-screen at the south end of the ground ...

Using the articles: indefiniteness

The indefinite article is likely to be common in varieties which are characteristically indefinite, where information is being introduced for the first time or where listeners and readers are assumed to be lacking in knowledge.

Stories

Jokes, nursery-rhymes, limericks, and story-telling often begin in this way:

I remember a chap who had a car like that ...
There was an Englishman, an Irishman ...
There was an old woman who lived in a shoe ...
There was a young lady from Bolton ...

Definitions

Definitions in textbooks, dictionaries, and encyclopedias are characteristically of the form 'An X is a kind of Y which has attribute Z':

An adjective is a word that describes a noun.
chromium A hard, lustrous metal ...

Travel magazines

Items introducing us to new parts of the world rely on the indefinite article, as in this extract from a travel guide:

Take a hike into the Hawaiian hinterland and you are frequently rewarded with a waterfall and handy swimming hole. A favourite on Maui is Puohokamua falls, a 30-foot tumult tumbling into a perfect lovers-in-a-clinch pool in a lush fern-filled amphitheatre.

In literature

Important dramatic effects can be conveyed through the use of the articles. At the beginning of a novel, nothing is known, so we might expect the use of the indefinite article. This is how Philip Pullman begins *The Amber Spyglass*, Book 3 of his 'Dark Materials' trilogy:

> In a valley shaded with rhododendrons, close to the snow line, where a stream milky with meltwater splashed and where doves and linnets flew among the immense pines, lay a cave, half-hidden by the crag above and the stiff heavy leaves that clustered below.

But in Book 1 of the trilogy, *Northern Lights*, he opts for definite articles:

> Lyra and her daemon moved through the darkening hall, taking care to keep to one side, out of sight of the kitchen. The three great tables that ran the length of the hall were laid already, the silver and the glass catching what little light there was, and the long benches were pulled out ready for the guests.

It is an effective device. New information is presented as if it were familiar. It invites the reader's cooperation and active involvement. The reader has to do some work. Which hall? Which kitchen? Which guests? The definiteness conveys the impression of an already-existing reality, and helps readers build up a mental picture of the fictional world they are being invited to enter. It is a well-established effect. Here are the opening lines of Thomas Hardy's *Jude the Obscure*:

> The schoolmaster was leaving the village, and everybody seemed sorry. The miller at Cresscombe lent him the small white tilted cart and horse to carry his goods to the city of his destination ...

The titles of novels regularly use *The* for the same reason: *The Alien* is intriguing as a book title; *An Alien* much less so.

DESCRIPTIVE SUMMARY

In the noun phrase, **predeterminers** are words which can be used before the central class of determiners. They can be grouped into a very few types, shown here preceding *the* or *a*:

- Three basic quantifiers – *all, both, half*:
    all the time   both the cars   half the price
  (*All* and *both* are also used as central determiners, p.205.)
- A class of multipliers – *twice, double*, etc.:
    double the cost   three times the amount
- A class of fractions – *a quarter, two-thirds*, etc.:
  a quarter the cost   three-quarters the amount
  These are often followed by *of*.
- Two exclamatory items, *such* and *what*:
    I saw such a lot of people!   What an idiot!
  (For *what* in exclamatory clauses, see Chapter 7.)

Some adverbs (Chapter 52) can modify predeterminers, such as *not, only, almost*, and *just*.
    almost all the people   **precisely** twice the cost
    not even a quarter of the interest

EXPLANATION

The chief function of the predeterminers is to work along with the central class of determiners to express notions of quantity. Their meanings range from the universal sense of *all* to the highly particularizing senses of the fractions. Usually only one quantifying predeterminer is used in an individual noun phrase, but the various adverbial additions allow the sense to be narrowed down further.

When *of* is used, it changes the grammatical status of the predeterminers, making them more like pronouns:

two-thirds (of) the amount   half (of) the answers

The *of* draws attention to the way the head noun can be broken up into parts (a 'partitive' meaning). However, because the semantic difference between the two constructions is minimal, they are taken together in this chapter.

Using predeterminers

- The exclamatory items are common only in informal conversational contexts, though they will also be found in literary texts of varying formality:

    I never heard of such a thing.
    What a time we had at the show!
    What a rascal art thou ... (Prince Hal to Falstaff, Shakespeare, *Henry IV Part 1*, II.iv.344)

- The more general quantifying expressions also have a widespread use in conversational varieties:

    It's half a mile to the next roundabout.
    You can't please all the people all of the time.

    The more specific expressions tend to be restricted to domains where precise levels of quantification are expected. Most obviously, this includes the various fields of science and mathematics, as well as subjects which deal routinely in quantities, such as economics, surveying, geography, and history:

    Over half the men and two-thirds of the women were illiterate at the beginning of the century ...

- Any domain where it is important to give the impression of precision is likely to make great use of predeterminers. Advertising, for example, contains claims such as these:

    Twice the whitening power for half the price!
    A single portion gives you three-quarters of your daily requirement of vitamins B1 and B2.

In the noun phrase, **postdeterminers** are words which can be used after the central class of determiners (Chapter 35), but before other kinds of premodification (Chapter 39). There are four main types, shown here mainly following *the*:

- the **cardinal numerals** – *one, two*, etc.:
    the four main types
- the **ordinal numerals** – *first, second*, etc., along with some sequencing words, such as *last* and *next*:
    the third turning on the left   the last big event
- a set of quantifiers – *much, many, (a) few, (a) little, several*:
    the many answers   a few chances
- a set of phrasal quantifiers, consisting of noun + *of*:
    a **lot of** books   a **number of** signs

Some of the forms express degree (Chapter 48). This set occurs with count nouns (Chapter 30), such as *answers*:
    few / fewer / fewest   many / more / most
This set occurs with noncount nouns, such as *interest*:
    little / less / least   much / more / most

As with the other determiners, the chief role of postdeterminers is to enable us to express different kinds of quantification, at varying levels of precision. Two main semantic dimensions are involved:

Determinate vs. indeterminate

This contrast is offered by the choice between ordinal or cardinal numerals and the other items:
    I have **sixteen** copies.   I have **several** copies.

Paucal ('little') vs. multal ('lot')

This contrast is made within the indeterminate group of items: it distinguishes the forms of *few* and *little* from the other items in this group:

I have **few** copies.   I have **many** copies.

Some quite subtle contrasts of meaning can be expressed:

I have little chance of passing the exam. [pessimistic]

I have a little chance of passing the exam. [optimistic]

The postdeterminer use of *a little*, when used with noncount concrete nouns, must be distinguished from the adjectival sense of *little*, meaning 'small':

Mary had a little lamb. [adjective: her lamb was small]

Mary had a little lamb. [postdeterminer: she had a small portion]

Using postdeterminers

The same range of factors influences the use of postdeterminers as is found in relation to predeterminers (p.214). It is important to note the extent to which we rely on postdeterminers in many everyday contexts. We seem to be perpetually quantifying, as seen in these extracts. The first is from a business advertisement:

Nifco produces **over 18,000** different types of industrial plastic parts and components, and has expanded to a network of **sixteen** companies in **twelve** countries.

The second is from a newspaper report of an international tennis competition:

Rain postponed **four** women's matches and **three** men's matches on Wednesday and Thursday in the US Open. As a result, **two** suspended matches will continue to a **fourth** day, and the completion of **several** other matches due to begin on Friday is now in doubt.

DESCRIPTIVE SUMMARY

Premodification describes any words appearing between the determiner set (including postdeterminers) and the head of a noun phrase. They are of four main types:

- Adjectives (Chapter 48), sometimes accompanied by intensifying adverbs, such as *very*:

    a big green car   a very pretty flower
- Participles (Chapter 16), both -*ing* and -*ed*:

    the approaching train   the adopted children
- Nouns (Chapter 28):

    a garden chair   my summer vacation
- Phrases and clauses:

    a ready-to-wear suit   a do-it-yourself mentality

Indefinitely long sequences of items may occur:

In the market I found some amazingly cheap, really pretty long green summer dresses.

Coordination (Chapter 64) also appears:

a green and red costume   a cheap but pretty dress

EXPLANATION

Both premodification and postmodification (Chapter 40) add descriptive detail to the noun phrase. The same meaning can be expressed using either option:

a plastic spoon   a spoon made of plastic

that political report   that report about politics

These examples illustrate the basic difference between the two types: premodification is a much more condensed style of expression compared with postmodification. The same thing is being said in fewer words.

Being succinct: benefits and costs

Succinctness has its benefits, but also its consequences. What we gain in brevity, we lose in explicitness. Because the speaker or writer has chosen the less explicit option, the burden is on the listener or reader to work out exactly what meaning is intended. This is especially the case with premodification using a noun: any sequence of two nouns needs to be interpreted.

We're expecting more foreign contributions.

[contributions from foreign countries?

contributions to foreign countries?]

The postmodifying equivalents shown in the brackets clarify the relationship between the nouns.

Most noun + noun sequences present no problem:

safety belt   football fan   market reports

However, the less familiar or more abstract the meaning, the more we may find difficulty:

union actions   education proposals   Oslo accords

What *are* Oslo accords, exactly? Agreements made *in* Oslo, *about* Oslo, *for* Oslo? Several possibilities arise.

For this reason, sequences of premodifiers are not as commonplace as we might expect. If *Oslo accords* is inexplicit, so much more so is:

the forward-looking 1990 Oslo accords

[several interpretations are possible, such as:

the accords of a forward-looking 1990s Oslo?

the forward-looking 1990 accords from Oslo?]

With each extra premodifier, the interpretations multiply.

Of course, if the speaker/writer has gauged the knowledge of the audience correctly, there is no problem. A politician writing for politicians could assume that everyone would know what the *Oslo accords* were. But someone writing for a general readership would be wise not to make such an assumption, and to opt for the more explicit postmodifying expression.

Ordering premodifiers

As soon as we opt for a sequence of premodifiers, we find we must arrange them in a particular order. The factors governing the order are all semantic in character, but they are not easy to define precisely, and usage varies somewhat.

There is no theoretical limit to the number of possible premodifiers, so that the following sequence – although unlikely ever to occur – is grammatical, and in the most likely order:

> I love those stunning valuable huge old red German gold-plated grandfather clocks.

Each premodifier here represents a semantic class:
- Nearest to the head noun is the attribute which most closely identifies the **type** of noun it is:
  > grandfather clock (vs. *alarm/carriage/cuckoo*, etc.)

  Other examples: *photo album, lap-top computer.*
- Next comes any reference to the **substance** of the noun, such as the material from which it is made, or the state of that material, or (in the case of abstract nouns) the most salient feature of their character:
  > gold-plated ... clocks (vs. *silver/wooden*, etc.)

  Other examples: *steel rail, carved pillar, broken wheel, increased risk, developing nation, opening hours.*
  Participles, as the last three examples show, fall into this class of premodifier.
- Next comes any reference to **provenance**:
  > German ... clocks (vs. French/eighteenth-century, etc.)

  Other examples: *Anglo-Saxon mentality, Welsh tourism.*
- Next comes any reference to **colour**:
  > red ... clocks (vs. *green/bright blue*, etc.)

  Other examples: *orange shoes, red-brown gate.*
- Next comes any reference to **age**:
  > old ... clocks (vs. *new/ancient/classical*, etc.)

  Other examples: *old-fashioned hat, pre-War ideas.*

- Next come the vast majority of adjectives – all the items identifying **general** attributes of the noun, such as its size, dimensions, and other properties:

    huge ... clocks (vs. *tiny/circular/octagonal*, etc.)

    Other examples: *intelligent answer, kind offer, tasty meal, vast area, tall buildings, inaudible message.*

    If more than one adjective is selected from this class, they may appear in any order – though phonetic factors (such as rhythm) may be influential:

    an intelligent, thoughtful, sensitive reply

    a sensitive, thoughtful, intelligent reply, etc.

Very few adjectives are place-sensitive in front of this general class. But two further groups tend to appear at the very front of the noun phrase:

- Immediately in front of the general class would come any adjectives expressing the speaker/writer's **evaluation** of the noun:

    valuable ... clocks (vs. *nice/lovely/ugly*, etc.)

    Other examples: *boring speech, gorgeous dress.*

- At the very front come **absolute** or **intensifying** items:

    stunning ... clocks (vs. *marvellous/unbelievable*, etc.)

    Other examples: *sheer brilliance, fantastic concert.*

Coordinating premodifiers

Any pair or group of premodifiers can be coordinated, the effect being to make the items equivalent in their contribution to the meaning of the noun phrase:

    I had a tasty and expensive meal.

    = I had an expensive and tasty meal.

Without the coordination, we tend to see one adjective as more closely related to the head noun:

    a tasty, expensive meal [an expensive meal which is also tasty]

    an expensive, tasty meal [a tasty meal which is also expensive]

Using premodifiers

Premodification has two main functions: it adds descriptive detail to the noun phrase, often with the aim of making a vivid or dramatic impact; and it is the construction of choice whenever there is a constraint on length or a concern for succinctness. It is much more common in writing than in speech. However, long sequences of items are rare at any time; we usually find premodifiers used singly or in pairs, often with an accompanying intensifier.

Providing a vivid description

We have already seen a good example of adjectival description on p.187, in the extract from *Possession*. Premodification is the primary means of providing a great deal of detail in a succinct way, so it is widely employed to build up a picture of people and places in fiction. The earlier example was of a scenic location. Here is a corresponding use of adjectives in character description – of Captain Ahab, in Herman Melville's *Moby Dick* (Chapter 28):

His **whole high, broad** form seemed made of **solid** bronze, and shaped in an **unalterable** mould, like Cellini's **cast** Perseus. Threading its way out from among his **grey** hairs, and continuing right down one side of his **tawny scorched** face and neck, till it disappeared in his clothing, you saw a **slender rod-like** mark, lividly **whitish**. It resembled that **perpendicular** seam sometimes made in the **straight, lofty** trunk of a **great** tree, when the **upper** lightning tearingly darts down it ...

This extract also includes an adjective in postmodifying position (*whitish*): see p.228. A further use of adjectives in character description is illustrated on p.259.

Providing a tempting description

Advertising is the one major exception to the generalization that premodifier sequences are uncommon. Ads are trying to do two things at once: grab your attention and convey the salient features of the product. Both require brevity, especially in settings where the consumer's attention is curtailed – such as on a TV screen, or when passing a poster at speed in a car.

- The catch-phrase or slogan with just two premodifiers is especially common, particularly in television jingles.
  Golden, toasted cheese.   A rich coffee taste.
  The ultimate driving machine.
- There is often alliterative support and a bouncy rhythm:
  Chunky, crunchy crisps.   A light, lingering perfume.
- Adjectives may even be repeated:
  A big big burger.   That rich rich flavour.
- In many cases the first adjective is emotional and the second descriptive:
  delicious refreshing drink   exciting citrous flavour
  fantastic new recipe   elegant tapered slacks
- When the product identity is clear from the context, the premodifiers can carry the whole weight of the message:
  Reassuringly expensive.
  Cool ... thirst-quenching ...
- Adjective comparison (Chapter 51) is commonplace:
  The smoothest ride you ever had.
  The country's most wanted Christmas toy.
  A more elegant dress for those special occasions.
- The possibilities offered by indefinitely long sequences are occasionally exploited, as in this 1973 advertisement for Pepsi-Cola:
  Lipsmackin' thirstquenchin' acetastin' motivatin' good buzzin' cooltalkin' highwalkin' fastlivin' evergivin' coolfizzin' Pepsi.

Providing an academic description

The brevity of premodification makes it a construction of choice
in subject-areas where there is a need to present several attributes
in quick succession, such as biology and medicine. We can see the
gain in succinctness in this encyclopedia definition of *agave*:

An **evergreen** perennial with **very short, tough** stems and
thick, fleshy, waxy, sword-shaped leaves, forming a rosette.

To express these notions using postmodification would add an
undesirable wordiness:

... with stems which are very short and tough ...

Because academic writing is always comparing and contrasting
properties, most nouns need to be premodified. Here is an
example from *The Cambridge Encyclopedia of Earth Sciences*
(Chapter 14):

The **chemical** characteristics and the **compositional** variations
with space and time outlined for **volcanic** rocks above also
characterize **intrusive** rocks of **destructive** margins. However,
the relationship of **extrusive and intrusive** rocks is not
unequivocal; **young intrusive** rocks are not yet exposed by
erosion, and **exposed** intrusions may not represent **magmatic
liquid** compositions or may be hydrothermally altered because
of **slow** cooling in the presence of **meteoric** water.

The extract also shows a use of an adjective after the verb
(*unequivocal*): see Chapter 48.

Coordinated premodifiers such as *extrusive and intrusive* are
especially common in academic writing, where they convey the
required impression of balanced, thoughtful judgement:

during the late fifteenth and early sixteenth centuries
the analysis of animal or plant remains
in Roman, Greek, and Egyptian settlements

Providing a succinct description

Constraints on the length of expression are at the heart of all news reporting. Radio and television broadcasters are sensitive to the pressures of time; newspaper and periodical journalists to those of space. The two mediums particularly favour the use of premodifying nouns, especially in the plural:

drinks merger   profits growth   talks proposals

and especially with those nouns further modified or supported by an adjective:

dirty-tricks campaign   new divorce laws
foreign affairs committee   human rights issues

Several such phrases appear in this extract from a front-page news report:

The **interim government** yesterday scrapped the **controversial anti-subversion legislation** that sparked an **unprecedented political crisis** in the summer and brought a million **civil rights protesters** onto the streets of the capital. **Pro-democracy legislators** welcomed the move, which they said was long overdue. A **government spokesman** said that a **special working group** would be set up to study the **enactment implications**.

HEADLINES

Premodifiers are often seen in headlines. Here are four from a single front-page:

Hong Kong scraps **subversion** bill
US economic recovery fails to revive **job market**
Police arrest **Shanghai tycoon** on **financial charges**
Annan calls for overhaul of **world security system**

They will often be seen on a news-vendor's stand, where it is essential to be brief, even to the point of inclarity:

PENSIONS PROBE   TAX SHOCK

Of course, it is precisely the intriguing inexplicitness that arouses our curiosity, and makes us buy the paper!

Postmodification describes any words or constructions which appear after the head noun in the noun phrase. There are three main types:

- Prepositional phrases (Chapter 59):
    a guitar **on the floor**   the stars **in the sky**
- Nonfinite clauses (Chapter 17):
    There's a map **pinned to the wall**.
    See the guitar **lying on the floor**?
    That's the CD **to buy**.
- Finite clauses (Chapter 17):
    There's a map **which is pinned to the wall**.
    See the guitar **which is lying on the floor**?
    That's the CD **you should buy**.
- A few other word classes sometimes postmodify:
    two days **more**   the countryside **proper**
    the devil **incarnate**   a man **your age**
    a trip **abroad**   the people **themselves**

Sequences of postmodifiers also occur, often coordinated:
    I saw some **kids with red shirts who were playing football**.
    I saw some kids **wearing red shirts and playing football**.

EXPLANATION

The range of constructions available in postmodification allows us to introduce a huge amount of complex detail into a noun phrase, varying in explicitness and stylistic effect.

Varying explicitness

The relationship between the three main types of postmodification is one of increasing explicitness.

- Most explicit is the finite clause (the relative clause: Chapter 41), for this gives as much information as possible about who or what is involved, and especially about the time of an action:

  the clown who is dancing in the street [the action is happening now]

- Rather less explicit is the nonfinite clause, for this conveys only the nature of the action, telling us nothing about its time of occurrence (Chapter 17):

  the clown dancing in the street [is/was/will be popular]

- Least explicit is the prepositional phrase, for this does not even tell us what action or state there might be:

  the clown in the street

In fact we do not usually need to be very explicit, because extra information comes from other parts of the sentence or from the nonlinguistic situation. Prepositional phrases, accordingly, are by far the commonest form of postmodification, accounting for two-thirds or more of all postmodifiers in all varieties. *Of* and *in* are the most frequently used prepositions.

An even more reduced construction is seen in:

  fifty miles an hour   the events last year

These postmodifiers are noun phrases of speed, age, time, and location. They resemble prepositional phrases:

  fifty miles in an hour   the events of last year

In several other cases, the postmodification is a single-word adverb or preposition:

  my trip abroad   the road ahead   the way in

Some of these constructions might be expanded (e.g. *the road which lies ahead*), but it would result in a wordiness which most people instinctively avoid.

Varying stylistic effect

The normal place for adjectives is in front of the noun; used as postmodifiers, a stylistic contrast is inevitable:

The old haunted castle stood on the hillside.
The castle, old, haunted, stood on the hillside.

The postmodification draws attention to the adjectives, resulting in a more atmospheric description. If read aloud, as the commas suggest, they would be spoken as separate intonation units, further highlighting their meaning.

The effect can be enhanced by expanding the adjectives (Chapter 49), a technique common in fiction:

The castle, old as the legends, haunted by the spirits of kings, stood on the hillside.

The postmodifying option allows an alternative rhythm and rhyme in a poetic line:

Was a lady such a lady, cheeks **so round** and lips **so red**, –
On her neck the small face **buoyant**, like a bell-flower on its bed
(Robert Browning, 'A Toccata of Galuppi's')

Adding emphasis

Sometimes the effect of switching from premodification to postmodification is simply to add emphasis:

two more days! → two days more!
the 1812 overture → the overture 1812

The effect can be slightly archaic, and is often formal or rhetorical. This is especially the effect which arises when referring to domains of subject-matter:

I've money **enough**.   We talked of matters **political**.
In years **past**, we would ring the church bells.
The meeting will deal with all things **Welsh**.
Let's turn now to the countryside **proper**.

Some of these expressions, through longstanding use, have become fixed phrases:

the body politic   the devil incarnate   whisky galore

Using postmodifiers

Postmodifiers are most frequently used in formal writing – especially writing in which the thought is of some complexity. They are therefore a feature of academic writing, where strings of postmodifying elements can be found – especially of prepositional phrases – expressing a characteristic density of information.

Releasing hormone is stored by the neurones of the median eminence of the hypothalamus in response to stimuli from the brain. [everything after *neurones* is postmodification]

The subject-matter in such cases is typically non-human.

There is also an association between the different types of postmodifier and certain verbs:

- Nonfinite -*ing* clauses often have a verb of inclusion, such as *being, containing, using*, and *involving*:

    We prepared a solution containing all four elements.

- Non-finite -*ed* clauses often have a verb expressing the result of a process, such as *based, given*, and *produced*:

    The clinic developed an approach based on two early studies by American researchers.

Fostering parallelism

When writers use more than one postmodifier, the items tend to be of the same structural type – two prepositional phrases, for example, or two -*ed* clauses:

the response of the people to the new law ...
the idea, formulated by Jones and tested by Brown ...

It has long been thought stylistically elegant to compose postmodifying constructions which are rhythmically, grammatically, and semantically symmetrical. These properties combine in the epigraph to J.R.R. Tolkien's *The Lord of the Rings*:

One Ring to rule them all. One Ring to find them.
One Ring to bring them all and in the darkness bind them.

Watching out for ambiguity

We need to take care when using more than one postmodifier in the same noun phrase because it is easy to slip into ambiguity or give a confusing impression:

I'd like the car in the showroom with the red front.

Which has the red front – car or showroom? A simple re-ordering avoids any possible ambiguity:

I'd like the car with the red front in the showroom.

A particular danger is to separate a nonfinite clause from its head noun, so that it is unclear which noun it refers to. This is the so-called 'dangling participle' (p.125):

A plane looked out for sharks flying over the beaches.

Sharks fly? Here, too, re-ordering solves the problem:

A plane flying over the beaches looked out for sharks.

If a sequence of postmodifiers contains structures of different kinds, any relative clause (Chapter 41) is likely to be placed later rather than earlier in the sequence. This is because the greater explicitness of finite clauses makes them easy to recognise and relate to the head noun, even when separated from it:

The mayor sympathized with the <u>response</u> of the objectors <u>which was widely reported in the press</u>.

The singular *was* clearly links the clause to *response*. Reversing the order of postmodifiers could result in ambiguity, because there is nothing in the prepositional phrase showing which noun it relates to:

The mayor sympathized with the response which was widely reported in the press of the objectors.

Does *of the objectors* refer to *response* or *press*?

The first order also respects the principle of end-weight (p.344): a finite clause is always going to be 'heavier' than a prepositional phrase, and will feel rhythmically more appropriate if it follows the shorter postmodifier.

The noun phrase

Elegant construction

Although academic writing makes most use of the more developed forms of postmodification, they can be found in any variety of speech or writing which is trying to convey structured thinking of any complexity. The interplay between content, structural balance, and rhythm to achieve a clear and elegant result is not easy to control, however. Most writers need to rewrite their drafts of complex noun phrases, and it requires oratory of some skill to do justice to intricate postmodification in speech. In these examples the head noun is in bold, and the postmodifiers are underlined.

From journalism

This extract is from a sports page item on golf:

Five places will be decided by a separate qualifying points **table**, amassed from tournaments anywhere on the globe, and launched this week at the European Masters in Switzerland.

From religion

Many prayers use complex postmodification:

O **God**, unto whom all hearts are open, all desires known, and from whom no secrets are hid, cleanse the thoughts of our hearts ... (Book of Common Prayer, *Holy Communion*)

From public speaking

These powerful lines are from a speech made by Winston Churchill in June 1941. It is written text read aloud.

I see the Russian **soldiers** standing on the threshold of their native land, guarding the fields that their fathers have tilled from time immemorial. Any **man or state** who fights on against Nazidom will have our aid. Any **man or state** who marches with Hitler is our foe.

DESCRIPTIVE SUMMARY

The most complex kind of postmodification in the noun phrase (Chapter 40) is the finite clause, usually called the **relative clause**. Each clause is introduced by a word which 'relates' the clause to the preceding head noun (or **antecedent**): these are either **relative pronouns** (*who, whom, whose, which, that*) or **relative adverbs** (*where, when, why, while, whence, whereupon*, etc.):

The official who visited me was very helpful.

I visited the place where I grew up.

There is concord between the relative pronoun and the antecedent (Chapters 14 and 33):
* *who(m)* and *whose* refer back to personal nouns;
* *which* refers back to nonpersonal nouns;
* *that* refers back to either personal or nonpersonal nouns.

When the subject of the relative clause is present, the pronoun may be omitted:

I opened the parcel which John sent.

I opened the parcel John sent.

EXPLANATION

The semantic relationship between a postmodifier and its noun can be viewed in one of two ways, and this contrast is most clearly illustrated with reference to relative clauses. The contrast goes under various labels, such as **restrictive** vs. **nonrestrictive** (the terms used in this book) or **defining** vs. **nondefining**. The terms refer to the type of semantic relationship between the clause and the head noun.

- In a restrictive relationship, we need the relative clause in order to identify the reference of the noun.

I am your uncle...
I have come from France....
I have written a book....
The book I have written is out next week..
Would you like to see a copy of the book I have written...

- In a nonrestrictive relationship, we do not need the clause, because the identity of the head noun is already known.

Either it has been previously identified in the linguistic context or its identity is a matter of general knowledge.

The contrast is signalled in writing through punctuation, and in speech through intonation (Chapters 75 and 76).

We can illustrate the contrast in meaning through a pair of examples:

My uncle who lives in France has written a book.

Gloss: I have other uncles who do not live in France. Where he lives is therefore crucial to his identity, in this sentence. The clause restricts the meaning of the noun.

My uncle, who lives in France, has written a book.

Gloss: I have one uncle, and I'm just happening to mention that he lives in France. Where he lives is not really an issue. The clause does not restrict the meaning of the noun.

It is the nonrestrictive relationship which needs to be marked by punctuation – commas, dashes, or parentheses.

Using relative clauses

Restrictive postmodification directly affects the semantic identity of the head noun. We come to rely on it as a means of expressing the core of what we want to say, in the noun phrase. It is therefore much more common than nonrestrictive postmodification.

Nonrestrictive clauses contain information which is tangential to the meaning of the head noun. They could be omitted without this seriously affecting the core meaning of the noun phrase. Nonrestrictive clauses therefore tend to be most used in varieties where a value is placed on adding tangential information.

In news reporting

News items are always trying to add extra interest to their content. The main piece of news can often be reported very briefly, and nonrestrictive clauses then provide a convenient means of elaboration. Their content is deemed newsworthy, but it is nonetheless content that has been 'tacked on'. In this news item on a business merger, the essential content is reported in the main clause:

   The deal included the sale of Smith's …

The item might have ended there, but it did not. The sentence continued, after a comma:

   … which had already been offered for sale a year ago.

This strategy is a major stylistic feature in all kinds of journalism. Here is an extract from a business page about a Liberian firm (nonrestrictive clauses are underlined):

   It took over in 2000 after the previous managers fell out with the government of former president Charles Taylor, <u>who went into exile in Nigeria last month</u>. Liser is based in the US, reflecting the links between the US and Liberia, <u>which was founded by freed US slaves more than 150 years ago</u>.

Neither clause is strictly necessary, but they add interest.

In informal speech

In informal speech, nonrestrictive relative clauses are often inserted later in a sentence, away from their head noun (as a **supplementary** relative clause). The usage reflects the lack of forward planning which is typical of spontaneous speech. The speaker introduces an extra point after the noun phrase is completed – simply adding it on, as a kind of parenthesis, later in the sentence. At the very end of a sentence, the meaning usually relates to the sentence as a whole (a **sentential** relative clause):

- I told John about your suggestion for a loan – **who's more than happy to oblige, by the way** – and then Sara raised a problem ...
- so in the end he returned everything to the shop – **which really surprised me**.

Usage issues

The relative clause has attracted a surprising amount of usage controversy, some of the issues dating back centuries. Among the earliest is the objection to a preposition being separated from its relative pronoun and placed at the end of a sentence (p.296), and the use of *whom* instead of *who*:

That is the man I was referring to.
That is the man to whom I was referring.
That is the man whom / who I saw.

Most issues of this kind relate to distinctions of formality. Some usages (such as the use of *whom* instead of *who*) are associated with formal discourse; others with informal. The prescriptive tradition was highly dismissive of the informal usages, and strongly recommended the formal alternatives for all occasions. Today, we are learning to respect the choice between the two levels of style which the language makes available to us.

Pronoun vs. no pronoun

In the case where the relative pronoun can be omitted (p.232), formal English prefers the pronoun to be present; less formal English generally omits it:

A firm decision is the response which we wanted.

A firm decision is the response we wanted.

The zero usage is especially common in conversation and fictional dialogue. By contrast, academic writing tends to make the relationship explicit, and this can actually aid comprehension in complex sentences. In the following example, the use of *which* helps the reader to follow the organization of the sentence:

The exposure index may differ from the film speed the manufacturer prints on the side of the box.

The exposure index may differ from the film speed which the manufacturer prints on the side of the box.

WH- VS. THAT

In cases where we could use either a *wh-* form (*which, who*) or *that*, formal British English prefers the *wh-* forms; *that* is more common in informal English. American English prefers *that* in all styles:

A firm decision is the response that we wanted.

That is rare in both British and American English when the clause is nonrestrictive, and style manuals dislike it:

I went to get my car, that was left in the garage.

OF WHICH VS. WHOSE

If we want to express a possessive relationship after an inanimate noun (Chapter 33), we have a choice of pronouns:

I saw the book whose cover was very badly torn.

I saw the book of which the cover was very badly torn.

The former is the more natural construction, used in all styles; but some do not like to use a personal *whose* after an inanimate noun, and opt for the *of which* construction. The effect conveyed is one of extreme care, but most people find this usage artificial and awkward.

A similar choice can be seen in this pair of sentences:

It was a situation where anything could happen.

It was a situation in which anything could happen.

The former is widely used, in all styles; but some people find the use of the locative *where* uncomfortable after a noun which does not express a physical location, and opt for the *in which* construction in formal styles, especially in academic writing.

WHERE, WHEN, WHY VS. *WHICH/THAT*

The relative adverbs *where, when,* and *why* reinforce the meaning of the preceding noun, and are widely used in speech and writing:

This is the place where we saw the deer.

It was a time when the country was in turmoil.

This is the reason why we made progress.

However, some people object to the apparent tautologies involved in such examples. Because *place*, for example, already expresses a location, they feel *where* duplicates it, and they would then opt for an alternative in formal style, despite its awkwardness:

This is the corner at which we saw the accident.

Most criticism has been focused on *the reason why*, with a *that*-construction preferred:

This is the reason that we made progress.

Nonstandard constructions

Regional dialects offer several alternatives to the range of constructions found in Standard English. They include the use of different relating words:

He's one person **as** will go.

That's the ticket **what** I bought.

We also find the omission of the pronoun where it is expected:

There's people think Jack's to blame.

Anyone wants this can have it.

42 Noun phrases in apposition

When two or more noun phrases (NPs) act together as a single element of clause structure, each having the same reference, they are said to be in **apposition**:

We saw Mike's **sister**, **Jane**.
I visited **Vienna**, **the capital of Austria**.

The two parts are sometimes linked by a word or phrase emphasizing their identity, such as *that is*, *namely*, or – when the meaning warrants it – *for example*.

EXPLANATION

The semantic identity of the two NPs is crucial to the notion of apposition. In this respect, the construction contrasts with coordination (Chapter 64), where there is no such identity:

We saw the grocer and Mr Jones.

Here, two people were seen, whereas in the appositional equivalent, there is only one:

We saw the grocer, Mr Jones.

The semantic relationship between the NPs can be of several kinds:

- Equivalence – one NP names the other:
  This is my friend, Arthur Jones.
- An attribute – one NP characterizes the other:
  I asked the guard, a helpful fellow.
- An inclusion – one NP illustrates the other:
  I read some classic novels, such as 'Emma'.
- A rewording – one NP rephrases the other:
  He's a pediatrician – a child specialist.

The noun phrase

Using apposition

The relationship between appositional NPs is usually nonrestrictive (p.232): one NP provides information not absolutely essential to the intelligibility of the clause. In each of the above examples, one of the NPs could be left out. We can therefore think of apposition as a kind of postmodification which has been maximally abbreviated:

We saw Mike's sister, (who is called) Jane.

In news reporting

Apposition packs information into the noun phrase, and is thus a frequent choice in varieties where space or time is at a premium, such as news reporting, where it is the usual way of providing further data about people:

Iwan Llewelyn-Jones, the pianist, is playing ...

A Labour spokesman, James Smith, said ...

Ninety per cent of appositions in news contain a proper name.

In academic writing

The compression provided by apposition makes it widely used in academic or professional writing, where one NP glosses the other NP in some way, often in parentheses:

- Providing an explanation: *the task (Project No. 32)*
- Providing an acronym: *the British Medical Association (BMA)*
- Providing a convenient abbreviation – as in the opening sentence of this chapter: *noun phrases (NPs).* This is very common in science writing: *the point P in the diagram*
- Providing a symbol in a formula: *water, H_2O*
- Providing a list of specifications with several NPs: *the product contains the required vitamins (B1, B2, C).*

Academic writing also makes some use of the rare cases of restrictive apposition, where the second NP is a linguistic illustration of the first: *the word 'happy', the term 'verb'.*

Pronouns are words which stand for a noun or noun phrase (Chapter 27) or which refer directly to some aspect of the speech situation:

I wore black **shoes** and Jo wore brown **ones**.
I bought **black shoes** and put **them** on.
That was close!

Pronouns are of several different types (Chapter 44), each of which displays individual properties. Among these properties we find:

- a contrast between personal and nonpersonal gender (Chapter 33) and between male and female: *who* vs. *which, he* vs. *she* vs. *it*
- a contrast between singular and plural number (Chapter 31): *I* vs. *we, she* vs. *they*
- a contrast between subject and object case (Chapters 34 and 46): *I* vs. *me, he* vs. *him, who* vs. *whom*
- a contrast between persons (Chapter 45): *I* vs. *you* vs. *he,* etc.

EXPLANATION

Pronouns are ways of achieving economy of expression.

Mr Brown showed Mr and Mrs Smith around his house in Baker Street. **They** asked **him** when **he** had bought **it**.

Without pronouns, the second sentence would become absurdly wordy and repetitive:

Mr and Mrs Smith asked Mr Brown when Mr Brown had bought Mr Brown's house in Baker Street.

Pronouns simplify the task of speakers and writers, enabling them to express their meaning in as few words as possible. But pronouns make listeners and readers work harder, because each pronoun presents them with the task of identifying what is being referred to. Things can go wrong, if the speaker makes too many assumptions about the listener's knowledge:

A: I wish he'd phone. B: Who?   A: John Smith.

The noun phrase provides the needed explicitness.

In writing, where there is no immediate feedback of this kind, a loose use of pronouns can make a sentence unclear or impossible to follow:

The king and his brother fled to France, but he was caught and executed.

Who was executed? We cannot ask the writer – though teachers might add a rhetorical 'Who??' in the margin of a student essay. Great care needs to be taken when we use pronouns in writing, to ensure that the target of the cross-reference (the **antecedent**) is clear.

Using pronouns

We use pronouns to establish a chain of reference throughout what we are saying or writing. The reference can point in five directions:

POINTING TO THE DISCOURSE PARTICIPANTS
First- and second-person pronouns are the chief ways of orientating the discourse between the speaker/writer and the addressee(s):

I said I'd lend Di **my** bike if **you** could lend **me yours**.

A few other forms can also be used in this way (p.249).

POINTING TO THE IMMEDIATE SITUATION OF THE PARTICIPANTS
Third-person pronouns, demonstrative pronouns (Chapter 44), and some others can refer directly to the situation surrounding the speakers:

Did you see **that**? **They**'ve given **each other** a kiss!

This use is rare in writing, unless the writer refers directly to some property of the page:

Look at **that**! Another crossing-out!

POINTING TO THE GENERAL SITUATION OF THE PARTICIPANTS
Several of the personal pronouns can be used in a general ('generic') sense, referring vaguely to 'life' or 'people':

You just can't tell.   How's **it** going?   **One** never knows.

They say the president will resign. **It**'s a difficult time.

Apart from the case of *one* (p.251), these uses are typically informal.

POINTING TO EARLIER PARTS OF THE DISCOURSE
This is by far the commonest use of the third-person pronouns – to refer backwards (an **anaphoric** use):

The tree has lost *its* leaves. *It* looks very bare.

POINTING TO LATER PARTS OF THE DISCOURSE
A third-person pronoun can refer forwards (a **cataphoric** use) – a feature most commonly found in formal writing:

Before **they** left for London, the king and his ministers spent three days in France.

Using pronouns distinctively

Pronouns are so frequent and 'ordinary' that they are hardly noticeable in the stream of speech (p.178):

> ... anyway **I** decided **that** wasn't **something I** wanted to ask **her** about – but then **I** changed **my** mind and gave **her** a call and **she** was just delighted **you** know ...

They are extremely common in informal conversation, where they are motivated by the fact that the participants share the same discourse situation. Three-quarters of the subjects in all clauses are pronouns.

Pronouns are less common in contexts which present a high density of information, such as news reporting, descriptive fiction, and academic prose. But even here they are an important means of economy – as with the use of *they/their* in this paragraph – and their cross-referring properties can be stylistically exploited.

ADDING ANTICIPATION

Several varieties use a third-person pronoun in the first clause of a text to make a dramatic impact, arousing curiosity and making the reader 'wait for it'. Here are examples from a broadcast news report, a newspaper article, and an advertisement:

- **He**'s done it again! Schumacher romped home ...
- A Number One hit with **his** last single has meant lots of publicity for Aled Jones ...
- Try **it** now! The soup cube with a difference. Soupo!

ADDING INTRIGUE

An opening pronoun in fiction immediately involves the reader, because it is temporarily unclear what is going on. Here are the first lines of a short story and a poem:

- There was no hope for him this time: it was the third stroke. (James Joyce, 'The Sisters')
- A cold coming we had of it. (T.S. Eliot, 'Journey of the Magi')

Most pronouns are **definite**, referring to specific, identifiable entities. The central class expresses contrasts of person, gender, and number (Chapter 47). There are three types:

- **personal** pronouns (*I/me, you, she/her,* etc.) have the commonest use, and are treated in Chapter 45:

  She saw **them** there. [said of Jo and her parents]

- **reflexive** pronouns – *myself, yourself, himself, herself, itself, ourselves, yourselves, themselves*:

  The cat has hurt **herself**. [= the cat]

- **possessive** pronouns – *mine, yours, his, hers, its, ours, theirs* are used on their own; the possessives *my, your,* etc. are used as determiners (p.205):

  Is this paper *yours*? [= your paper]

The other definite pronoun classes are:

- **reciprocal** pronouns – *each other, one another*:

  Di and Jo saw **each other**. [= Di and Jo]

- **relative** pronouns – *who(m), whose, which, that* – see Chapter 41:

  Jane saw the official **who** visited her. [= the official visited]

- **interrogative** pronouns – *who(m), whose, what, which*:

  What's the name of that animal? [= an ibyx]

- **demonstrative** pronouns – *this/that, these/those*:

  [of a computer operation] **That** is extremely fast.

Indefinite pronouns are of two types:

- **compounds** – *every-, some-, any-, no- + -one, -body, -thing*:

  No-one saw **anything**.   **Somebody** shouted.

- ***of-* pronouns**, such as *all, both, each, some, a few, none, little, more, most* (cf. determiners, p.205):

  All of the guests had **some**. [of the pie]

As the glosses in brackets show, the pronouns provide an economical way of referring to associated noun phrases. But each class performs a different semantic role.

REFLEXIVES
Reflexives, as their name suggests, 'reflect' the meaning of a noun or pronoun elsewhere in the clause.
- The basic use is seen in *The cat hurt herself*, where the pronoun completes the meaning. *The cat hurt* makes no sense, and *The cat hurt her* would refer to another entity.
- There is also an emphatic use, where the pronoun acts as an optional extra, reinforcing the meaning (it is in apposition, p.238): *Jo herself told me*. In this role, there is some mobility for the pronoun: *Jo told me herself*.

There are some interesting regional variations:
Is herself at home? (Irish English)
We're getting us a new car. (informal US English)
And literature provides some distinctive uses:
I celebrate myself, and sing myself
(Walt Whitman, 'Song of Myself')
Ourself will mingle with society (Shakespeare, *Macbeth*, III.iv.3)

POSSESSIVES
Whether used as determiners or as separate pronouns, the term 'possessive' is misleading, in that these items express far more than a concept of ownership (as do genitives, p.201). For example, *The problem is yours* is a problem which affects you rather than being owned by you. *That bag is mine*, on the other hand, is clearly possessive.

Possessive meaning can be intensified by (*very*) *own: my book → my very own book*. The contrast can be important in avoiding ambiguity:
The organizers are hoping that members will travel in their cars. [the organizers' cars? the members' cars?]
The organizers are hoping that members will travel in their own cars. [= the members' cars]

RECIPROCALS

'Reciprocal' means exactly what it says. In *Di and Jo saw each other / one another*, Di saw Jo and Jo saw Di. There is no difference in meaning between the two expressions – even though the old prescriptive tradition tried to insist that the former should be used between two people and the latter for more than two. The following mean the same thing:

The children asked each other the question.
The children asked one another the question.

However, the two are not quite the same stylistically: *each other* tends to be used in less formal contexts, and is much more commonly used; *one another* is more formal.

INTERROGATIVES

These pronouns express two semantic contrasts:
- a **gender** contrast of personal (the *who* series) and nonpersonal (*what, which*):

Who is in the woodshed?   What is in the woodshed?

- a contrast of **definiteness**: indefinite *what* contrasts with definite *which* – the latter always implying a choice made from a limited number of alternatives:

What was the winning number? [you must recall it]
Which was the winning number? [you have a list]

Note also the use of *what* to ask about role or status:

What is her father? [a politician]
Which is her father? [in the photograph]

DEMONSTRATIVES

These express proximity – *this* for nearness (**proximal**), *that* for distance (**distal**). The meaning is usually spatial, but can also be temporal or more abstract:

This is the road. [the one we have reached]
That is the road. [the one some distance away]
This is the day to start my new project. [today]
That is the day to start my new project. [another day]
This / that is a rumour I'm paying no attention to.

Demonstratives are always definite in meaning, and usually nonpersonal, but there are some special uses.

- The definiteness can sometimes be rather vague:

    I never felt like **that** before.   **Those** were the days.

- The nonpersonal associations can be added to persons, usually resulting in disparagement:

    You're not going out with **that**! [referring to Mike]

    But there is no disparagement if used in introductions:

    Yes, **this** is Dave. [on the phone]   **This** is Dr Smith.

The use of *this* and *these* is very common in academic writing, because they mark immediate textual reference, important in texts containing a high density of information. There are two instances in this extract from an encyclopedia entry on fluoridation:

Water supplies often contain fluorine naturally in sufficient concentrations to increase the resistance of teeth to attack. **This** has led the authorities to recommend the addition of fluorine to reservoirs deficient in the element. While **this** is done in many instances, a vociferous minority of the population who object to adding 'chemicals' to water have succeeded in preventing it from becoming universal.

INDEFINITES

All indefinite pronouns refer to entities which we are unable or unwilling to specify in an exact way. They are especially used in conversational settings. All of them express quantity – from universality (*every-*) through partitivity (*some-*, *any-*) to absence (*no-*). In addition, they display:

- a contrast of assertiveness in *some* vs. *any*:

    Did something happen? [it probably did]

    Did anything happen? [it probably didn't]

- a stylistic contrast: *-body* is more informal, and is found more in conversation, especially in American English usage; *-one* is more formal (as with *one*, p.251).

DESCRIPTIVE SUMMARY

Three persons are represented in the personal pronoun system:
- The **first** person: singular *I, me, mine, myself;* plural *we, us, ours, ourselves;* related are the determiners *my* and *our.*
- The **second** person: *you, yours, yourself, yourselves,* related is the determiner *your.* In older Standard English, and still in some regional dialects and religious usage, we find *thou, thee, thine, thyself.*
- The **third** person: singular *he, him, his, himself; she, her, her(s), herself; it, its, itself; one;* plural *they, them, theirs, themselves;* related are the determiners *his, her, its,* and *their.*

EXPLANATION

The term 'personal' arose because the system chiefly refers to the people involved in the act of communication – speaker(s)/writer(s), addressees, and third parties. It is slightly misleading, however, because these pronouns also include *it,* which is typically nonpersonal (p.197), and *they,* which can be either personal or nonpersonal. *I/me* and *you* are the most frequently used pronouns, because of their use in conversation.

In normal usage, the first person refers to the sender of the message, the second person to the receiver, and the third person to anyone else referred to. But each person also has special uses which convey important stylistic effects.

Special uses of the first person

These all relate to *we (us,* etc.), which in its normal use is a plural referring to the speaker/writer plus others.
- *We* is **inclusive** if it includes the addressee:
  We should all go right now, Mary.

- *We* can be 'hopefully' inclusive, as in the approach of the policeman:

  We don't want any trouble, do we, sir?
- *We* is **exclusive** when it excludes the addressee:

  We can do it without your help.
- *We* can exclude the speaker, as in the often patronizing address used by carers, or in references to third parties.

  How are we today? [= How are you today?]

  We are in a bad mood! [= He or she is in a bad mood]
- *We* can refer to an unknown number of participants, as in a legal document or a prayer:

  We the undersigned do solemnly affirm ...

  We thank you, O Lord, for all your benefits ...
- The most inclusive use of *we* refers to everyone:

  We are not paying enough attention to climate change.

  Science tells us that we should be cautious.

We can also be used with singular reference, when a writer wants to avoid an egotistical impression:

As we showed in Chapter 3 ... [cf. *As I showed* ...]

But it is especially used to suggest that author and reader are both involved in a joint enterprise (the 'authorial' *we*):

As we saw in the last chapter ...

The use of *you* here would sound abrupt or distancing:

As you saw in the last chapter ...

It is unusual to hear the authorial *we* in speech, unless someone is reading aloud. And the old 'royal *we*' (as in Queen Victoria's *We are not amused*) is obsolete.

Us has some informal singular uses, as in *Let's have a look* (p.71) – the only contracted pronoun form in English. Its use in such sentences as *Give us a lift* [= 'Give me a lift'] is considered nonstandard.

Special uses of the second person

You almost always refers to addressees, singular or plural. It can however be used in a third-person way, to refer to people in general:

> You never know what the weather's going to be like.

This is always informal, and sometimes very much so, as reflected in nonstandard spelling:

> Well, whaddaya know! [after a surprise encounter]
> Have you got the whatchacallit? [what-do-you-call-it]

Special uses of the third person

- Speakers and writers can refer to themselves in the third person. In speech, this is found only in informal and usually jocular contexts:

  > A [to child]: Where's your mother?
  > Mother [having heard]: She's in the kitchen.

  In literary writing, it is a formal and somewhat self-conscious way of referring to the author:

  > This reviewer has to say that he has never seen such a bad performance.

- Speakers and writers can refer to their addressee(s) in the third person. In speech, this is usually heard in a professional context, and is often thought patronizing:

  > Doctor: And how is Mr Smith this morning?

  In literary writing, it is a formal and somewhat self-conscious way of referring to the reader:

  > Readers of this column will not be surprised to learn ...

  And it can become part of a literary style, as when Tristram Shandy switches from his usual mode of address (*you*) into the third person (Laurence Sterne, *The Life and Opinions of Tristram Shandy, Gentleman*):

  > The reader will be content to wait for a full explanation of these matters till the next year, – when a series of things will be laid open which he little expects.
  > (the closing lines of Book 2)

One is chiefly used to avoid the informal or intimate tone of one of the other personal pronouns:

- Avoiding *I*, in a narrative:
    One is reminded of the French cave paintings ...
- Avoiding *you*, in instructional settings:
    Next one pours the mixture into the bowl ...
- Being unspecific about who is involved:
    This is not how one ought to behave.
  Who is behaving badly, here? It could be the speaker, the addressee, or a third party.

In all cases, the use of *one* is formal, and in speech it can reach the point of pretentiousness, as in the upper-class usage typified by *One fell off one's horse* [= I fell off my horse].

THE USES OF *IT*

- A dramatic, anticipatory use:
    It's surprising how often we miss that bus.
  This is especially common in news reporting:
    It's absolutely crazy. The government's latest plans for education reform won't please anyone.
- It has also developed several special meanings, such as:
    You're it. [next to play]   She's certainly got it. [appeal]
- It can also express no meaning (**empty** or **prop** *it*) in talking about time, distance, or atmospheric conditions (p.92):
    It's 2 o'clock / a long way / dark.

Pronoun modification

Several styles manipulate pronouns for special effects.
Premodification is always informal and rhetorical:
    Good old you!   Silly me!
Postmodification is more varied:
- in literature: *She Who Must Be Obeyed* (John Mortimer)
- in proverbs: *He who laughs last, laughs longest.*
- in impolite directives (p.70): *You with the hat on!*

DESCRIPTIVE SUMMARY

Five of the personal pronouns and one of the relative pronouns are the only items in English to show three case forms: subjective, objective, and genitive (Chapter 34):

I/me/mine   he/him/his   she/her/hers
we/us/ours   they/them/theirs   who/whom/whose

The **subjective** form is used when the pronoun acts as the subject of a clause (Chapter 9):

I was sleeping.   **She** was sleeping.   **They** were sleeping.

The **objective** form is used when the pronoun acts as the object (Chapter 10) or occurs after a preposition.

Di asked **me**.   Di asked **her**.   Di asked **them**.
Di spoke to **me**.   Di spoke to **her**.   Di spoke to **them**.

EXPLANATION

The purpose of the objective case is to mark pronouns as having the same semantic function as nouns in object position. But unlike other objects, variation in pronoun case usage has long been widespread, and it was an aim of prescriptive grammar to eradicate it. This was to be done by insisting that English followed the usage of the equivalent pronouns in Latin. There, a pronoun following the verb *to be* had to be in the subjective case.

The rule was insistently taught, though few people followed it. Usages such as *It was I* did achieve some currency in formal speech and writing, instead of the everyday *It was me*. But most subjective forms were rarely if ever used in this context, and have no currency today:

It's only I.   That'll be they.   It's we.

Centuries of pedagogical sensitivity over the issue have left their mark on our intuitions, however, so that today we encounter pockets of usage variation. The contrast is always in the same direction: the subjective pronoun is more formal than the objective, and more likely to be seen in writing.

- In comparatives (Chapter 68)
  The choice appears after *than* in a comparative clause:
    [of John] Mary is better qualified than he / him.
- In cleft sentences (Chapter 71)
  The choice appears after *be* in a cleft sentence:
    It was he / him who was in the car.
- Postmodified pronouns
  The choice appears when a pronoun is postmodified by a relative clause (Chapter 41):
    It was they / them who went to London.
  The use of *them* with *that* is very informal:
    It was them that went to London.

Sometimes the variation is surprising, such as the use of pronouns after transitive verbs (Chapter 8). After all, there is no uncertainty about these constructions:

    John saw Mary.   John saw me.   not: ~~John saw I.~~

So theoretically, there should be no uncertainty over the coordinated construction:

    John saw me and Mary.   John saw Mary and me.

There is no problem over the former. But variation appears in the latter case, where the pronoun is politely placed last (as it would be in subject position too), so that in formal styles we can find:

    John saw Mary and I.

Presumably it is the distance of the pronoun from the verb which allows such usages to emerge.

This sort of sensitivity has led to a further development, in recent years, using a reflexive (p.244):

    John saw Mary and myself.

But many people still consider this to be nonstandard.

A contrast of male and female **gender**, based mainly on the sex of a person or animal (Chapter 33) is found in two of the third-person singular pronouns:

he / she   him / her   his / her(s)   himself / herself

The other pronouns are sex-neutral: *I, you, it* (referring to animates, p.197), *we*, and *they* can be either male or female.

The choice of pronoun in relation to nouns has become a contentious issue in recent years because of the widespread concern to maintain parity of esteem and opportunity between the sexes, especially in the context of employment. Sexism affects a great deal more than the use of pronouns, of course – it is also reflected in the choice of vocabulary, such as when we use *salesman* or *saleswoman* instead of the neutral *sales assistant*. But pronouns have attracted particular attention because they are so frequent.

The problem has focused on dual-gender nouns such as *student, candidate, doctor,* and *everyone,* which would traditionally have been referred to as *he*:

A doctor should spend time with his patients.
I expect everyone to do his duty.

Because we know that doctors and 'everyone' can be either male or female, people who want to avoid gender bias have developed other usages. There are now seven options.

- We can continue with *his* – which is what people do who are unaware or unimpressed by the gender issue.
- We can replace *his* by *her* – which is what people do who want to make a feminist point.

    A doctor should spend time with her patients.
- We can use both pronouns, which although clumsy is quite widely used in formal writing, is common in formal speech, and is increasingly heard in informal speech.

    A doctor should spend time with his or her patients.

    We cannot use this option with words like *everyone*:

    I asked everyone to do his or her duty.

    Usages with the *she/her* element first are unusual. The *his or her* usage is especially widespread in academic writing (where we might expect awareness of the gender issue to be strongest), and where we find a number of other forms: *his/her, s/he, (s)he*.
- We can use *they*, the commonest informal spoken usage. However, this attracts criticism from people who do not like the thought of *they/their* referring to a singular noun.

    A doctor should spend time with their patients.

    But this is the only option with words like *everyone*:

    I asked everyone to do their duty.

    No-one felt they could leave.

    This singular usage of *they* is growing. It is, after all, what has already happened to the pronoun *you*, which has been used for both singular and plural for 500 years.
- We can invent a new sex-inclusive pronoun, such as *thon* or *ho*, but such usages have never caught on.
- We can try to balance the use of *he* and *she* in a text (e.g. *he* for speakers and *she* for addressees), but the artificiality of the exercise makes this option little used.
- We can avoid the whole issue, by rephrasing – usually by making the noun plural:

    Doctors should spend time with their patients.

    I asked all the people to do their duty.

DESCRIPTIVE SUMMARY

Adjectives have these grammatical characteristics:

- They can premodify a noun (Chapter 39) – in **attributive** position – and occasionally postmodify it:
  a small room   red shoes   things French
- They can occur as a complement (Chapter 11) – in **predicative** position – either alone or postmodified:
  That room is **small**.   Plums are **good to eat**.
- They can be premodified by intensifying adverbs, such as *very*:
  a very small room   an extremely small room
- They can express **degree** of comparison (Chapter 51), using either *-er/-est* endings or *more/most*:
  small   smaller   smallest
  desirable   more desirable   most desirable
- Several adjectives have distinctive suffixes, such as *-less, -able, -ish, -al*, and *-ous*:
  hopeless   loveable   boyish   political   tremulous
- There is a close relationship between adjectives and adverbs. Many adjectives form adverbs by adding *-ly*:
  sad → sadly   definite → definitely

EXPLANATION

Adjectives express a property or attribute of a noun. They allow us to make subtler distinctions than could be made by the noun alone. For example, the word *train* by itself, in its sense of 'vehicle', has a very limited meaning, but adjectives allow us a huge range of further possibilities:

express / goods / comfortable / late ... train

Adjectives help us to talk about nouns in two main ways: they can describe and they can classify.

Describing

Adjectives enable us to describe nouns, by referring to their inherent colour, size, age, and all the other properties that we can perceive or evaluate (p.220):

a red chair   a big building   an old car
a clear view   a good concert   a splendid time

Most of the commonly occurring adjectives in this category are monosyllables. They are typically **gradable** – that is, the property they express can be possessed to various degrees:

That house is big ... bigger ... very big ... extremely big

Classifying

Adjectives enable us to **classify** nouns, by placing a noun into a particular category. There are three main types:

- expressing source or affiliation:

  Chinese   Irish   Christian   Anglo-Saxon

- expressing a group or subject (especially ending in *-al*):

  chemical   legal   official   social   human   public

- expressing the way a noun relates to other nouns:

  different   basic   entire   previous   maximum   total

These adjectives are typically **nongradable** – the meaning does not easily allow intermediate degrees, unless we are being funny or making a special point. We can find contexts which allow us to say:

That's very Irish.   It was a more human response.

but we cannot say, when talking about *our entire staff*,

~~Our very entire staff went on strike.~~
~~Our staff is more entire than theirs.~~

Relational adjectives operate in pairs or small sets, the senses of the items defining each other. We learn their meanings by seeing how they contrast:

same/different   initial/final   general/particular
simple/complex   previous/subsequent

Exploiting adjective position

Most adjectives can appear in either attributive or predicative position, and this provides an opportunity to use them in stylistically contrasting ways. We do not usually use attributive position for more than one or two adjectives at a time (p.222); predicative position, on the other hand, is ideally suited for longer sequences, especially if there is coordination or adverb modification. This follows the principle of putting longer ('weightier') information towards the end of a clause (p.344).

Character writing relies heavily on adjectives, as we saw in Chapter 39. But it is important not to let the description become mechanical by the repetitious use of a single construction, as in this constructed example:

> The tall stranger had a broad face with a high forehead and bushy eyebrows. He had blue eyes, a pointed nose, and a wispy beard. He was wearing a bowler hat, a bright scarf, and a green coat with black lapels, and on his small hands there were pink gloves.

The writing is vivid enough, but its unremitting use of single attributive adjectives soon makes it pall. We sense the need for variation, either in attributive position, or in predicative position – or, ideally, in both.

We can see the two syntactic positions being fully and professionally exploited in the description of Dismal Jemmy in Chapter 3 of Charles Dickens' *The Pickwick Papers*. The style alternates between the two positions, and avoids the repeated use of a single premodifying structure, thereby giving variation to the pace and rhythm of the narrative. We see several types of premodifying structure – intensifiers, adjective sequences, compound adjectives – and use made of most of the semantic classes of adjective outlined in Chapter 39. Boredom could never set in when such a range of the language's resources is being exploited.

- In the first sentence, the adjectives are almost entirely attributive (in bold), allowing a series of vivid details to be presented in quick succession. Even though some of the adjectives are themselves modified, each noun phrase refers to only one feature of the face.
- We then have a sequence of predicatives (underlined) allowing a more leisurely passage of description. Each of the facial features now has two adjectives – with the jaws given a specially lengthy comparison (45 words).
- This is then followed by another sequence of succinct attributives, allowing the clothing to be described in a further series of quick brush-strokes.

It was a **care-worn looking man**, whose **sallow** face, and **deeply sunken** eyes, were rendered still <u>more striking</u> than nature had made them, by the **straight black** hair which hung in **matted** disorder half way down his face. His eyes were <u>almost unnaturally bright and piercing</u>; his cheek-bones were <u>high and prominent</u>; and his jaws were <u>so long and lank</u>, that an observer would have supposed that he was drawing the flesh of his face in, for a moment, by some contraction of his muscles, if his **half-opened** mouth and **immovable** expression had not announced that it was his **ordinary** appearance. Round his neck he wore a **green** shawl, with the **large** ends straggling over his chest, and making their appearance occasionally beneath the **worn** button-holes of his **old** waistcoat. His **upper** garment was a **long black** surtout; and below it he wore **wide drab** trousers, and **large** boots, running rapidly to seed.

Note that not all nouns need adjectives. For example, nouns to do with entities which underlie the description, such as *nature*, *flesh*, and *muscles*, are left unmodified. To give every noun an adjective would be, as the nineteenth-century idiom said, to 'over-egg the pudding'.

DESCRIPTIVE SUMMARY

Some adjectives are restricted in what they can do.
- Some are found only in attributive position:
  the chief reason   not: ~~the reason is chief~~
- Some are found only in predicative position:
  The boy felt faint.   not: ~~the faint boy~~
- Some can appear only after a noun (Chapter 40):
  We have apples aplenty. not: ~~aplenty apples~~

Adjectives have three other major functions:
- They can be the head of an adjective phrase:
  I'm **very glad**.   Your car's **cleaner than mine**.
  In some cases, the adjective **has** to be postmodified:
  We were **loath to do it**.   not: ~~We were loath~~.
- They can act as an abbreviated clause:
  Tired and happy, the children got on the bus.
  This function is discussed in Chapter 62.
- They can appear as a complement to the object:
  I found her work **brilliant**.
  This function is discussed in Chapter 11.

EXPLANATION

There is usually no semantic difference between the attributive and predicative uses of an adjective: *I have a fat cat* means *I have a cat that is fat*, and vice versa. But:
- sometimes the two uses do change the meaning
- adjectives which are attributive-only or predicative-only belong to certain semantic classes
- the semantic 'weight' (p.344) of adjective phrases tends to make them predicative.

Changing the meaning

From a semantic point of view, adjectives can relate to their nouns in two ways:
- they can refer to an inherent or permanent characteristic of the noun:

    I've got a red coat. [the coat is red and stays red]
- they can refer to a non-inherent or temporary condition affecting the noun:

    I've got a new car. [the car will not always be new]

Sometimes the same adjective can be used in both ways. This is the basis of such utterances as the following:

    Late buses leave Victoria on the hour through the night. Get there on time, because they're not usually late.

Late buses are not usually late? The attributive use is expressing an inherent property ('a bus whose nature is to run late at night'); the predicative use is a non-inherent property ('depending on circumstances, this bus might be on time or late'). A similar contrast distinguishes *the late king* (definitely a permanent property) and *the king was late* (in arriving). Another example:

    My novel is complete rubbish. [its nature is awful]
    My novel is complete. [it is finally finished]

The late king ... the king was late.

Attributives tend to express inherent meanings

Several adjectives tend to be used only as attributives:
- those which express an absolute notion of quantity:
    a total stranger   not: ~~a stranger who is total~~
    Other examples: *perfect idiot, utter fool*
- those which express a time or place relationship:
    a former pilot   not: ~~a pilot who is former~~
    Other examples: *current interests, southern hemisphere*
- those which identify a group or topic (p.257):
    chemical weapons   not: ~~weapons which are chemical~~
    Other examples: *criminal lawyer, foreign office*
- those which express the manner or degree of a process:
    a strong advocate   not: ~~an advocate who is strong~~
    (changes the meaning of *strong*)
- those which express modal meanings (Chapter 26):
    a would-be writer   not: ~~a writer who is would-be~~
    Other examples: *actual cause, possible reason*
- those which delimit or particularize:
    the main objection   not: ~~the objection which is main~~
    Other examples: *chief reason, first concern*
- those which express a strong emotion (expletives):
    a bloody fool   not: ~~a fool who is bloody~~
    Other examples: *poor chap, blasted idiot*

Predicatives tend to express non-inherent meanings

Several adjectives tend to be used only as predicatives:
- those which express a temporary state of poor health or physical condition:
    ill   faint   poorly   unwell   drunk   bereft
- those beginning with *a-*, also expressing temporary states:
    afraid   asleep   awake   alert   alone
- those requiring postmodification, usually expressing a state of affairs existing at a particular time:
    She's loath to go.   He was apt to ask questions.

Using adjectives

Varieties display preferences for different kinds of adjectival construction.

LISTS

Lists of properties, especially if they have a complex structure (through compounding or postmodification), are usually predicative. They are common in fiction.

> The soldiers were strong, well-trained, extremely well equipped, and ready to take on anyone.

The points can be in any order, but they usually follow the end-weight principle (p.344), increasing in length.

COMPOUNDS

A good way of compressing information is to use an adjectival compound. These are very common in time- and space-constrained settings, such as news reporting:

> a racially motivated attack   the second-round match

The alternative, to use a relative clause, is much wordier:

> an attack which was racially motivated

They are also common in literary passages: see *care-worn looking* and *half-opened* in the extract on p.259.

REPETITIONS

The same adjective can be repeated (p.223) – usually twice, sometimes three times, rarely more, except in very informal conversation:

> It was a big, big mistake.
> I hope it's a long long long time before that happens.
> He grew stronger and stronger as the days went by.

In writing, such sequences are common only in children's literature. They seem somewhat patronizing in writing aimed at adults.

Only gradable premodifiers (p.257) can be used in this way. We do not say:

> ~~It was a complete complete complete mess~~.

We have to rephrase, and say something like:

> complete and utter mess.

DESCRIPTIVE SUMMARY

Not all words fit neatly into the various word classes of the
language. In particular, some adjectives resemble nouns, verbs, or
adverbs:

* Resembling nouns (Chapter 39):
  This is a country road.   The road is in the country.
  Some adjectives can even act as the head of the noun phrase
  (Chapter 27):
  the Welsh   the good   the biggest
* Resembling verbs:
  Some adjectives have the form of participles (Chapter 16), and
  look just like verbs.
  His work was intriguing.   His work was intriguing me.
* Resembling adverbs (Chapter 52):
  I caught the early train.   I finished work early.

Words beginning with *a-* are a special problem, because some of
them behave like adjectives (e.g. they can take *very*), and some
like adverbs:
  They are alert.   They are very alert.
  They are abroad.   They went abroad.   not: ~~very abroad~~.

EXPLANATION

Our need to add descriptive detail to nouns is so persistent, it
seems, that virtually every word class has been pressed into
adjectival service at some time or another. The result has been to
introduce a much greater richness of semantic expression into the
noun phrase, and fresh possibilities for making stylistic contrasts.

Adjectives

Increasing semantic expressiveness

- The premodifiers which resemble nouns introduce the kind of specificity we normally associate with that word class:

  country road   drinks merger   music industry

- Participles introduce the dynamic characteristics of verbs. Adjectives are typically static (p.163): we can say that *John is tall* but not that ~~John is being tall~~. Participles, however, add a sense of activity and involvement:

  a developing situation   the intriguing proposal
  the escaped prisoner   an unexpected delivery

- The *a*-words identify states, but introduce a hint of the 'how' meaning we associate with manner adverbs:

  We were alone / asleep / aghast / aware / ashamed.

- Other word classes can achieve adjectival status too – even pronouns, prepositions, and conjunctions:

  the It girl   a through train   an either/or situation

Exploiting semantic expressiveness

This range of examples illustrates the way in which the adjective class offers further opportunities for creative expressiveness. In particular, we have the choice of exploiting the nominal or verbal associations of words in order to make noun phrases increasingly precise or dynamic. Compare the different stylistic effects in these three sentences:

A bell sounded an alarm.

An alarm bell sounded.

An alarming bell sounded.

In the first sentence, it is just 'a bell', of no particular kind; the narrator reports what it did, but the statement has no emotion. In the second sentence, the adjectival use brings the meaning of 'alarm' into the forefront of our attention, and the short sentence adds a sense of urgency. With the dynamic participial usage in the third sentence, the narrator's emotions are thoroughly involved.

Most adjectives can be compared. The property they express can be related to a higher degree, to the same degree, or to a lower degree.

- We express higher comparison either by adding an *-er/-est* ending (the **inflectional** form) or by using a construction with *more/most* (the **periphrastic** form). The *-er/more* forms express a moderate (**comparative**) increase in degree; the *-est/most* forms express a maximum (**superlative**) increase.

  Di is tall. Ed is taller. Jo is tallest. not: ~~more/most tall~~
  an intricate task   a more intricate task a most intricate task
  not: ~~intricater   intricatest~~

- Comparison to other degrees offers fewer options. The same degree is expressed by *as ... as.* A lower degree is expressed by *less/least.*

  Di is as tall as Jean.   Jean is less tall.
  a less intricate task   the least intricate task

EXPLANATION

The availability of two forms of higher-degree comparison offers several opportunities for stylistic contrast. Normally, *-er* and *-est* are used with adjectives of one syllable in length (*older*, *blackest*), *more* and *most* are used with adjectives three or more syllables in length (*more/most interesting*), and two-syllable adjectives are variable (*polite* → *politer*, *more polite*). There are many exceptions, but also some general trends, as these next three illustrations show.

Adding emphasis

An adjective which normally compares using inflection can appear with *more/most* if we want to add extra dynamic emphasis or make the degree of the comparison more prominent:

The tank is fuller now. The tank is a bit more full now.

Double marking

Is it possible to use both forms of comparison at the same time? There are many examples in Shakespeare: Hamlet says *more richer* (*Hamlet*, III.ii.313), Mark Antony *most unkindest* (*Julius Caesar*, III.ii.184). But in modern English such usages are always nonstandard, heard only in jocular contexts or in regional dialects.

more nicer   the bestest

In fiction, an inflected polysyllabic adjective (e.g. *finickiest*) is usually the sign of a rustic, uneducated, or down-to-earth character. Such people can also be highly idiosyncratic in their usage. Here is Mrs Day in Thomas Hardy's *Under the Greenwood Tree* (Book 2, Chapter 6) inventing several comparatives:

The parishioners about here ... are the laziest, gossipest, poachest, jailest set of any ever I came among.

Being cautious – or not

The cautious claims of academic writing are expressed through the frequent use of the comparative degree and a reluctance to use the superlative. There is a tentativeness in the first sentence here which is missing in the second:

A more appropriate analysis was proposed by Smith.

The most appropriate analysis was proposed by Smith.

Academics have to be very certain of their position before they dare to use a superlative. By contrast, a superlative is common in advertising (Chapter 68) and promises interest in a news report:

The strongest earthquake in the area for several years rocked the city of Tokyo yesterday.

DESCRIPTIVE SUMMARY

Adverbs have several functions:

- Most act as an **adverbial** (Chapter 12) in clause structure, carrying out various functions (Chapter 55):
  We ran **quickly**.   **Happily**, we were on time.
- A group of **intensifying** adverbs premodify another word or phrase (Chapter 39):
  extremely happy   **very** quickly   **quite** a party
- A few adverbs postmodify a word or phrase (Chapter 40):
  my visit **away**   everyone **else**   the week **afterwards**
- Many adverbs can be compared for degree:
  more happily / most happily   sooner / soonest

When modified themselves, as in *very quickly*, adverbs form the head of an **adverb phrase**.

EXPLANATION

Just as adjectives express subtle semantic distinctions in relation to nouns (p.256), so adverbs immensely enlarge the range of meanings expressed by verbs. However, adverbs comprise a much more heterogeneous and versatile word class. They can affect the meaning not only of verbs in clauses, but also of adjectives in phrases, and even of whole clauses.

Adverb phrases, prepositional phrases, and certain kinds of clause all perform the same range of functions as do the adverbs which modify verbs and clauses:

We ran **quickly**.   We ran **very quickly**.
We ran **in the street**.   We ran **where it was safe**.

They are therefore dealt with together, as adverbials, in this part of the book.

We have already seen in Chapter 12 just how frequent adverbials are. They are especially common in conversation and fiction dialogue, because these are uses of language where the clauses tend to be short. They therefore employ a correspondingly large number of verbs, and this allows for more opportunities to modulate meaning through the use of adverbials.

Adverbs modifying nouns?

No single generalization covers the full range of the adverb's semantic or pragmatic functions – unless it is the negative observation that they have little directly to do with nouns. A few adverbs can modify noun phrases – especially *quite* and *rather*:

We had quite a nice time.   It was rather a mess.

And the informal usages *sort of* (*sorta*) and *kind of* (*kinda*) can appear before the noun phrase too, as well as within it:

That was kind of a joke, wasn't it? ... a kinda joke.

But an adverb immediately before a noun is indeed unusual. We never say:

~~the quickly man~~   ~~an extremely car~~   ~~a soon film~~

A rare example of an adverb taking on adjectival properties is:

He's the very man I want. [= precisely the man I want]

It is because this kind of usage is so unusual that it can be exploited for stylistic purposes. An example from advertising is the description of a perfume as:

the anytime, anywhere fragrance

But probably the most famous use of an unusual adverb premodifier is in the Beatles' *Sergeant Pepper* album, where we were introduced to the 'Nowhere Man':

He's a real nowhere man
Sitting in his nowhere land
Making all his nowhere plans for nobody.

Intensifying adverbs

The intensifiers, which modify adjectives and adverbs, are rather different from the other adverbials, because they relate to each other in a special way. We can locate them impressionistically along a scale of intensity, between a maximum and a minimum.

- Adverbs around the mid-point on this scale simply express extra emphasis (**emphasizers**):

    I'm interested.   I'm definitely interested.
  Other examples: *certainly, very, by all means*

- Adverbs which intensify upwards (**amplifiers**) suggest that the adjective is above a norm:

    I'm greatly interested.
    [= more interested than I would normally be]
  Other examples: *totally, completely, a great deal*

- Adverbs which intensify downwards (**downtoners**) suggest that the adjective is below a norm:

    I'm hardly interested.
    [= less interested than normal]
  Other examples: *almost, scarcely, more or less*

Adverbs and adverbials

Using intensifiers

Intensifiers are especially valuable in varieties where it is
important to think of qualities as if they were degrees along a
scale.

IN ADVERTISING

Intensifiers are a natural means of heightening the appeal of an
adjective in advertisements. Many are simply alternative,
attention-grabbing ways of expressing the notion of 'very':

exceedingly good cakes   fantastically comfortable

Often they add a descriptive meaning:

noisily crisp celery   [toothpaste] tastes minty good
a mouthwateringly tangy orange drink

The intensifers are almost always amplifiers and emphasizers. We
are unlikely to see downtoners in an ad:

It has a more or less exciting taste.

You'll get an almost clean wash.

Intensifiers are not often used as part of the lead slogan,
advertising a product, but they are common within the body-copy,
as in these extracts:

At the end of a specially hard day ...
A brand new collection ...   Really effective hand care ...

IN WEATHER FORECASTING

Probably no area of everyday human existence is perceived more
in terms of degree than the weather. We are constantly quantifying
the various possibilities for rain, sunshine, wind, and fog, and we
use the full range of intensifiers to do it. Professional weather
broadcasters rely on them greatly, as shown by these extracts from
a single two-minute radio broadcast:

we have a **more-or-less** east–west split in the country
temperatures will be **nearly** normal for March
we'll see light winds and **largely** clear skies
it's going to become **extremely** unsettled in the south
it'll be **very much** milder in the north

DESCRIPTIVE SUMMARY

The adverbial element is highly mobile within the clause. It can appear initially or finally, and within the clause in a variety of places:

Slowly the ship passed through the lock.

The ship passed through the lock **slowly**.

The ship **slowly** passed through the lock.

The ship passed **slowly** through the lock.

The ship will **slowly** pass through the lock.

Many adverbials can appear in all possible places; but some are less flexible. *Also*, for example, usually appears before the verb; *as well*, at the end of the clause.

The ship also passed through the lock.

not: ~~The ship passed also through the lock~~.

The ship passed through the lock as well.

not: ~~The ship as well passed through the lock~~.

EXPLANATION

In the above example, *slowly* did not change its meaning, as it moved around the clause, and most adverbials are like that. An example of an adverbial which *does* change its meaning is *naturally*:

I took the picture naturally. [without any artifice]

Naturally I took the picture. [of course I did]

Adverbials of this kind tend to be of the type discussed in Chapters 56 and 57.

However, the position of an adverbial in a clause is not random. A variety of factors influence both how many adverbials we use and where we put them.

Adverbials at the end

The vast majority of adverbials in both speech and writing occur at the end of a clause.

> I saw Mary **at the bus-stop in the high street**.
> We got home **at six in the morning**!

End position is where we usually put an adverbial which adds new information, the other clause elements leading up to it as a kind of natural climax. This is reinforced in speech by the way we usually make the last bit of information in a clause intonationally prominent (Chapter 75).

Adverbials at the beginning

Most adverbials, if we wish, can be placed at the beginning of a clause. But there has to be a reason.

- We can bring an adverbial forward if we want to draw special attention to it:

    > **Six in the morning** we got home!

    This would be very likely if someone had doubted us:

    > A: We got home at six in the morning.
    > B: No, it was five.
    > A: Six in the morning we got home!

- We can bring an adverbial forward if it expresses a general viewpoint or adds some kind of contextualizing information:

    > **As a matter of fact**, I thought it was six o'clock.
    > **At the concert the week before**, she played really well.

    As the definite articles here suggest, the first part of this sentence is referring to 'given' information – something the participants already know.

Adverbials in the middle

In longer clauses, there are several possibilities for adverbials to appear in medial position. These focus our attention on particular parts of the clause, and can express some very subtle nuances of meaning:

> He was **really** sad. [stressing the degree of his sadness]
> He **really** was sad. [stressing the fact that he was sad]

Adverbials with preferences

Although in theory most adverbials can appear initially, medially, or finally in the clause, in practice there are major semantic and stylistic trends which cause one position to be preferred to another.

The weight of the adverbial

If an adverbial is short – a single-word adverb or a brief adverb phrase – it is more likely to turn up at various positions in the clause

(quickly) we (quickly) ran (quickly) to town (quickly).

Longer adverbials – prepositional phrases or finite clauses – are much less mobile, and tend to appear at the end.

We ran to town **as quickly as we could manage it**.

We could front the adverbial here, but this would force our addressee to wait for the information needed to interpret it.

As quickly as we could manage it ... [who? what?]

We could also try this adverbial in medial position, but the result would be some very awkward constructions:

We ran **as quickly as we could manage it** to town.

We **as quickly as we could manage it** ran to town.

Initial and medial adverbials tend to be short – single adverbs or brief phrases. Single-syllable adverbs (e.g. *then, now, well, so*) are very commonly initial:

So I said to John ...   **Well** it was late ...

These are especially common in conversation, but they have a certain formal or literary use too, as this extract from the King James Bible shows (John, 4.43):

Now after two days he departed thence, and went into Galilee. For Jesus himself testified, that a prophet hath no honour in his own country. **Then** when he was come into Galilee, the Galilaeans received him, having seen all the things that he did at Jerusalem at the feast: for they also went unto the feast. **So** Jesus came again into Cana of Galilee ...

The meaning of the adverbial

The type of adverbial also affects whether it moves away from end-position. 'Type' here refers both to the meaning of the adverbial (Chapter 54) and to its grammatical class (Chapters 55 to 58).

INITIAL POSITION
Initial position has three main functions:
- It connects to what has gone before (Chapter 58):
    However, I managed to complete the work on time.
- It introduces a personal attitude (Chapter 57):
    Frankly, I wonder why we bother.
- It sets the scene:
    Everywhere in the grounds, people were strolling.

Time adverbials tend to appear at the beginning, because they are a way of maintaining the momentum or direction of a narrative:

In the morning we got up early.

Then we saw the car.   **Later on** the sun came out.

By contrast, space adverbials tend to appear at the end:

We met our friends **in the park**.

I like it **here**.   I've just been **to Japan**.

MEDIAL POSITION
Medial position is very much associated with adverbials which have a strong relationship to the action expressed by the verb, such as those of mood, manner, and degree:

They will **probably** leave the car in the garage.

I **carefully** screwed the top into place.

John **increasingly** found the going hard.

Putting a modality adverb at the end is a real sign of casual or unplanned expression:

They will leave the car in the garage, **probably**.

Adverbials which intensify or focus the meaning (p.268) are also typically medial:

I **completely** agree with what you say.

I **merely** wanted to ask a question.

Ordering adverbials

It is very common to find several adverbials within the same
clause. We often want to talk simultaneously about where, when,
how or why something happened, at the same time incorporating
expressions of our attitude and showing a connection with a
previous sentence:

However / we / unfortunately / didn't get / there / with the car /
because we had a breakdown.

Five adverbial meanings are expressed in this example:
connection, attitude, location, means, and cause.

Increasing length

This example also illustrates the major factor governing the normal
order of adverbials, when a cluster is used at the same position in
a clause: the shorter items in the cluster tend to precede the longer
ones. This is well illustrated in the above sentence:

... there / with the car / because we had a breakdown.

One word ... three words ... five words. As a general rule, single-word
adverbs tend to precede phrases which tend to precede subordinate
clauses. Nonfinite clauses (Chapter 17) tend to precede finite clauses:

Di went out / to call Jack / because she wanted a lift.

Sequencing meanings

There is also a strong tendency for the different semantic categories
of adverbial (Chapter 54) to fall into a set sequence. Usually
adverbials which express a process precede those expressing space
and these precede those expressing time, as in this example:

We arrived / safely / in London / on time.

Any adverbials of respect tend to appear at the beginning of a
sequence:

I was advised / about the issue / seriously / last week.

Adverbials of contingency tend to be at the end:

I ran in the marathon / last year / for charity.

Overriding factors

CLARITY

Sometimes the position of an adverbial can cause ambiguity – in which case we need to relocate it, regardless of our normal expectations about meaning and length. This next sentence is fine if the meeting referred to was held on Sunday:

Jane wrote the letter after our meeting on Sunday.

Here, Jane might have written the letter on Monday. But if we want to make it clear that the letter was actually written on Sunday, we need to rephrase:

She wrote the letter on Sunday after our meeting.

This now allows the possibility that the meeting might have been held on an earlier day.

STYLISTIC FACTORS

There are certain adverbial sequences which we do not like to use, regardless of their type, meaning, or weight.

- We don't like repeating an adverbial in the same clause:

I definitely think you definitely should go.

And this extends to adverbials which are very similar in meaning, so that we sense a tautology:

I definitely think you certainly should go.

People who waffle do this all the time, of course.

- We don't like two *ly* items together, unless the first is an intensifier:

We'll drive slowly certainly.

but: We'll drive extremely slowly.

Nor do we much like a direct sequence of prepositional phrases which begin with the same preposition:

I spoke to them on the phone on the road.

- We don't like having a series of medial adverbials:

The bus was of course indeed definitely late.

For examples of the use of adverbials in different varieties, see Chapters 54 and 58 (pp.291–3).

DESCRIPTIVE SUMMARY

Because adverbials express such a wide range of meanings, their grammatical treatment always includes a semantic classification.

- **Space** (or 'place') adverbials express position, direction, and distance:
  They live **in London**.   They ran **to town**.
  The path was **about a metre wide**.

- **Time** adverbials express position, duration, frequency, and the relationship between times:
  They left **on Monday**. We went **for a month**.
  I **sometimes** swim.   We visited Bath **next**.

- **Process** adverbials express manner, means, instrument, and agent:
  We argued **loudly**.   We travelled **by train**.
  I cut it **with a knife**. It was made **by hand**.

- **Respect** adverbials express 'with respect to':
  I'm advising John **about his rights**.

- **Contingency** adverbials express a wide range of meanings to do with cause, reason, purpose, result, condition, and concession:
  I'm late **because of Fred**.   I did it **for fun**.
  You'll get there **if you hurry**.

- **Modality** adverbials express different kinds of emphasis, approximation, and restriction:
  I **definitely** agree.   It was **roughly** a mile.

- **Degree** adverbials express the extent to which an event took place:
  I **fully** understand.   I **almost** cried.   I did **enough**.

The notions of time, space, and process are especially frequent and wide-ranging across varieties of English, because they are central to defining the circumstances surrounding the verb. In particular, time adverbials are intimately involved with the expression of tense (Chapter 23) and agent adverbials with voice (Chapter 22). But any of the semantic classes might appear in any variety, depending only on what people want to say or write.

At the same time, we would not expect adverbials from the different semantic classes to appear with equal frequency in all uses of language. Their choice and distribution will be influenced primarily by the subject-matter of the discourse, but they will also be affected by the variety's level of formality and by the nature of the interaction between the participants.

Historical writing

Adverbials of time are to be expected in historical writing, but also adverbials of space — for events have to happen somewhere. This extract summarizing the events of the American Revolution is taken from *The New Penguin Encyclopedia*. Time adverbials are shown with continuous underlining; space adverbials with broken underlining:

Fighting began at Lexington and Concord, MA (Apr 1775), and lasted until the surrender of Lord Cornwallis to Washington at Yorktown, VA, in 1781. Military conflict centred on Boston until the British withdrew (Mar 1776). From August 1776 until the beginning of 1780, the main theatre was the states of New York, New Jersey, and Pennsylvania, with major engagements at Long Island, at such New Jersey sites as Princeton, Monmouth, and Trenton, and at Saratoga in upstate New York.

Geographical writing

Adverbials of space always relate to the question 'where?'. They are therefore critical in descriptions of locations, as this guide-book extract about Amsterdam illustrates. After an opening scene-setting clause, the piece depends entirely on its often coordinated space adverbials (underlined):

The Jordaan is a tranquil part of the city, crammed <u>with canal houses, old and new galleries, restaurants, craft shops and pavement cafés</u>. The walk route meanders <u>through narrow streets and along enchanting canals</u>. It starts <u>from the Westerkerk</u> and continues <u>past Brouwersgracht</u>, <u>up to the Ij river and on to the Western Islands</u>.

Scientific writing

Science is concerned with causes and effects, hypotheses and measurements. We would therefore expect to find particular use made of adverbials of respect, contingency, modality and degree. *If-* clauses are the primary expression of a hypothesis:

If X is the case, then *Y* will be the consequence.

And any account of experimental results will be full of qualifications, using degree adverbials of amplification, such as *highly*, *extremely*, *strongly*, and *relatively*. The connection between ideas, so important in scientific reasoning, will also foster a sophisticated use of conjuncts (Chapter 58), such as *secondly*, *therefore*, *alternatively*, and *i.e.* The adverbials are underlined in this passage from a journal article:

<u>With respect to group A</u>, a major finding was the high number of cases dying <u>from malnutrition</u>. <u>Although we had expected some rise in frequency</u>, we did not expect the results here to exceed those in group B <u>so significantly</u>. <u>Generally</u>, the reverse is the case.

Instructional writing

Process adverbials are to be expected in instructional writing, as they generally answer the question 'how?'. They are given continuous underlining in this cooking recipe for *tagliatelle con prosciutto*. In the context of cooking, we also find time adverbials to be important (broken underlining). We would be less likely to encounter these in, say, a manual for fitting a thermostat.

Cook the tagliatelle in fast-boiling water in the usual way for about 10 minutes. Meanwhile lightly fry the ham in a little butter for 2–3 minutes. Drain well, mix with the butter and ham and serve on a hot dish, sprinkled with the cheese.

If we were to leave all the adverbials out, we would end up with a very bare passage indeed:

Cook the tagliatelle ... fry the ham ... Drain ... mix ... and serve.

This example also highlights the way some adverbials blend meaning from two semantic classes. For example, is *in a little butter* an adverbial of space or of manner? Does it answer the question 'where?' or 'how?' The answer is: a bit of both – but because the phrase means '*in* a little butter' the dominant element in the sense seems to be one of space.

Conversation

The informal and interactive nature of conversation motivates several distinctive adverbial uses:
- colloquial items, such as *sort of* (*sorta*) and *as well*
- colloquial variants, such as *real good* (for *really*)
- expletive items, such as *bloody interesting*
- situation-dependent adverbs, such as *here* and *now*
- reaction signals, such as *yeah* and *mhm*
- initiating adverbs, such as *well* and *oh*
- vague adverb compounds, such as *maybe* and *anyway.*

DESCRIPTIVE SUMMARY

Adverbials perform four types of grammatical role within a clause, acting as adjuncts, subjuncts (Chapter 56), disjuncts (Chapter 57), and conjuncts (Chapter 58). Adjuncts are by far the largest class. They relate either directly to the meaning of the verb (**predication adjuncts**) or to the sentence as a whole (**sentence adjuncts**). Both types can be seen in this sentence:

Last week I went **by coach** to see a show.

- The action of both the main clause and the subordinate clause took place 'last week'. The time adverbial *last week* is a sentence adjunct.
- The process adverbial *by coach* is a predication adjunct, as its meaning applies only to the action of going. The seeing of the show did not take place in a coach.

EXPLANATION

Because it is the nature of predication adjuncts to modify the meaning of the verb, they tend to stay close to the verb. Their most natural position is at the end of a clause, specifying the verb meaning in some way.

She **readily** loaned me the money.

I drove the car **very slowly**.

By contrast, it is the nature of sentence adjuncts to modify a whole sentence, regardless of how many clauses it has. They therefore tend to appear at the sentence periphery – at the very beginning or very end.

In the morning, we got up and went into town.

We got up and went to town **in the morning**.

Telling the difference

The distinction between predication and sentence adjunct is important, because it conveys a difference in meaning. Compare these two sentences.

Jo heard a noise **in the kitchen**.

In the kitchen, Jo heard a noise.

The first contains a predication adjunct, telling us where the hearing took place. The second contains a sentence adjunct, telling us about something that happened in the kitchen. The separateness of the sentence adjunct is reinforced by the use of a comma. This is not possible in the first sentence. We do not write:

~~Jo heard a noise, in the kitchen.~~

That would break the link between the predication adjunct and its verb. The two sentences allow different interpretations. In the first one:

- We don't know where Jo is – probably not in the kitchen.
- The noise is probably coming from the kitchen.

In the second one:

- We do know where Jo is – she's in the kitchen.
- We don't know where the noise is coming from – it may well be from outside.

Another example

I packed my clothes in a case in London.

Here the two adjuncts are in the same sentence, but they relate differently to the verb. The case and the packing go closely together whereas the packing and London do not. We can easily separate *London* from the verb:

In London, I packed my clothes in a case.

but we cannot separate *the case* from the verb:

~~In a case, I packed my clothes in London.~~

This is because *in London* is a sentence adjunct, and *in a case* is a predication adjunct.

For other ordering issues, see Chapter 53. For examples of adjuncts in use, see pp.292–3.

The term **subjunct** refers to a type of adverbial (Chapter 55) which plays a **subordinate** role in relation to a whole clause or to one of its elements (Chapter 3).

- A whole clause: in this example, the main meaning is built up out of a subject (*everyone*) a verb (*should be*), and two adjuncts (*there, on time*). The subjunct *certainly* is not part of the clause, but adds a gloss to it – increasing the intensity, in this case:
  Certainly, everyone should be there on time.

- A clause element: in these examples, the subjunct *only* applies to just one of the elements:
  Only the chief clerk sent a fiver. [no-one else did]
  The chief clerk sent **only** a fiver. [no larger amount]

EXPLANATION

In essence, a subjunct adds a semantic slant to what has been said in the associated clause. There are two broad types.

A slant on the clause as a whole

- To make the clause content sound more courteous or polite, using such words as *kindly*, *graciously*, and *please*:
  Please would you sit down.
  Apart from the commonly occurring *please*, these subjuncts tend to be rather formal and formulaic, especially when used with the passive (Chapter 22):
  Customers are kindly requested not to smoke.
  A formulaic use also appears at the ends of letters:
  Sincerely ...   With cordial greetings ...
- To convey a point of view about the clause content:
  Militarily, we're in a good position.
  Other examples: *psychologically*, *socially*

These are usually adverbs ending in *-ly*. An informal use of *-wise* also exists, especially in American English:

Weatherwise, things are not looking so good.

A slant on a part of the clause

- To add an attitude about the relationship between the subject and the verb:

  Resentfully, the boy left the room.

  Other examples: *bitterly, with unease, reluctantly*
- To add a sense of time to a clause element:

  They're still in the back garden.

  Other examples: *already, yet, just, forever*
- To emphasize a clause element, locating it within a scale of intensity higher or lower than normal:

  Emphasizing: It's actually a type of duck.

  Scaling upwards: I see your position perfectly.

  Scaling downwards: I sort of see your position.

  Other examples: *really, indeed, of course; utterly, deeply, well; somewhat, almost, kind of, a bit*
- To focus on a clause element:

  Adding to it: I asked John to write as well.

  Restricting it: I asked John alone.

  Other examples: *also, even, too; only, just, merely*

Positioning a subjunct

Most subjuncts can move about the clause, so we need to attend to their location, to ensure that their slant applies to the element we intend. But we must respect context. This next sentence is unambiguous, even though *only* is separated from its point of focus:

I only left the car in the garage for a week.

However, in self-consciously formal usage people generally place *only* next to its focal point:

I left the car in the garage for only a week.

For examples of subjuncts in use, see pp.291–3.

DESCRIPTIVE SUMMARY

The term **disjunct** refers to a type of adverbial (Chapter 55) which plays a **superior** role in relation to a clause. Disjuncts, as it were, look down from above on a clause, making a judgement about what it is saying or how it is phrased.

- About what it is saying: **content** disjuncts make an observation about the truth of a clause or make a value judgement about it:
    Without a doubt, we left the papers behind.
    Annoyingly, we left the papers behind.

- About how it is phrased: **style** disjuncts comment on the style or form of what is being said:
    To put it bluntly, I think he should leave.

In a word, disjuncts express our **stance**.

EXPLANATION

The term 'stance' well summarizes the point of a disjunct. We regularly need a way of giving an assessment of what we are saying. In particular, we often find ourselves wanting to make three kinds of judgement:
- We want to say how certain we feel about the content of a clause:
    - by expressing our conviction about it:
        undeniably   indeed   obviously   clearly   to be sure
    - by expressing our doubt about it:
        conceivably   perhaps   maybe   supposedly   possibly
    - by commenting on its truth or reality:
        actually   really   ideally   theoretically   essentially

- We want to express our evaluation of the content of the clause – a judgement that can be of several kinds:

Adverbs and adverbials

- we view it as right or wrong:
    rightly   wrongly   correctly   incorrectly   justly
- we view it as wise or foolish:
    cleverly   foolishly   sensibly   wisely   cunningly
- we view it as unexpected (often followed by *enough*):
    strangely   amazingly   ironically   oddly
- we view it as appropriate or expected:
    appropriately   inevitably   naturally   predictably
- we view it as satisfying or dissatisfying:
    pleasingly   disturbingly   annoyingly   refreshingly
- we view it as fortunate or unfortunate:
    fortunately   happily   luckily   tragically
- we view it has having a positive outcome:
    hopefully   significantly   thankfully   mercifully

Some examples:

Rightly or wrongly, he was freed by the jury.
Foolishly, we took the wrong turning.
To my surprise, there were no problems.
What is even more pleasing, we didn't have to pay.

- We want to comment on the way we are expressing the content of the clause:
  - by drawing attention to what is being said:
      candidly   frankly   put simply   to be blunt   in short
  - by withdrawing our commitment ('hedging'):
      generally speaking   personally   metaphorically   strictly
    Clauses are common here, especially in conversation:
      if you ask me   since you want to know   putting it in
      words of one syllable   to be perfectly frank about this

Reviews and arguments make great use of disjuncts. It would be unusual to hear an academic or legal dispute without such words as *patently*, *purportedly*, and *manifestly*. Levels vary from formal *assuredly* to everyday *maybe*. On the other hand, we would be surprised to hear them from the presenter of the six o'clock news. For examples of disjuncts in use, see pp.291–3.

DESCRIPTIVE SUMMARY

The term **conjunct** refers to a type of adverbial (Chapter 55) which connects ('conjoins') independent grammatical units, chiefly clauses, sentences, and paragraphs. Conjuncts work along with conjunctions (Chapter 66) to provide the connectivity required for the smooth, coherent running of a discourse. All types of adverbial structure can be used: adverbs, adverb phrases, prepositional phrases, and adverbial clauses:

> meanwhile   more precisely   for instance   to conclude

Conjuncts usually occur at or towards the beginning of a clause, and some (e.g. *besides*, *still*) are hardly ever found in other locations. But conjuncts in the middle or end of a clause are certainly possible:

> So you think, **in other words**, that she'll resign?
> I said I'd go, **anyway**.   What do you think, **though**?

Also, conjuncts often follow conjunctions:

> and **furthermore** ...   but **instead** ...   or **else** ...

For simplicity, all examples in this chapter will be of conjuncts linking sentences.

EXPLANATION

We do not speak or write in sentences; we write in discourses (Chapter 73). And conjuncts enable us to express certain kinds of meaning relationship as we move from one sentence to the next. We might think that there is an indefinite number of ways of doing this. In fact, we can group the semantic functions of conjuncts into eight basic types.

- Adding an extra piece of information, especially by way of reinforcement:

  Moreover, the door was open.

  Other examples: *furthermore, also, what is more*
- Adding an element in a list:

  Next we need to look at the balance sheets.

  Other examples: *first, second, to begin with, then, lastly*
- Summarizing a state of affairs:

  In conclusion, I think we should vote for the motion.

  Other examples: *overall, therefore, thus, to sum up*
- Restating or illustrating:

  In other words, I think we should go by bus.

  Other examples: *namely (viz), for example (e.g.)*
- Expressing a result:

  Hence three people must have been in the car.

  Other examples: *therefore, thus, as a result, accordingly*
- Expressing an inference:

  Otherwise there would be no point in going.

  Other examples: *else, then, in other words, in that case*
- Expressing various sorts of contrast

  reformulating an idea: *rather, better, more precisely*

  replacing an idea: *alternatively, again, instead*

  opposing an idea: *by way of contrast, conversely*

  conceding an idea: *however, nevertheless, at any rate*

  An example: **On the other hand**, it was a good game.
- Shifting attention to a new topic:

  By the way, have you heard from Pete?

  Other examples: *incidentally, meanwhile, meantime*

Some conjuncts fall into more than one of these categories. For example, a word like *then* has a wide range of conjunct uses, including:

First find the pilot light. Then use a spanner to … [next]
There's nothing more we can do, then! [to sum up]
If we are agreed, then we can move on. [in that case]
We might go. Then again, we might stay. [in contrast]

Using conjuncts

Most varieties use conjuncts sporadically. In particular, the unplanned nature of conversation makes many types of conjunct unlikely. We do not spend much time, in everyday chat, carefully reformulating (*more precisely*), contrasting (*nevertheless*), or enumerating (*thirdly*). However, as soon as we launch into a monologue, or start to argue, or change the topic, conjuncts start to flow:

all the same   by the way   anyway   in other words ...

The exploitation of the full range of conjuncts is likely to be found only in those varieties which deal with complex argumentation, such as academic speaking or writing.

Any comparison of conjuncts between speech and writing shows great variation in levels of formality. At the formal end of the scale we find such items as:

thus   hence   furthermore   conversely   nonetheless

At the informal end:

then   so   by the by   anyhow   for a start

There is also some regional variation – for example, these are primarily informal American English:

second of all   anyways   [final] too (You did too!)

And the stylistic variation can be exploited – as in Lewis Carroll's *Alice Through the Looking Glass* (Chapter 4). There is humour in the choice of a rare formal conjunct contrasting with the informal *nohow*.

'I know what you're thinking about,' said Tweedledum; 'but it isn't so, nohow.'

'Contrariwise,' continued Tweedledee, 'if it was so, it might be ...'

Conjuncts can also be overused. In theory we can insert as many as we like into a sentence. In practice, this gives a rambling impression it is wise to avoid:

And so, to sum up, in other words, I think that, all in all, we should nevertheless look to the future ...

Combining adverbials

Conjuncts, along with adjuncts, subjuncts, and disjuncts (Chapters 55 to 57), provide us with the mechanisms we need to modulate the meaning of verbs and to orientate the meaning of clauses and sentences within a discourse. None of these four categories works in isolation. At the same time, differences of subject-matter, situation, and intention can result in major differences in the frequency and type of adverbial used in a particular variety.

In court

The information-gathering purpose of a lawyer's cross-examination results in a heavy concentration of adjuncts, especially of time and place, as this extract from a US trial illustrates:

LAWYER: Did you have occasion to be working <u>at or about 12 o'clock midnight</u>?

WITNESS: Yes sir, I did.

LAWYER: Uh, <u>on the night of June the ninth and the early morning hours of June the tenth</u>?

WITNESS: Yes sir.

LAWYER: <u>How many hours</u> had you been <u>on duty</u> <u>that day</u>?

WITNESS: <u>Eight</u> <u>hours</u>. We were <u>just ready</u> to go <u>off duty</u> <u>when</u> a <u>call came in</u>.

LAWYER: <u>At that time</u>, did you have occasion to go <u>to a residence on Sheridan Avenue</u>?

WITNESS: Yes, sir, we did.

LAWYER: <u>Where</u> was that sir?

WITNESS: <u>Four-twelve West Sheridan</u>.

The other adverbial types are uncommon, apart from the occasional use of introductory *now* (from the lawyer) and *well* (from the witness). It is the adjuncts which give substance to the interaction.

In sports commentary

Because we cannot see the action, radio commentaries have to provide the kind of descriptive detail which a televisual account would take for granted. More than space and time is involved, however. Commentators also have to describe the manner of action, and to express their opinion about what is going on, thus motivating the use of value-judgement disjuncts (p.287). And sports commentaries are of course known for their scaling up in intensity, warranting further disjuncts. (Conventions: <u>adjuncts</u>; *disjuncts*; <u>con</u><u>junc</u><u>t</u>s)

Smith passes <u>beautifully</u> <u>to Gray</u>, who heads it <u>very firmly and deliberately</u> <u>to – Pritchard</u>, who *obviously* wasn't expecting anything to come <u>his way</u> – but *luckily for him* he's unmarked – and <u>now</u> he's got a chance – <u>down the left side of the field</u> – Garner is keeping a close eye <u>on him</u>, *very sensibly* – but Smith's <u>up there with him</u> – and *really* this is looking dangerous <u>now for United</u> ...

The coordinated adverb phrase (*very firmly* ...) is a convenient means of filling in time while the commentator awaits the outcome of an action. The overall atmosphere is very largely a creation of the adverbials. If we omit the vivid words, there is very little left.

In public speaking

It is the balanced interaction between the various types of adverbial which produces some of the most effective styles of speaking or writing. Written language, offering repeated opportunities for reflection and revision, permits a greater range and sophistication in adverbial use. But it is remarkable what can emerge from the mouth of a competent speaker.

Here is an example from an experienced public speaker, arguing with considerable conviction for increased financial support for the arts in Britain. We should note the way he adds content to his speech with <u>adjuncts</u>, attitude and emphasis with *disjuncts* and **subjuncts**, and structural organization with <u>conjuncts</u>. The integration and balance achieved is typical of the genre – and is all the more noteworthy when we reflect that such speeches are usually spontaneous, using few if any notes or other support materials:

> So, <u>to sum up</u>, are the arts getting the government support they need in this day and age? *In a word*, no. *Certainly* we have seen <u>in some circles</u> a raising of the profile. **Indeed**, <u>as I have said</u>, my own local authority has **really** been quite generous, <u>by comparison with other parts of the country</u>. But they are *undoubtedly* the exception. <u>In our region</u>, **virtually** all the other bodies have either kept their grants <u>at the same level</u> or offered minimal increases. Two, **even**, have reduced the level of funding. **Socially as well as artistically**, this is a recipe <u>for disaster</u>. So I am arguing <u>today</u> <u>above all</u> <u>for a major rethink of national policy</u>, and I would like, <u>if I may</u>, to make three suggestions – *briefly*, <u>as I see my time is running out</u>. <u>First</u>, each arts centre should have <u>at least</u> one guaranteed post – <u>in other words</u>, a post paid for <u>by the local authority</u> and giving the holder – and **of course** the centre – a chance to plan <u>ahead</u>. ...

DESCRIPTIVE SUMMARY

Prepositions provide a means of linking noun phrases, and a few other constructions (some adverbs, adjectives, and clauses), with other parts of the clause. The item governed by a preposition is called its **complement**, and the elements combine into a **prepositional phrase**.

Examples of prepositions and their complements:

- noun phrase: *in the garden, on time*
- adverb: *until recently, by now*
- adjective: *for dead, at worst*
- clause: *We agreed **on where to go**.*
- another phrase: *The noise came **from in the garden**.*

Prepositional phrases have three functions:

- they postmodify nouns (Chapter 40):

    We saw a car with a red roof.

- they act as adverbials (Chapter 12):

    I saw John on the train.

- They complement a verb or adjective (Chapter 48):

    They are in the garden.   I was ready for food.

EXPLANATION

The main function of prepositions is to express meaning relationships – especially of space and time – between a noun phrase (Chapter 61) and other parts of the clause. They are the *only* regular way in which such meanings can be expressed. No other word class has the same kind of close relationship with a noun phrase. Adverbs do not govern noun phrases, and only four adjectives do:

    It's worth a lot.   He's (un)like you.   I'm due a refund.

Some uses of a preposition express little or no meaning, as they are there only as part of a structural relationship (and the prepositions are sometimes called 'particles' for that reason). This is the case when *by* is used in the passive construction (Chapter 22) and when *of* is used in the *of-* genitive (Chapter 34):

Tim was chased by a dog.   I had the time of my life.

We can sense the lack of meaning for the prepositions here if we contrast their use with clauses where there is a clear meaning:

Let us talk of cabbages and kings. [= about]

The cat was sleeping by a dog. [= next to]

Prepositions which are completely dependent on a preceding verb or adjective (Chapter 20) also have little or no independent meaning:

I relied on John. [not: ~~in John~~, ~~with John~~, etc.]

I'm fond of Mary. [not: ~~fond with~~, ~~fond for~~, etc.]

These constructions have to be learned as idioms.

Varying prepositional positions

We can sometimes vary the placement of a preposition relative to its complement, and this always carries with it some sort of pragmatic contrast.

Postpositioning the preposition

In just a few instances, we find prepositions occurring *after* their complement. The effect is usually to increase the formality – even if the usage is already very formal:

Notwithstanding the manager's objections, ...

The manager's objections notwithstanding ...

Other examples: *apart* (*from*), *aside* (*from*):

Aside from late trains ... → Late trains aside ...

The following type of example carries some regional resonance. All varieties of English use the first, but the second is typically British:

Last Monday I saw Sue.   Monday last I saw Sue.

Stranding the preposition

With many clauses introduced by a *wh-* word (p.59), it is normal to place the associated preposition at the end – in a 'deferred' or 'stranded' position:

What's he up **to**?   What did it smell **like**?

It is impossible to bring the preposition forward in such cases. No-one ever says, ~~To what is he up~~? or ~~Up to what is he~~? or ~~Like what did it smell~~?

But in other cases, movement *is* possible, and then the alternatives convey an important contrast between informal and formal style:

Which country is Paris the capital of? [informal]
Of which country is Paris the capital? [formal]

The latter would be normal in careful writing, and in speech would be typical of serious occasions, such as a crucial moment in a television quiz. These usages can sound extremely official or solemn:

For whom are you looking?
To what were you referring?

Sometimes the meaning can change. A clause like *What did they sell it for*? is actually ambiguous. It can mean 'Why did they sell it?' or 'How much did they get for it?'. *For what did they sell it?* would mean only the latter.

Many people are worried about placing the preposition at the end of the clause, because they have heard of the so-called 'rule' that it is wrong 'to end sentences with a preposition'. Originally a preference of the poet John Dryden, and enthusiastically adopted by prescriptive grammarians in the eighteenth century, it was taught in grammar classes as the only desirable usage to generations of children. But the deferred preposition has always been part of English, allows us to make an important stylistic contrast, and is frequently found in the most respected writing.

Possibly the most famous speech in English makes use of deferred prepositions (Shakespeare, *Hamlet,* III.i.56):

> To be or not to be – that is the question …
>> To die, to sleep –
> No more – and by a sleep to say we end
> The heartache and the thousand natural shocks
> That flesh is heir **to**. …
>> Who would these fardels bear,
> To grunt and sweat under a weary life,
> But that the dread of something after death,
> The undiscovered country, from whose bourn
> No traveller returns, puzzles the will,
> And makes us rather bear those ills we have
> Than fly to others that we know not **of**?

These are perfectly neutral stylistic uses of the deferred preposition. The usage is neither informal nor formal. There is no possibility of contrast: Hamlet could not have said ~~to that flesh is heir~~ or ~~of that we know not~~.

Both attached and deferred positions were present in Early Modern English. Their use in Shakespeare and other poets is not always associated with formality, however. Rather, the choice is often made to suit the demands of the metre. For example, both *with whom* and *who … with* are spoken by the same character, Joan la Pucelle, on formal occasions in Shakespeare's *Henry VI Part 1* – first to the Duke of Burgundy (III.iii.62) and then to the assembled lords (V.iv.86):

- Then lead me hence: **with whom** I leave my curse.
- **Who** joinest thou **with** but with a lordly nation …?

But when characters speak prose, this factor is irrelevant. In Shakespeare's *Measure for Measure*, when Lucio, the opportunistic man-about-town, speaks prose, he uses an informal style, and deferred prepositions are his norm:

- here comes the rascal I spoke of (V.i.281)
- This is he I spoke of (V.i.302)

DESCRIPTIVE SUMMARY

Most commonly used prepositions are **simple**: they consist of only one word. Prepositions which consist of more than one word are **complex**.

- Simple prepositions:
    after   at   by   for   from
    in   on   through   up   with
- Two-word prepositions:
    ahead of   because of   except for   near to
- Three-word prepositions:
    as far as   in accordance with   in front of
- Four-word prepositions:
    as a result of   for the sake of   in the light of

EXPLANATION

The number of simple prepositions is very limited – about 70. Complex prepositions allow us to express a wider and more subtle range of meanings than those offered by the simple set. As a consequence, many complex prepositions are found only in relation to particular kinds of subject-matter or in specialized stylistic settings. An example is the English we associate with legal documents, courtroom speech, and official pronouncements. This is characterized by usages which, in other contexts, would sound very formal or distant:

    in pursuance of   with respect to   in case of

Such varieties also use formal simple prepositions:

    pending   concerning   touching   save

However, most simple prepositions are stylistically neutral: words like *in* and *with* can be found anywhere.

For such a small word class, a surprising number of prepositions vary across dialects and styles.

Variation across regions

Several differ between American (A) and British (B) English,
though the influence of American English in Britain is increasing
the amount of shared usage, especially in informal speech:

toward (A) / towards (B) the wall
in (A) / on (B) behalf of the company
in back of the house (A) / behind the house (B)
among the crowd (A) / among(st) the crowd (B)
We go there Mondays (A) / on Mondays (B)
It's a quarter of four (A) / quarter to four (B)
We met the winter of 83 (A) / in the winter of 83 (B)

Local regional usage in Britain includes:

Scottish *agin* ('against'), *outwith* ('outside')
Northern *while* ('until'), *out* ('out of')

Some regional usages, such as *off of* and *irregardless of*, are felt
to be nonstandard.

Variation across styles

Some prepositions are restricted by subject-matter.
• Only in mathematical expression do we find:
less, minus, plus, times, over (as in *five over three*)
though *minus* and *plus* have developed a general informal usage
for non-numerical entities:

We'll come minus the kids – and plus Uncle Joe.

• Foreign borrowings add greatly to a style's formality:
From Latin: *qua, versus, via, pace* [pah-chay]
From French: *sans, vis-à-vis, à la, apropos*
• There are also some poetic and archaic prepositions:
'tween, 'twixt, ere [before], *unto*
Archaisms are not restricted to biblical contexts, but appear in
quotations and other allusions:

DO UNTO OTHERS ... [newspaper headline]

DESCRIPTIVE SUMMARY

Prepositions enable a noun phrase to enter into a particular semantic relationship with another part of the clause. The kinds of meaning can be grouped into several broad types, each containing literal and figurative uses.

* The most frequent and wide-ranging type expresses spatial meaning, with over twenty items locating noun phrases in any of three physical dimensions – point, line or surface, area, or volume: *at Brown's hotel, on a chair, in the sea.*

Other prepositions express such notions as:

* Time: *at three, on Monday, during May*
* Cause: *for charity, because of my interest ...*
* Manner: *by bus,* [tasting] *like a pear*
* Accompaniment: *with my friend*
* Support and opposition: *for / against the idea*
* Possession: *a woman of charm, a dog with a collar*
* Concession: *in spite of the problems, despite that*
* Exception: *except for Jim, besides the mayor*
* Addition: *as well as a book, in addition to Di*

EXPLANATION

The literal meanings of prepositions operate in a very straightforward way. Replacing one preposition by another between noun phrases directly alters our understanding of the way the entities in the real world relate to each other. If we see a book and a box, one must be in a spatial relationship to the other, and the preposition tells us which it is – *by, near, under, on* (etc.).

Extended meanings

It is more difficult to understand prepositional meaning when the items are used in abstract, figurative, or idiomatic expressions. Why do we say that a train is *on time* and not *at time*? Why do we *slow down* and not *slow up*? *freak out* and not *freak on*? Often the reasons are unknown or even unknowable – a consequence of some linguistic event that happened early in the history of the language, for which we have no written evidence. But sometimes we can see a process of reasoning at work.

Why *start up* and *slow down*?

Hundreds of idiomatic expressions use the prepositions *up* and *down*, and most of them can be seen as extensions of the two basic meanings, where *up* is seen as operating at or towards the higher end of a vertical scale, and *down* at or towards the lower end. The notion of physical height naturally extends to notions of size, activity, energy, nearness, status, and so on.

- *Up* is used where we want to convey an increase:
  wake up   start up   blow up   look up to
- *Down* is used where we want to convey a decrease:
  calm down   slow down   let down   look down on

By further extension, *up* is used to express emergence, such as approaching, coming into existence, or completing a process:
  loom up   dream up   settle up   use up   sum up

Why do people *freak out*?

Out (of) basically expresses a change of physical state – usually one of emergence, as in *We went out of the house*. It is therefore often used for general notions of something coming into existence, such as a solution or an ordering (*work out, find out, sort out*), of something going out of existence (*drown out, blot out, run out*), or of a mind altering its state (*black out, knock out, come out* – and *freak out*).

DESCRIPTIVE SUMMARY

We can make sentences smaller in two ways. (For processes which make them bigger, see Chapter 63.)

By using pro-forms

A **pro-form** is a word that replaces or refers to a longer construction:

- **Substitution** uses indefinite pronouns (p.246) such as *one*, *some*, and *many*, a few adverbs (e.g. *so, thus*), and the verb *do*:

    I wanted a screwdriver and Jo found **one** for me.
    Mike went by bus and we **did** too.
    You're going to be late – I told you **so**.

- **Coreference** uses definite pronouns (p.244) such as *she, they*, and *that*, and a few adverbs (e.g. *then, there*):

    My aunt paints fine portraits – and **she** sells **them**.

By using ellipsis

Ellipsis occurs when an identifiable part of a sentence is left out (at a location here shown by ⋏):

    I tried to fix the car but I couldn't ⋏. [fix the car]
    John started with soup and then ⋏ had fish. [John]

EXPLANATION

We shorten sentences because we do not want to repeat ourselves. It is not a special way of communicating, but a routine practice, as we see if we expand an abbreviated sentence. The full form is absurd.

- Jane saw Jim at the concert and tried to speak to him, but he left before she could.
- Jane saw Jim at the concert and Jane tried to speak to Jim, but Jim left before Jane could speak to Jim.

Using abbreviation: the benefits

Pro-forms and ellipsis avoid redundancy of expression and introduce a desirable economy into what we say and write. Our language can actually increase in clarity and effectiveness, as a result. By omitting information which is already known ('given') from earlier in the utterance, we place the remaining ('new') information into sharper relief. Also, especially if the earlier information is complex, the abbreviation saves listeners and readers having to process unnecessary material, as in this example:

Mrs Smith said she had expected the minister to publish the results of the public enquiry at the earliest opportunity, but he had not.

The ellipsis helps us to focus all our attention on the contrast between *earliest opportunity* and *not*. It results in a succinct, dramatic statement – an effect which would be reduced if the construction were in its full form:

Mrs Smith said she had expected the minister to publish the results of the public enquiry at the earliest opportunity, but the minister had not published the results of the public enquiry at the earliest opportunity.

Abbreviation is a welcome device especially in those varieties of language where time or space is at a premium, such as news broadcasting and newspaper journalism. But economy of expression is widely felt to be a benefit for *any* area of language use. It is unusual to find people consciously dragging out their sentences in the manner of the above example – but not impossible. If we change the speaker – say, to a minister answering a parliamentary question – we find that sentence expansion ('inflation' would perhaps be a better word) is routine:

We were hoping to publish the results of the public enquiry at the earliest opportunity, and we **intend** to publish the results of the public enquiry at the earliest opportunity.

(The end of the sentence is often drowned out by supporting cheers!)

Using abbreviation: the costs

The downside of abbreviation – of any kind – is that it makes listeners and readers work harder. Even with simple lexical abbreviations such as *BBC*, users assume that addressees know what is being referred to. If addressees do not, then communication breaks down.

It is the same with sentence abbreviation. Each element we omit, and each item we introduce as a cross-reference, imposes an extra demand on our listeners and readers. It makes our sentence less explicit. Pro-forms are a little more helpful than ellipsis, in this respect:

Ellipsis: I could visit her, but I don't want to ⅄.
Pro-forms: I could visit her, but I don't want to do so.
Neither: I could visit her, but I don't want to visit her.

But both processes make listeners and readers work that little bit harder.

We are all easily able to cope with a considerable amount of abbreviation. No-one would have had difficulty handling the above examples. But we must beware of pushing these tolerances too far.

• We need to take care not to elide too much, especially in the middle of the clause. It is not too demanding to cope with ellipsis at the beginning or end of a clause:

He went home and ⅄ wrote a letter.
John wrote a letter and so did I ⅄.

But ellipsis in the middle of a clause ('gapping') is much more difficult to process:

John went to France and Mary ⅄ to Italy.

If repeated, it can rapidly become uncomfortable:

During the play, Mary marries Fred, Jane Tom, Arthur Emily, and Evelyn Michael.

And even initial ellipsis can be ambiguous if there is more than one possible subject preceding:

Jo spoke to Di who went home and wrote a letter.

Who wrote the letter?

- We need to take care that we do not introduce an ambiguous pro-form:

  After the Duchess named the ship, she slid down the slipway.

This is not a problem of intelligibility, because our world knowledge tells us that duchesses do not usually slide down slipways. But it *is* a distraction, prompting humour where we might not have wanted it.

In the next example, the ambiguity is real:

  A union spokesman expected a meeting with the minister, and he would issue a statement afterwards.

Who will issue the statement? This sort of error is common in immature writing. People fail to check which item the third-person pronoun refers back to.

In all such cases, we can solve the problem by increasing the explicitness (perhaps using punctuation for the purpose), or by rephrasing, or both:

- Jo spoke to Di, who went home and wrote a letter.
- Jo spoke to Di, who went home. Jo then wrote a letter.
- Jo spoke to Di, who went home, and she (Di) then wrote a letter.

People who are aware of the possible ambiguity often gloss their pro-forms as in the last example.

Avoiding repetition

We usually find repetition unnecessary or boring, and avoid it whenever we can. But it does sometimes have a communicative function, such as to play for time, emphasize a point, or express irony. Here, a politician is piling on the rhetoric:

  We shall ask for support in the north of England. We shall ask for support in the south of England.

(He might have said: ... *ask for it in the south*.) And here the speaker is using mock babytalk (half-addressing Jim):

  I bought Jim a lovely birthday present, and Jim liked his lovely birthday present, didn't Jim!

Exploiting abbreviation

Abbreviation is a core feature of the language, and all varieties display it to some degree. But different kinds of abbreviation do tend to characterize particular styles.

In conversation

Initial ellipsis is very common in conversation, especially in British English, where the situation makes it clear what has been left out.
Λ Going to town? [are you]
Λ Raining again. [it is]
End ellipsis can also be found:
How could you Λ! [do what has just been noticed]
But medial ellipsis is rare. This is much more likely in situations which permit some degree of forward planning – formal speaking and writing:
I will acknowledge Λ but you must reply to her letter.

The highly elliptical character of informal conversation can be seen in this piece of question–answer dialogue from the film *The Third Man* (1949). There is also reliance on pro-forms:

MARTINS: You and I were both friends of Harry Lime.
WINKEL: I was his medical adviser.
MARTINS: I want to find out all I can.
WINKEL: Find out?
MARTINS: Hear the details.
WINKEL: I can tell you very little. He was knocked over by a car. He was dead when I arrived.
MARTINS: Who was there?
WINKEL: Two friends of his.
MARTINS: You're sure ... Two?
WINKEL: Quite sure.

Writing of this kind displays a rhythm and pace which well illustrates the dramatic effectiveness of a maximally economic style.

In advertising

Advertising avoids sentence complexity, and relies greatly on abbreviation to make its utterances easy to assimilate and remember. Ellipsis often relies on the visual context:

And all because the lady loves Milk Tray.

Because I'm worth it. [L'Oréal]

Sometimes the meaning is deliberately left open:

'X' washes whiter. [presumably, than all other powders]

Pro-forms also often refer to the context, or to some vague 'universal' he or she:

Does she or doesn't she? [use Clairol]

I bet he drinks Carling Black Label.

It is. Are you? [for *The Independent* newspaper]

In literature

Literary writing often exploits the ambiguity inherent in abbreviation. In Dylan Thomas's *Under Milk Wood*, a child tells her mother about meeting a local character.

Nogood Boyo gave me three pennies yesterday, but I wouldn't.

An end-ellipsis is unexpected, and leaves it to the imagination what activity Nogood Boyo had in mind.

The ambiguities inherent in abbreviated language are exploited to fullest effect in writing which tries to represent a person's thoughts, such as the 'stream-of-consciousness' technique. Here is a paragraph from Mr Bloom's long soliloquy in the middle of James Joyce's *Ulysses*. Bloom has just written a letter *I* in the sand:

Some flatfoot tramp on it in the morning. Useless. Washed away. Tide comes here a pool near her foot. Bend, see my face there, dark mirror, breathe on it, stirs. All these rocks with lines and scars and letters. O, those transparent! Besides they don't know. What is the meaning of that other world. I called you naughty boy because I do not like.

Simple sentences contain only one clause. Sentences which can be immediately analysed into more than one clause are **multiple** sentences. There are two types:

- In **compound** sentences, clauses are in a relationship of **coordination** (also called **parataxis**), chiefly by using the linking words (**conjunctions**) *and, or,* or *but*. Each clause can stand alone as a simple sentence – once any ellipsis (Chapter 62) has been 'filled out':

  Jane washed the car and I washed the potatoes.
  Jane washed the car and [she] went to town.
  → Jane washed the car.   She went to town.

- In **complex** sentences, clauses are in a relationship of **subordination** (also called **hypotaxis**), using such conjunctions as *if* and *until*. In a complex sentence, a **subordinate clause** (underlined) is dependent on the **main clause**, and cannot stand alone:

  Jane washed the car <u>until it was gleaming</u>.
  → Jane washed the car. [main clause]
  but not: <s>Until it was gleaming.</s>

  A subordinate clause always expands the whole of an element of clause structure – S, O, C, or A (Chapter 3).

EXPLANATION

It would be a simple grammatical world if we spoke only in simple sentences. In practice, such a restriction would leave us highly frustrated, for we would be unable to express most of what we want to say. We need complex sentences to express complex thoughts.

Reducing and expanding sentences

This need emerges in young children at around age three. Before that, sentences typically have just one clause. But towards the end of the third year they begin to string these clauses together to produce primitive narratives, proudly (though somewhat nonfluently) making use of their first conjunction, *and*. This is part of a three-year-old's reply to 'Where have you been?':

we went on a bus and – and we went to the shops – and – I got an ice-cream – and we did – we did see a big teddy in a shop ...

The thoughts come tumbling out, often rather erratically and not always with mature grammar, but with a clear intention to create a discourse. The nonfluency is a natural feature of language development at this age. It is not to be confused with stammering, even though the hesitancy is sometimes quite marked and persistent. Normal nonfluency is a phenomenon which appears in all children, as they move from simple to complex sentences, and it dies away as they develop confidence in processing larger units of information.

Other conjunctions soon appear – such as *but*, *'cos* [because], *when*, *before*, and *after* – expressing an increasingly complex set of meanings to do with time, space, and causality. It takes children several years to master the full range. Some notions – such as hypothesis (*if*) and concession (*although*) – do not become routine until around school-age.

Even though by five children are able to use quite sophisticated multiple sentences, they retain their core preference for *and* – and this remains the natural narrative preference in adult speech. It is automatically carried over into children's writing, when they begin to construct early stories, and the replacement of *and* by a more specific form of linking expression becomes a major stylistic target of early teaching (p.368).

DESCRIPTIVE SUMMARY

Sentences can be made bigger by coordinating units, either by explicitly using one of a small set of **coordinating conjunctions** (**coordinators**) or by linking clauses through punctuation (in writing) or intonation (in speech). When the coordination is explicit, it is called **linked** (or **syndetic**) coordination; when it is implicit, it is called **unlinked** (or **asyndetic**) coordination.

In coordination, the units to be joined have to be grammatically alike – for example, all noun phrases, or adjectives, or clauses. Virtually anything can be coordinated, and the process can go on indefinitely.

- I saw a cat and a dog and a cow and a hen and ...
- It was red and dirty and old and horrible and ...
- The day is fine and the sun is out and the beach is inviting and ...

We cannot coordinate different kinds of units:

It was red and a cat and the day is fine and ...

The coordinators are *and, or, but, nor*, and the correlative pairs *both ... and, either ... or*, and *neither ... nor*.

EXPLANATION

We coordinate units because we are thinking of them as being in a closer semantic relationship than if they appeared as separate sentences. Compare:

- John bought a car. I bought a lolly.
  John bought a car and I bought a lolly.
- I've a map. I've a torch.
  I've a map and a torch.

In *Rediscover Grammar*, coordinator meanings are dealt with in Chapter 66.

Coordinating the units suggests that we are thinking of them as 'together' in some way. The first example suggests, perhaps, a reflection on the unfairness of life ('... and all I got was a lolly'). The second suggests that I have thought out what I need in advance.

If we are going to coordinate units, we need to make sure they have enough semantically in common to justify our making the connection. Although there is no grammatical rule which stops us saying the following sentence, it is unlikely on semantic grounds:

I'm going to the cinema and it's raining in Norway.

Special circumstances do of course permit such bizarre sentences to be used: for example, imagine someone rushing in, just off the Norway plane ... But on the whole we avoid them, because they place too great a demand on the listener's interpretive ability.

We can see the increasing closeness of the semantic link if we compare sentences where the level of the coordination varies. Compare these four versions of the same sentence:

A I painted the house and I painted the garage.
B I painted the house and painted the garage.
C I painted the house and the garage.
D I painted the house and garage.

- A and B are clause coordinations, the second with an ellipsis of the subject (Chapter 62). They are the most explicit versions, but also the most repetitive. They suggest that two very separate actions are involved.
- C and D are phrase coordinations. These versions do not just add succinctness. They suggest a closer association between the noun phrases. In the case of D, it is much more likely that the house and garage is a single integrated unit, or at least one which I am thinking of as a unit. This is probable, but a little less likely, in C. It is much less likely in A or B.

Semantic structures

Because coordination suggests a close semantic link, we have to be careful when we coordinate more than two clauses with *and*. We can use a notation to show the possibilities with three clauses:

A and B and C   (A and B) and C   A and (B and C)

- The first version is used when all three clauses are semantically equal:

    I drank juice and Ted drank milk and Jo drank water.

- The second version expresses a closeness of meaning between the first two clauses, and contrasts them with the third. In speech, the sentence would probably be said by rhythmically linking the first two clauses; in writing, a comma can help to reinforce the structure:

    The bus was late and it was full, and I was tired.

- The third version links the last two clauses:

    I finally finished the page at six, and Jo typed it out and Di took it to the printers.

We also have to be careful when we use minimal phrasal coordination. If the nouns are so close in meaning that they could apply to the same entity, it may be unclear whether we are talking about one entity or two.

    John had a discussion with his accountant and golf partner about the cost of new clubs.

How many people did John talk to? One or two?

The semantic problem is potentially greater when the first noun in a pair of coordinated noun phrases is premodified (Chapter 39). If either noun could accept the premodifier, it can be unclear which it applies to:

    I love the old walls and bookshops in that town.

Are the bookshops old? Rephrasing avoids the problem.

    I love the old walls and old bookshops in that town.
    I love the bookshops and old walls in that town.

Types of semantic relationship

Coordination between clauses expresses several kinds of semantic link. The second clause can relate to the first in such ways as the following:

- It expresses a result or reason:

  The signal was at red and the train stopped.
  The train stopped; a signal was at red.

- It expresses a contrast:

  Jane wore a blue coat, and Jack wore a red one.
  Dick took the exam, but he failed.

- It expresses a condition, often a promise or a threat:

  Let me borrow your coat and I'll take the letter.
  Don't be long or you'll miss the train.

- It expresses an alternative:

  You can travel by bus or you can walk.

- It expresses an additional related point:

  The suspect wears glasses and he walks with a limp.

- It adds a comment or afterthought:

  We'll start the show at six – but that's good.
  They're enjoying themselves – or they seem to be.

End-position prominence

Although coordinate clauses are grammatically equal, the clause at
the end is always a little more prominent than the others – especially
in speech, where it usually carries the intonational emphasis (Chapter
75). We therefore tend to place second the information which is new
or which we feel to be of special importance. In this sentence, it is the
result which is important, so it goes in end position:

Dick took the exam, but he failed.

We are less likely to say:

Dick failed after he took the exam.

Even when the meanings of the two clauses are apparently equal,
it is the second one which carries a little more semantic weight
(p.344). These two sentences convey slightly different nuances:

You can travel by bus or you can walk.

You can walk or you can travel by bus.

In the first sentence we are highlighting the possibility of walking;
in the second, of going by bus.

Order-of-mention

Coordination is also influenced by a simple rule: order-of-mention.
The order in which the units are mentioned corresponds to the
order in which the events take place in the real world. If we say:

(A) I heard a noise and I went into the kitchen

we mean that the noise took place first. If it had been the other
way round, we could have said it this way:

(B) I went into the kitchen and I heard a noise.

However, with a little linguistic manipulation we can keep the
order of sentence B while expressing the meaning of sentence A.
To do this, we need to use an appropriate subordinate clause or
adverbial (Chapter 58):

I went into the kitchen **after** I heard a noise.

I went into the kitchen; **earlier**, I heard a noise.

When we do this, we 'break' order-of-mention (p.316).

Adding or omitting coordinators

It is because order-of-mention is the 'default reading' that we can omit the conjunction without harm.

Di watched the news; Jo watched the sport.

The succinctness of these sentences conveys an impression of deliberate contrast, and is often associated with terse, controlled communication: 'you, A, do this; you, B, do this; you, C, do this'.

In fact it is normal to omit all conjunctions except the last, in a sequence of more than two:

I bought some juice, crisps, jam, and cheese.

Jo went by bus; Di went by train; Tim went by car; and Fred went by plane.

Punctuation usage varies, in such cases – notably, whether there should be a comma before the *and* (the so-called 'serial comma', p.385). But, with or without a comma, the function of the conjunction is clear-cut: it signals the last item in the list.

We do not have to omit these non-final conjunctions. However, if we don't, we give the sequence a more urgent, dramatic, or 'breathless' tone:

I bought some juice and crisps and jam and cheese.

Jo went by bus and Di went by train and Tim went by car and Fred went by plane.

While such sequences are quite common in speech, they would generally be avoided in writing.

Beware *but*

There is no limit to the number of times we may use *and* or *or* in a sentence. However, *but* is a special case. It is restricted to a single use, at a given level:

Jo went by bus but Di went by train.

~~Jo went by bus but Di went by train but Tim went by car.~~

Inserting an extra *but* or two is a common error in immature writing.

Breaking order-of-mention

There are times when it is desirable to break order-of-mention, and times when it is not.

Desirable: in historical narrative

We might expect a historical narrative, focusing as it does on chronological order, to favour an order-of-mention style; but in fact history books regularly add stylistic variety by getting away from a bare sequence of events – 'this happened, then this happened, then this happened'. Here is an example from an information book aimed at junior-age schoolchildren:

> There were two closely associated disasters in London in the mid-1660s. In 1666 there was a great fire; the year before there had been a great plague. The fire put an end to the plague.

The writer evidently wanted to give special focus to the plague, so he placed it at the end of the sentence. But the plague is the *earlier* event, so he then needed to restore the correct semantic relationship. This he did by using a time adverbial, *the year before*.

While this poses no problem to a competent reader, it is a regular source of confusion for children who are learning to read or for those with persistent reading difficulties. Asked 'What happened first?', readers who do not notice the adverbial will inevitably say 'the fire'. 'What happened next?' – and they answer 'the plague'. They are then, of course, unable to say how the fire 'put an end to the plague'.

Rewriting textual material of this kind immensely eases the task of reading comprehension:

> There were two closely associated disasters in London in the mid-1660s. In 1665 there was a great plague; a year later there was a great fire. The fire put an end to the plague.

Other order contrasts involve subordinate clauses, especially those using *before* and *after* (Chapter 66).

Undesirable: in instructions

We are unlikely to break order-of-mention when it is important to get a sequence of events exactly right, such as in an instruction manual or a set of experimental procedures. It is not difficult to see the accident waiting to happen if a series of instructions were to be written like this:

Remove the four screws carefully in the order A, C, B, D, and before doing this ensure you cover the drainage hole.

'Right, I've taken out the screws. What was that second bit again? Oops!' That outcome is unlikely to happen if the instructions were written like this:

Make sure you cover the drainage hole, and take out the four screws carefully in the order A, C, B, D.

Writers of instruction manuals are usually scrupulous to follow order-of-mention, and this is especially important when instructions are being given orally, and there is no opportunity to 'read ahead'.

Fixed orders

We often have no choice about the order of a coordination.

- Some clauses begin with a formulaic expression, and this always appears first:

    Be sure and come early.

    Be an angel and buy me one.

    He's gone and left the tickets at home.

- Some phrases follow an order of perceived precedence in the real world:

    earlier before later: *sooner or later, life and death*

    higher before lower: *up and down, head and shoulders*

    positive before negative: *yes and no, right or wrong*

    status: *duke and duchess, employers and employees*

    Reverse order is not possible: we do not say *later or sooner, no and yes,* and so on.

Using coordination

All varieties of English coordinate units, but there are some notable differences in the type of coordination used. The loose linking of clauses with *and* is a major characteristic of conversation, but much less noticeable in formal writing, where *but* and *or* are more likely. Conversely, phrasal coordination is very common in formal writing and uncommon in conversation. Phrasal links are especially useful when considering alternatives and explaining things – important features of academic and technical writing. This paragraph provides examples:

very common ... and uncommon   academic and technical

Informal style

Informal speech and writing readily use loosely appended or interpolated coordinations:

I like veggie food – and Jo does too.

She said – and I agreed – that it was a shame.

These are signalled by prosody in speech (Chapter 75) and by punctuation (such as the dash) in writing.

We also find several kinds of approximation and emphasis:

two or three   more or less   more and more

and the like   and so on   and so forth

Nobody, but nobody can tell me what to do!

Advertising

Advertising slogans tend to avoid coordination, because of the length involved. Ads need to be short and snappy. But certain patterns do have some use, such as those which recommend people to 'do X and Y will happen'. Jingles also help to support any grammatical complexity:

Reach out and touch someone. [AT&T]

A Mars a day helps you work, rest, and play.

It takes a licking and keeps on ticking. [Timex]

Usage issues

Successful coordination relies on bringing the same kind of units together, and there can be comprehension difficulties if unlike units are coordinated – something which is quite common in careless writing. Here is an example of a phrasal coordination going wrong:

> The suspect was of medium height, of dark complexion, with a broken arm, and a Scots accent.

The way to check whether the units are appropriate is to take them one at a time:

- The suspect was of medium height. [no problem]
- The suspect was of dark complexion. [no problem]
- ~~The suspect was with a broken arm~~. [problem]
- ~~The suspect was a Scots accent~~. [problem]

To fix the sentence there needs to be some rephrasing, such as:

> The suspect was of medium height and of dark complexion, had a broken arm, and spoke with a Scots accent.

And here is a clausal coordination going wrong:

> I read the letter, discussed it with Hilary, and she answered it.
> I read the letter. [no problem].
> I discussed it with Hilary. [no problem]
> ~~I she answered it.~~ [problem]

This has to be something like:

> I read the letter and discussed it with Hilary, and she answered it.

Or, if we want to avoid a sequence of two *ands*:

> After I read the letter and discussed it with Hilary, she answered it.

The original sentences would probably pass unnoticed in speech, but they appear careless and inelegant in writing, and some stylists pay careful attention to even quite subtle distinctions (as in the second example).

DESCRIPTIVE SUMMARY

Sentences can be made bigger by linking clauses which – unlike coordination (Chapter 64) – do *not* have the same grammatical status. The link is usually made by using one of a small number of **subordinating conjunctions** (**subordinators**), such as *if, when*, and *so that*. These identify **subordinate clauses**, which are dependent on a single **main clause**.

Any clause element except the verb can be represented by a subordinate clause. The items in brackets show the way the clause can be replaced by a single word.

- Subject clauses (Chapter 9):
  What Mary said was really sad. [cf. <u>It</u> was sad]
- Object clauses (Chapter 10):
  Mary said **that I would be late**. [cf. Mary said <u>this</u>]
- Complement clauses (Chapter 11):
  A car is **what I want**. [cf. A car is <u>nice</u>]
- Adverbial clauses (Chapter 12):
  Call **when you're ready**. [cf. Call <u>soon</u>]

Subordinate clauses can also be found within certain phrases, after nouns, adjectives, and prepositions (see especially Chapter 41).

EXPLANATION

By its nature, subordination marks semantic inequality: the information in the subordinate clause is considered to be background information compared to what is in the main clause.

The contrast is with coordination. In the first sentence below, the two clauses each provide some new information; in the second sentence, only the second clause does:

Mike has bought cake and Jane has bought juice.
When Mike bought cake, Jane bought juice.

The second sentence says, in effect: 'you already know about Mike buying cake ... well, Jane bought juice at the same time'. The information in a subordinate clause is 'given'. The speaker assumes it is already known.

Omitting the subordinator

In nonfinite clauses (Chapter 17), it is sometimes possible to omit the subordinator:

- When asked to arrive at six, Ted said he would try.
  Asked to arrive at six, Ted said he would try.
- While driving along the lane, we had a puncture.
  Driving along the lane, we had a puncture.

The choice most often appears in clauses of time. We tend to choose the shorter option in conversation, and the more explicit form in writing or in spoken contexts where it is important to be clear, such as news broadcasting. The conjunction can actually add a desirable clarification, as these examples show:

Leaving the meeting, the prime minister said ...
While leaving the meeting, the prime minister said ...
Before leaving the meeting, the prime minister said ...
After leaving the meeting, the prime minister said ...

Omitting the verb

A subordinate clause can also be reduced by omitting the verb – usually a form of the verb *be* (**verbless** clauses, p.125):

Whether a wise or a foolish decision, John will go.
[= Whether it is a wise or a foolish decision ...]
Where possible, we should have extra help.
[= Where it is possible ...]

This sort of compression is often found in literary style.

DESCRIPTIVE SUMMARY

Subordinate clauses are so many and varied in type that they need a separate chapter to discuss their meanings and uses. They contrast with coordinating conjunctions (Chapter 64), whose functional range is quite restricted.

Adverbial clauses, especially, are very versatile:

- They are mobile, occurring initially, medially, or finally in relation to a main clause:
  - **Even though the roads would be busy**, the company made a decision to travel to Bath by bus.
  - The company made a decision, **even though the roads would be busy**, to travel to Bath by bus.
  - The company made a decision to travel to Bath by bus, **even though the roads would be busy**.

- They readily occur in sequences, the last item sometimes explicitly linked to the others (p.315):

  We left as soon as we could, after the concert finished, [and] while the traffic was light.

- They readily occur like Chinese boxes, one inside another. There are four in this example:

  I'll meet you **where** Di was working **when** she was saving up **because** she needed cash **to** buy a bike.

EXPLANATION

The functions of subordinate clauses are just the same as those expressed by the individual words or phrases which share their clausal role. Adverbial clauses also follow the same general semantic principles relating to position and order as already discussed in Chapter 53.

The functional identity between subordinate clauses and other units can be seen in these sentences. In each case we have an adverbial: a word, a phrase, and a subordinate clause.

I saw Mary **there**.

I saw Mary **at the hotel**.

I saw Mary **when she checked in at the hotel**.

The essential difference is the increase in explicitness that takes place. We get more information as we move from single words to phrases to clauses. (For the difference in explicitness between finite and nonfinite clauses, see Chapter 17.)

Some commonly used subordinators are listed below, grouped according to their meaning:

- **Time sequence**: *after, before, since, until*
  The letter arrived after I'd gone to work.
- **Time duration** or **simultaneity**: *as, when, while*
  The meeting ended when the clock struck one.
- **Place**: *where, wherever*
  I'll meet you wherever you want.
- **Condition**: *if, unless, in case*
  If you leave now, you'll be there on time.
- **Concession**: *(al)though, if, even though, whereas*
  Even though John apologised, I was still angry.
- **Reason**: *because, since, for, as*
  The traffic stopped because the road was flooded.
- **Purpose**: *to, in order to, so as to*
  I'm going to London to get a new job.
- **Result**: *so, so that*
  The electricity went off, so everything stopped.

Other meanings include **similarity** (*as, like*), **contrast** (*whereas, while*), and **exception** (*except, save that*). More complex subordinators include several ending in *that* (e.g. *granted that, in order that, now that*) and in *as* (e.g. *as long as, as soon as, insofar as*).

Problems of ambiguity

When two subordinate clauses appear in sequence after the main clause, there can be ambiguity. The usual interpretation is for the first subordinate clause to modify the main clause and for the second subordinate clause then to modify the first, as in this formula:

MAIN CLAUSE « SUB CLAUSE « SUB CLAUSE

I've asked John **if** he'll lock up **when** we've all gone.

'Going' relates to 'locking up', and both relate to 'asking'.

But in a sequence such as this, the future time reference allows a second interpretation:

I'll ask John **if** he'll go **when** the doctor arrives.

This could mean, following the above formula: 'I'll ask John this question now; I want him to leave when the doctor arrives.' Or it could mean: 'I'll ask John this question later on, when the doctor arrives'.

If we intend the second meaning, then we need to place the subordinate clause where it will not cause any ambiguity:

I'll ask John, when the doctor arrives, if he'll go.

When the doctor arrives, I'll ask John if he'll go.

Any problem of interpretation would of course be easy to solve in conversation; but unless the context made things very clear, the ambiguity would remain in writing.

The problem of *as* and *since*

As the list on p.323 shows, a few conjunctions are used with more than one meaning. We must therefore be careful not to inadvertently cause an ambiguity:

The vote was taken as people were shouting.

[= 'because' or 'while' they were shouting?]

There have been no problems since Tom resigned.

[= 'because' or 'since the time' he resigned?]

In such cases, the easiest solution is to rephrase, using the unambiguous conjunctions.

Using subordinators

There are very few regional or stylistic biases in the use of subordinators, but we should note:

- *Whilst* is a minority alternative to *while*, especially in British English.
- *Directly* and *immediately* are informal, and especially used in British English.

  I'll go directly the post arrives.
- Some subordinators have nonstandard uses:

  I can't do anything without the manager comes in complaining.

  I told him about there's a lot of rubbish in the park.

  I'm going now on account (of) I have to be there at six.
- *Lest* is more widely used in informal contexts in American English. It is often formal or solemn in British English, as in the expression used in war-memorial contexts:

  Lest We Forget.
- Many people find *like* meaning 'such as' to be informal and American, and they try to avoid it in writing, preferring an alternative:

  Some people prefer examples like this.

  Some people prefer examples such as this.
- In the series ending with *that*, the *that* may be omitted:

  Given (that) he was only sixteen at the time ...

  Granted (that) they are new to the business ...

  Assuming (that) we can all go ...

  The shorter version tends to be found in less formal contexts.
- Several of the *as-* series are formal, usually restricted to legal contexts: *inasmuch as, insomuch as, forasmuch as.*
- There are some archaic subordinators still used in formal or literary writing, and occasionally in speech: *albeit, whence, whereat, wherefore, whither.*

Using subordinate clauses

All varieties of English make use of subordinate clauses, but there are some notable differences in the type of clauses used.

Advertising

As with coordination (p.318), advertising slogans tend to avoid subordination. But constructions using *when* and *if* are quite common, as they focus on the perceived need of the potential customer. The main clause is often taken for granted, because the visual context makes it clear what is being advertised.

You know when you've been Tango'd.

When it absolutely, positively, has to be there overnight. [Federal Express]

When you care enough to send the very best. [Hallmark]

If you want to get ahead, get a hat. [Hat Council]

If it's on, it's in. [*Radio Times*]

With an appropriately catchy jingle, even a sequence of subordinate clauses can be found:

You'll wonder **where** the yellow went **when** you brush your teeth with Pepsodent.

News reporting

There are several semantic priorities governing the reporting of news, such as specifying the time-frame of the event, providing information about causality, and giving relevant background information. The subordinate clause is ideally suited to providing background (Chapter 65), so sequences such as the following are common in both newspaper and broadcast journalism:

After another night of shelling, the city of Baghdad is eerily quiet. [TV news]

When the merger was announced, shares in both companies rose sharply. [newspaper article]

Instructional writing

It is perhaps unexpected to think of subordinate clauses in relation to repair manuals and other instructional texts, with their 'do this and then do that' orientation. But such works are constantly concerned with diagnosis, causes, and effects. A guide to plumbing contains several *if-* and *when-* clauses in its section on 'How to clear an air lock':

If knocking is heard in a pipe, there is an air lock ...
When a cold-water pipe is airlocked ...
If the air lock cannot be cleared in this way ...
When all the air has spurted free ...

Academic writing

The nature of academic writing is reflected in its use of adverbial clauses which express processes of reasoning and attitudes of cautious interpretation. There is a focus on causes and conditions, results and exceptions, contrasts and similarities. The opening paragraph of an article in *The Cambridge Historical Encyclopedia of Great Britain and Ireland* includes three adverbial clauses (continuous underlining) – perhaps surprisingly, none to do with time. The *although-* clause concedes a point, the *if-* clause qualifies a point, and the *as-* clause makes a comparison. The tightness of expression is reinforced by the two *wh-* clauses (broken underlining):

Although there is much that is controversial and uncertain about social change between 1450 and 1625, there is one feature on which most historians would agree: that over that time-span a period of relative stability was replaced by one of obvious instability. Society in 1520 was still very like what it had been in 1450. By 1625, on the other hand, it had changed, if not fundamentally then at least visibly and tangibly. As late Elizabethan and Jacobean literature shows, people at the end of the period saw themselves in a society beset with uncertainties ...

In poetry

There are probably as many ways of starting a poem as there are grammatical constructions in English, but certain techniques do recur. The use of a subordinate clause in the opening line is quite a common way of providing an initial orientation:

Before the Roman came to Rye or out to Severn strode,
The rolling English drunkard made the rolling English road ...
(G.K. Chesterton, 'The Rolling English Road')
If I should die, think only this of me ...
(Rupert Brooke, 'The Soldier')
As I walked out one evening,
Walking down Bristol Street,
The crowds upon the pavement
Were fields of harvest wheat.
(W.H. Auden, 'As I walked out one evening')

Any subordinator could be used in this way, but *when* is a particular favourite, either initially or finally:

When I consider how my light is spent ...
(John Milton, 'On His Blindness')
My heart leaps up when I behold
A rainbow in the sky ...
(William Wordsworth, 'My heart leaps up')

The technique is as old as English poetry. Chaucer's *Canterbury Tales* begins with *when that*, a time subordinator equivalent to simple *when* today:

Whan that Aprille with hise shoures soote ...
[When that April with his sweet showers]

And an opening subordinate clause is a feature of Shakespeare, who uses one in over thirty of his sonnets. His two favourite subordinators are *when* and *if*:

When forty winters shall besiege thy brow ... (No. 2)
When I do count the clock that tells the time ... (No. 12)
If thou survive my well-contented day ... (No. 32)

In prose

Other popular literary subordinators, in both poetry and prose, are *as* and *like*, because of their role in introducing similes. While many similes are phrasal (*he roared **like a lion***), clausal comparisons are also widespread. Here are three from Falstaff in quick succession during Act V of Shakespeare's *Henry IV Part 1*:

Turk Gregory never did such deeds in arms as I have done this day.

I like not such grinning honour as Sir Walter hath.

I'll ... live cleanly as a nobleman should do.

With novels, a subordinate clause turns out to be a useful technique for getting the reader 'into' a work, because it provides a quick way of getting across some background information at the same time as introducing a salient point of character, setting, or plot. Once again, *when* is a popular choice.

- Agatha Christie's opening to her crime thriller *Evil under the Sun*:

When Captain Roger Angmering built himself a house in the year 1782 on the island off Leathercombe Bay, it was thought the height of eccentricity on his part.

- Evelyn Waugh's opening to *Brideshead Revisited*:

When I reached 'C' Company lines, which were at the top of the hill, I paused and looked back at the camp ...

- Charles Dickens' opening to *David Copperfield*:

Whether I shall turn out to be the hero of my own life, or whether that station will be held by anybody else, these pages must show.

Subordinate clauses are also found as intriguing or enticing titles of works and chapters:

- *Now That You're Back* (A.L. Kennedy)
- *As I Walked Out One Midsummer Morning* (Laurie Lee)
- 'How Tom Brangwen Married a Polish Lady' (the opening chapter of D.H. Lawrence's *The Rainbow*).

DESCRIPTIVE SUMMARY

A comment clause is a type of subordinate clause (Chapter 65) which is purely parenthetic in function and often lacks a subordinator. In speech, such clauses are marked by a parenthetic tone of voice. In writing, they are separated from the surrounding text by punctuation – usually commas or dashes. They may occur initially, medially, or finally in a sentence.

My computer, **as you know**, is not working very well.

To be honest, I think the decision was unfair.

It's going to take you a while, **you know**.

EXPLANATION

Comment clauses offer us the chance to add a qualifying or 'hedging' comment about what we are saying or how we are saying it – in the manner of disjuncts (Chapter 57). They express a wide range of meanings, from tentativeness (*I guess, it appears, I believe*) to certainty (*there's no doubt, I can say without contradiction*). Attitudes range from positive (*I'm delighted to say*) to negative (*I fear*). In many cases, the meaning is simply one of emphasizing or drawing attention to what has been said (*put plainly, as I've said, what is more, mind you*).

There are hundreds of these expressions in English, chiefly used in conversation. They are usually very short and formulaic, generally in the first or second person, and almost always in the present tense. They express a range of formality, from colloquial (*you see*) to formal (*it must be admitted*).

In speech

The natural home of the comment clause is conversation.
A phrase like *you know* performs several functions

  I got it at the shop – you know, the shop on the corner.

- It gives speakers time to marshal their thoughts.
- It gives listeners time to assimilate what has been said or to focus on what is about to be said.

If speakers are unclear in their thinking, or if they want to avoid addressing an issue directly, comment clauses quickly proliferate:

  the issue you raise, I must say, is one of those, it has to be acknowledged, which, frankly speaking, is of considerable importance ...

An overuse of comment clauses readily attracts criticism.

In writing

Some use of comment clauses is made in writing, even in academic contexts, where their tentativeness appeals:

  it was reported   one acknowledges   as we see it
  as is widely known   stated approximately
  it may be necessary to add   some authorities say

DESCRIPTIVE SUMMARY

The notion of comparison as expressed through the adjective (Chapter 51) or adverb (Chapter 52) can be extended by using comparative clauses. Several constructions are available:

Your house is older than mine (is).
Your house is more interesting than mine (is).
Your house is less interesting than mine (is).
Your house is (not) as interesting as mine (is).
Your car travels faster than mine (does).
Your car travels more rapidly than mine (does).

In each case we have a **comparative element** (*older, as interesting*, etc.) and a **comparative clause** introduced by *than* or *as* (with *like* a further option). The clause is either full or elliptical (Chapter 62), as shown in parentheses.

EXPLANATION

The purpose of the comparative clause is to express different degrees of equivalence and nonequivalence:
• the two notions are the same: *as ... as*
• one notion is 'less': *less ... than, not as ... as*
• one notion is 'more': *-er than, more ... than*

The different elliptical possibilities increase economy of expression but reduce explicitness. The more abbreviated versions are more common in conversation, accordingly:

Jo goes by car more than Di goes by car.
Jo goes by car more than Di does.
Jo goes by car more than Di.
Jo goes by car more.

Reducing and expanding sentences

Using comparative clauses

The most heavily abbreviated versions permit further interpretations, and thus possible ambiguity:

> Jo goes by car more than Di. [more than Di travels by bus? more than Di eats cakes?]

> Jo goes by car more. [than anyone? than she used to?]

However, it is this very ambiguity which makes abbreviated comparatives appeal to advertisers:

> X washes clothes whiter.

The implication, of course, is 'whiter than all other washing powders do'. But if someone were to challenge the makers of X, they could simply claim that they only meant 'whiter than X did before'.

The notion of comparison is at the heart of advertising, but it is also critical in several other domains.

IN ACADEMIC WRITING

Academics are always concerned about comparison as a mode of explanation. How does X compare or contrast with Y? The use of the *-er than* construction is especially common, often seen in the 'Results' section of journals:

> The bilingual children had a somewhat higher rate of pronoun usage than the monolingual children.

> The children's performance on Task 1 is only marginally better than their performance on Task 2.

IN IMAGINATIVE LITERATURE

The construction by writers of an imaginative reality is heavily dependent on the process of comparison, as suggested by well-established notions such as the simile (p.329). Comparative clauses abound:

> To be a queen in bondage is more vile
> Than is a slave in base servility

> (Shakespeare, *Henry VI Part 1*, V.iii.112)

> Mr Frodo is as nice a young hobbit as you could wish to meet.

> (J.R.R. Tolkien, *The Fellowship of the Ring*, Chapter 1)

We report what someone has said or written using a **reporting clause** (such as *she wrote, he said*). The speech or writing referred to is given in the **reported clause**. There is no particular limit to the number of clauses or sentences that can accompany a reporting clause.

> Di **said** that she was in town and would stay there until six and would then get the bus home. She would also be in the library for a while ...

- In **direct speech**, the exact words used by the speaker or writer are given, usually in quotation marks:

> Di said, 'I'm in town and will stay here until six.'

- In **indirect speech**, as in the earlier example, the words are presented as if reported by someone else:

> Di **said** that she was in town and would stay there until six.
> [= Di is in town and will stay there until six.]

In switching between direct and indirect speech, as these examples show, we need to make relevant changes to tenses, pronouns, and adverbs, as well as to punctuation.

EXPLANATION

Reported speech is an area of grammar which has a very clear semantic purpose.

- Reporting clauses enable us to identify all the participants in an interaction:

> 'Happy birthday,' said Gillian.
> 'Thanks,' Mark grunted.
> 'Happy birthday, mate,' muttered John.
> 'Don't worry,' said Mo, 'It'll soon be over.'

- The difference between direct and indirect speech expresses a difference in temporal perspective. Indirect speech is a step further back into the past.

  Mike said, 'Times are hard.'   Mike said that times were hard.
  The distancing of the clause content from the speaker is very clear when several words have to be altered:

  Mike said, 'I left this box here yesterday.'
  Mike said he had left that box there the day before.

Several factors affect the meaning of reporting clauses.

Choosing the reporting verb

The most frequent verb is *said*, but a dialogue can become boring if this is overused. Dozens of other 'reporting verbs' are available, each expressing a content which adds to the 'bare' act of saying:

admit   ask   assert   boast   confess   explain   observe
protest   recall   reply   shout   urge   warn   wonder   write

Several verbs comment on the manner of the speech:

laugh   mumble   mutter   snap   sneer   sob   whisper

Some of these indicate character: only bad guys sneer.

A few verbs are restricted to indirect speech:

believe   feel   imagine   mention   realize   suppose

We can say: *I believe that you know John.* But not: *I believe, 'You know John'.*

It is important to make reporting verbs suit the context. Overusing *urged* or *observed* is just as bad as overusing *said,* and an inappropriate use of a reporting verb can be unintentionally comedic: '*Hi', he snapped.*

Placing the reporting clause

The reporting clause can be initial, medial, or final:

Sue replied, 'I'm going and I'm taking Ted.'
'I'm going,' Sue replied, 'and I'm taking Ted.'
'I'm going and I'm taking Ted,' Sue replied.

The general stylistic preference is to use initial or final position. This keeps the quote intact and allows a greater opportunity for expanding the reporting clause (p.336).

EXPANDING THE REPORTING VERB

We can modify the reporting verb by giving details about the circumstances in which the speaking or writing took place or by specifying the tone of voice used:

Last Tuesday Sue admitted that she was tired.

'Sit down,' Tom said **angrily**.

The reporting clause tends to be expanded to the left, when it appears at the beginning of a sentence. It tends to be expanded to the right when it appears at the end.

Expansion in medial position can be awkward:

'I'm going,' Sue replied angrily to my innocent remark, 'and I'm taking Ted.'

We are more likely to see a lengthy expansion finally:

'I'm going and I'm taking Ted,' Sue replied, using the tone of voice which I'd heard many times before and which I knew brooked no argument.

Writers of fiction often employ this kind of style. It works because we can 'look back' if we need to, when we reach the end of the sentence, to check what was actually said.

By the same token, this style is not something likely to be heard in news reporting, where it is important to identify the source of a quotation as early as possible:

The Chancellor said today, 'There will be no further taxation increases during the lifetime of this parliament.'

We need to know that it is the Chancellor who made this remark. If the reporting clause is left to the end, we would have to wait before we could assess its significance:

'There will be no further taxation increases during the lifetime of this parliament,' the Chancellor said today.

We are likely to feel let down – or, at the very least, puzzled – if, upon reaching the end, we find the quotation attributed to someone of no political acumen:

'There will be no further taxation increases during the lifetime of this parliament,' David Crystal said today.

INVERTING

We can invert the subject–verb order in the reporting clause, but this is likely only in medial and final position:

'I'm going,' replied Sue, 'and I'm taking Ted.'

'I'm going and I'm taking Ted,' replied Sue.

It is a strategy very much favoured in news reporting:

'The economy in Germany is taking a turn for the better,' says our reporter in Bonn, Tom O'Hare.

And journalism is the place where we are most likely to see inversion in initial position:

Declared the 23-year-old striker, 'I have no intention of leaving the country.'

However, there are some restrictions on what can be inverted:

- The verb needs to be simple (Chapter 24); we cannot say:
  ~~'I'm going,' was replying Sue.~~
- The subject needs to be a noun; we can hardly ever invert if it is a pronoun:
  ~~'I'm going,' replied she.~~

Say is the only verb to allow pronoun inversion:

- *Said he/she* (and *saith he/she*) is an archaic usage:
  'The answer,' said he, 'lies in the mountains.'
- *Says* occurs idiomatically with *I*, *you*, *he*, and *she* in informal narration:
  So, says I, you want a life. Yes, says he ...

Inversion is especially likely in final position, because it enables us to give additional prominence to the subject. Compare:

'I'm going and I'm taking Ted,' Sue replied.

'I'm going and I'm taking Ted,' replied Sue.

Final inversion is especially found when there is a lengthy expansion. Examples such as the one on p.336 are actually much more likely to be inverted:

'I'm going and I'm taking Ted,' replied Sue, using the tone of voice which I'd heard many times before and which I knew brooked no argument.

Using reported speech

Reported speech is likely to be encountered only in conversation and fiction dialogue, and in varieties where quotation is an important part of the subject-matter. There is a big difference between the many voices which need to be represented in the two conversational settings and the single (rarely more than one) voice which is the focus of a quotation in such contexts as news reporting, biblical reference, and literary criticism. There are also several differences of style affecting individual varieties.

Varying formality

All the examples of indirect speech on earlier pages have displayed the conjunction *that*:

The manager told us that the shop was closed.

This is a stylistically neutral level, with respect to formality. But if the *that* is omitted, an increased level of informality is the result (as with relative clauses, p.236):

The manager told us the shop was closed.

Recapitulation

If there is a long sequence of reported clauses, news broadcasting often inserts a recapitulation, to remind listeners who the quotation has come from:

John Smith reported that there had been several expressions of interest in a merger between the two companies. He had received a number of letters from major shareholders offering full support. The result, **Smith claimed**, was a clear signal ...

Especially in newspaper reporting, the recapitulation is usually a more interesting descriptive phrase:

David Beckham said he was delighted to be playing for his new club, and was having no trouble adapting to the Spanish way of life. **The former Man United striker** also said he was very happy about the living arrangements which had been made ...

Avoiding nuance

In religious texts, such as the Bible, the utterances of the
characters are reported in a style which makes maximum use of
attitudinally neutral verbs. Even though biblical characters
presumably laughed, sobbed, and muttered, as everyone does, we
would never guess this from the way they are reported. The vast
majority of their utterances are introduced by the single verb *say*,
in its various forms. There is occasional use of other neutral verbs,
such as *ask* and *answer*, and – rarely – a stronger verb such as *cry*:

> And God said: Let the earth bring forth grass ...
> Thus saith the Lord God of Israel: Behold ...
> And they answered: John the Baptist ...
> The voice of one crying in the wilderness: Prepare ye the way of
> the Lord ...

The absence of a pair of quotation marks ('inverted commas') is
not unusual. Indeed, quotations lack distinctive punctuation in
several varieties where editors are anxious to avoid giving a
'cluttered' look to a page, as in this example from a popular
magazine:

> I will have to live with it, the prince said yesterday ...

Quoted matter also tends not to use quotation marks in newspaper
reports of speeches or court proceedings, and in any piece of
dramatic dialogue:

> Lord Denning: I cannot accept the submission.
> I put one question to her: What will you do?

Long quotations of several lines do not usually have quotation
marks at all, but are indented.

Quotation marks are not strictly needed for intelligibility, as long
as there is some means of separating the reporting and reported
clauses, as these examples illustrate. However, they are obligatory
in conservative styles of usage, and a great deal of attention has
been devoted in style manuals over how best to punctuate them.

Doing without reporting clauses

Standard novelist practice is to identify speakers with reporting clauses – something which is critical if more than two are involved, as we saw in the four-way dialogue on p.334. If we were to omit the reporting clauses there, the dialogue would soon become impenetrable:

'Happy birthday.'

'Thanks.'

'Happy birthday, mate.'

'Don't worry. It'll soon be over.'

We would find such a sequence only when the author is representing a situation where it is not important to identify the participants, such as a crowd scene in which everyone is talking at once.

However, with careful writing, a limited omission of reporting clauses is possible and effective. We can do without them for short stretches of dialogue if the context or subject-matter makes it clear who is talking. One technique is to build in the name of an addressee, after a few lines, to ensure that readers do not lose track of who is talking, as in this extract from Mary Wesley's *The Camomile Lawn* (Chapter 19):

Calypso watched Hector pack.

'Shall you grow a military moustache? It would make you very unattractive.'

'Would you mind?'

'I shan't be there to see it.'

'Calypso, darling, will you have Catherine?'

Omitting reporting clauses is also a safe practice if the voices are distinctive – one being a foreigner, perhaps, or a regional dialect speaker, or someone with a speech mannerism. The dialect difference makes it easy to follow the dialogue between Huck and the negro Jim in Mark Twain's *Huckleberry Finn* (Chapter 14):

'Looky here, Jim; does a cat talk like we do?'
'No, a cat don't.'
'Well, does a cow?'
'No, a cow don't nuther.'
'Does a cat talk like a cow, or a cow talk like a cat?'
'No, dey don't.'
'It's natural and right for 'em to talk different from each other, ain't it?'
''Course.'
'And ain't it natural and right for a cat and a cow to talk different from us?'
'Why, mos' sholy it is.'

The intelligibility is also aided by the fact that the participants have adopted distinct speech roles – one questioning, the other answering. A similar example from a spy novel is given on p.66.

Why should reporting clauses be omitted? It avoids the repetitiveness of the 'he said' type of construction, and it can add real pace to a dialogue. However, authors omit reporting clauses at their peril. When readers have to 'count back' to see who said what, the author has failed.

A footnote: playing with reporting clauses

The use of manner adverbials (such as *angrily*) is the basis of a genre of humour called 'Tom Swifties', named after an early twentieth-century boy hero. Tom Swift's reporting verbs were usually accompanied by a dramatic, atmospheric adverb, such as *Tom laughed harshly*, and a punning game developed based on the pattern.

'Go over there,' Tom said pointedly.
'I've no gin left,' Tom said dispiritedly.
'I must start the operation,' the surgeon cut in sharply.
'The needle has reached zero,' Tom said naughtily.
'We like fairy tales,' said Tom's brothers grimly.

DESCRIPTIVE SUMMARY

We can organize the information contained in a sentence or clause in a number of different ways, by varying the grammatical structure. If we see a picture of a clown holding a balloon, we might say:

A clown is holding a balloon.
There's a clown holding a balloon.
It's a clown who's holding a balloon.
A balloon, that clown is holding.
That clown, he's holding a balloon.
He's holding a balloon, that clown.
A balloon is being held by a clown.

All except the last (the passive construction, Chapter 22) are the subject-matter of Chapters 71 and 72.

EXPLANATION

There are four reasons why we 'package' information differently:
• We want to draw special attention to a particular point within the sentence.
• We want to clarify what we are saying.
• We want to convey a stylistic effect, such as adding extra suspense or mystery.
• We want to show how the sentence relates to previous sentences in the discourse.

Not all the techniques described in Chapters 71 and 72 are common. Some occur only in certain styles. But taken together we are unlikely to find a use of English which does not display some variations in information structure.

It is in the nature of communication to be informative. Correspondingly, it is natural for a sentence, which is the main way in which we make sense (p.8), to contain new information. But not everything in a sentence is new. A sentence is always part of a discourse, preceded by other sentences, or grounded in a shared physical situation or in a context of assumed knowledge.

The train's late again. [we know which train – we also know about trains]

Even the opening sentence in a discourse makes certain assumptions:

Mike, have you got some sugar I could borrow?

Here, the identity of *Mike* and *you* are given in the situation, and our knowledge of the world allows us to take *got* for granted – we know that people possess things.

Major sentences and the clauses which make them up, unless heavily abbreviated, always contain something old, or **given**, and something **new**. If we were to draw a graph of the information in a sentence, we would usually find a steady increase from left to right.

I ...
I want ...
I want the car ...
I want the car to be ready ...
I want the car to be ready by tomorrow.

Each element makes the reason for saying the sentence clearer, but it is only when we reach the end that we find out what the sentence is really about – what is really in the speaker's mind. *Tomorrow* is here the **focus** of the message. It provides the specific information which we need to take the discourse forward. It is the message's most important or relevant part. It contrasts with the information earlier in the sentence, the **theme**, which is relatively familiar. We know the identity of *I* and *the car*, and that there is something wrong with it.

Positioning the theme and focus

A clause usually puts the theme at the beginning and the focus at the end. We can have a single focus and varying theme:

I want to go **home**.
Will you go **home**?
Let's go **home**.
The children are going **home**.

Or we can have the same theme and varying focus:

I want to go **home**.
I want to go to **the circus**.
I want to go to **the shops**.

It is the last lexical item in the clause which usually carries the focus. And it is this position which usually attracts the clause element with greatest length and complexity – the 'weightiest' element. This is the principle of **end-weight**.

I want to go to the shops in the new arcade.

Bringing the focus forwards

The above is the usual situation. We can, however, bring the focus forwards if we want to make a special point. This happens when we want to draw attention to an element where we need to make a contrast of meaning. Virtually any element can be focused in this way:

- Di has paid Mr Jones to polish the **car**. [normal]
- Di has paid Mr Jones to **polish** the car. [not wash it]
- Di has paid Mr **Jones** to polish the car. [not Smith]
- Di has paid **Mr** Jones to polish the car. [not Mrs]
- Di has **paid** Mr Jones to polish the car. [not voluntary]
- Di **has** paid Mr Jones to polish the car. [not hasn't]
- **Di** has paid Mr Jones to polish the car. [not Jo]

In speech, the change would be signalled by the focused item carrying the intonation prominence (Chapter 75). In writing, we could use one of several conventions, such as bold face (as here), underlining, or italics. Especially on the Web, a contrasting colour provides a way of focusing.

Unexpected focusing

One word in the above sentence would not be focused:

Di has paid Mr Jones **to** polish the car.

This is because *to* is a particle whose function is purely grammatical, to mark an infinitive. It has no stateable meaning. But if it has no meaning, then there is no point in trying to contrast it with anything. Grammatical words, such as determiners, conjunctions, auxiliary verbs, and prepositions, do not usually receive a focus.

This is why many people get cross when they hear broadcasters placing extra stress on words which do not seem to warrant it. The prominence draws attention to the word and suggests the speaker is making a contrast of meaning – but no such contrast exists. This example from a sports commentary illustrates the practice:

He sends the ball high **over** the field to Smith ...

A semantic contrast is available for a focus on *high* – not *low* – but there is nothing possible for *over*. The usage is therefore criticised as misleading.

What is happening is interference from a second function of intonational prominence. Strong stress always has two possible functions: semantic contrast and the expression of emotion. The louder we speak the more emotionally involved we are. A sports commentator's job is to sound interesting and to convey the excitement of a game. The more variation in the voice, the more likely this aim will be achieved. Sometimes, as a consequence, the peak of pitch falls in unexpected places. Indeed, in the most excited renditions, every word could have a focus:

Oh, he-e – sends – the – ball – so-o – high ...

Everything is in focus here, and our normal semantic expectations are suspended by the mood of the moment. However, the usage is less easy to justify when we hear emotional contrast used for a topic which ought to be presented in a more low-key vocal manner.

DESCRIPTIVE SUMMARY

There are four ways in which we can alter the information structure of a sentence or clause.

- We can put something at the front that does not normally go there (**fronting**):

    Aristotle, his name is.

- We can put something at the end that does not normally go there (**postponement**):

    It's very nice, Paris.

- We can change the order of the elements (**inversion**):

    Down came the rain.

- We can precede the unit with a construction which alters its emphasis (**clefting**):

    It was yesterday I saw Jane.

- We can precede the unit with a construction which alters its status (**existential sentences**: Chapter 72):

    There's some juice in the fridge.

EXPLANATION

No single semantic or pragmatic generalization applies to all five techniques of variation. Each offers an alternative means of packaging information, and gives us a wide range of opportunities to vary our meaning and style. There are some overlaps in function, of course – for example, both fronting and inversion, as we shall see, exploit the expressive possibilities at the beginning and end of a clause, enabling us to focus (p.344) on two areas simultaneously. But each of the five strategies is unique in the range of functions it performs, and this makes it possible for them to play an important stylistic role.

Fronting

This strategy brings to the front of the clause an element that usually occurs after the verb, thereby giving it increased focus. Why should we do this? Most obviously, to give it extra prominence. But why should we want to give an element extra prominence? There are two main reasons: to highlight a connection with the preceding discourse, and to underline a contrast with something about to be said:
- **To this list of issues** we must add another point.
- **In Bath** I was born and **in Bath** I want to die.

Fronting is used only in declarative main clauses (Chapter 5), and is not very common in the language as a whole. However, some varieties use it regularly.

FOR SCENE-SETTING
Fronting is a useful strategy for varieties which need to set a scene in a vivid or dramatic way. For example, bringing forward an adverbial (Chapter 53) is often found in journalism, commentary, and other descriptions:
- **On the second day of the conference** the union leaders have openly expressed their opposition to ...
- **At the far end of the penalty box** there are no less than three players waiting for the corner kick.

FOR EMPHASIZING CONNECTIONS BETWEEN EVENTS
Tightly argued language often fronts an element in order to make the connection with earlier text clear. It is therefore found in academic writing and formal speech:
This second topic we will examine in Chapter 6.
The importance of this issue I wish to stress.

FOR MAKING AN INFORMAL IMPACT
In conversation and fiction dialogue, fronting conveys a wide range of informal emphatic effects, such as surprise and excitement:
- **Amazing** it was!   •   **In the garden** we found it.
- **The bigger** we make it, **the easier** it will be to ride.

Postponement

An element which normally comes at the beginning of a clause can be placed at the end to give it special focus, even though the information it contains is already known (given). This is one of the functions of the passive agent (Chapter 22), but we can achieve the effect in other ways.

BY EXTRAPOSING
When the subject or object is a clause, we can put the clause at the end (**extraposition**), and fill its original place with an 'anticipatory *it*':

Giving up your job won't help.

It won't help, **giving up your job**.

This helps to satisfy our expectation that the weightiest element should go at the end. In academic writing, where clauses are often lengthy, the technique can aid clarity:

It is notable that four of the children were unable to answer question three.

This is a much more natural expression than:

That four of the children were unable to answer question three is notable.

It is unwise to keep readers (or listeners) waiting too long before they get to the new information.

BY ADDING A TAG
The constantly evolving nature of conversation often makes it difficult to plan a structure in the most compact and integrated way. We therefore find a given element taken out of its usual place and tagged on at the end, with a pronoun marking where it would usually be:

Did **they** get there in time, **the children**?

It was a great film, **Sixth Sense**.

The strategy enables the speaker to clarify or check that the correct topic has been communicated. A similar strategy fronts an element, as a way of simplifying the content of what follows:

That picture of your mother, where did you put **it**?

Information structure

Inversion

Inverting the order of subject and verb has a very similar role to fronting (p.347). The crucial difference is that inversion allows the subject to be placed at the end of a clause, and thereby makes it, unexpectedly, the focus. But because the element at the front is also in an unusual position, there is some focus there too. Inversion is a clever way of giving prominence to two elements at once.

The secretary was **first to arrive**. [one focal point]

First to arrive was **the secretary**. [two focal points]

The second version tells us, in effect, that there are two interesting pieces of information in this sentence. The 'arriving' is the most novel point, but the fact that it was 'the secretary' is also of some interest.

It is this capacity to add extra interest which is the chief reason we use it when describing scenes and reporting events. But it also has an important role, like fronting, in organizing the flow of information so that the discourse remains cohesive.

INVERSION IN DRAMATIC NARRATIVE

Inversion helps to make a sudden event sound more urgent, and this effect makes it appeal especially to writers of fiction and dramatic poetry:

- In ran Bryce, his coat flapping behind him.
- Into the valley of Death / Rode the six hundred.
  (Tennyson, 'The Charge of the Light Brigade')

It is similarly used in descriptive commentary when wanting to express surprise or suspense:

And here comes the Queen, in her carriage of state ...

The third set was the turning-point in the match.

It is rare in conversation, apart from a few short or stereotyped utterances:

Away runs the dog ...   So say all of us.   Here's the bus.

Inversion requires quite a complex level of grammatical processing – something not typical of informal speech.

INVERSION IN SCENE-SETTING

Inversion is a common way of introducing a scene, especially in literature aimed at children:

At the end of the garden, in the trees, lay three dogs.

Adult writers tend to use the technique when they want to add an element of romance or mystery:

On the hilltop above me sat the rising moon ...

(Charlotte Brontë, *Jane Eyre*, Chapter 12)

J.B. Priestley uses inversions in a paragraph describing some English hills in *The Good Companions* (Chapter 2):

Here are pleasant green mounds, heights of grass forever stirring to the tune of the southwest winds ...

Over to the west, beyond the deep channels of the rivers, is the Welsh Border country, a Celtic place, with hills as dark and mysterious as a fragment of Arthurian legend. ...

Here is a place of compromise, for Nature has planed off her sharp summits and laid down green carpets ...

INVERSION IN POETRY

Poetry makes frequent use of inversion, often to meet the demands of a metre, but also to express a semantic contrast or parallelism. In Tennyson's 'Now Sleeps the Crimson Petal', half the lines display the pattern illustrated in the opening verse:

Now sleeps the crimson petal, now the white;
Nor waves the cypress in the palace walk;
Nor winks the gold fin in the porphyry frost:
The fire-fly wakens; waken thou with me.

INVERSION IN PRESENTING NEWS

Reporters, publicists, and others involved with news management use inversion to convey immediacy:

Present at the meeting was UN secretary-general Kofi Annan as well as several heads of state.

Billed to appear at the Centre next week is the Band of the Royal Marines ...

INVERSION IN DIRECTING ATTENTION

This is a common practice in guide books and travel literature, as in these extracts about a church in Paris:

By the south entrance is a sculpture carved by ...

On the south facade is a plaque dedicated to ...

In the east transept is the tomb of ...

The parallelism in the use of space adverbials helps the user to navigate. Sentences which do not begin in this way pose an unnecessary delay in our comprehension, especially if the subject is lengthy, as we have to read it through before knowing where to look for the location it refers to:

A mural of three revolutionary heroes, painted by an unknown artist, is on the west wall.

INVERSION IN ACADEMIC WRITING

Writing which is tightly packed with information often uses inversion (as well as fronting, p.347) to reinforce the sequence of ideas:

Among all these issues is a claim which has attracted particular attention.

Also problematic is the absence of a clear trend in the way Group A children responded to the stimuli.

Even more important are the results of experiment 2.

The style gives the impression of careful construction, and well suits the precision of expression we associate with academic research.

INVERSION IN FORMAL STYLE

Several inversions are archaic in tone. When used in literature they are very formal in style:

Be it proclaimed ...   Long may he remain with us.

When a clause begins with an element with a negative or restricting meaning, we always invert the subject and the first auxiliary in the verb phrase:

Hardly had John left when ...   So be it.

At no time did we leave the garden.

This is also largely restricted to writing or formal speech.

Cleft sentences

This construction, which appears in several variant forms, is the most elaborate grammatical means English has of making a clause element prominent. It is very common in speech, but it is also a convenient strategy in writing, because it offers writers flexibility over where to locate their focus. The construction is also easy to read aloud, as there is no uncertainty about where the centre of prosodic prominence goes.

The cleft sentence is a very easy way of highlighting different parts of a clause. The clause is 'cleft' into two components, related in the following way:
- At the beginning is the pronoun *it* followed by a form of the verb *be*.
- After the verb comes the focus of the cleft sentence (shown in bold below).
- This is then postmodified by a clause containing the rest of the information in the original sentence.

To illustrate this, here is a clause where the elements are in the expected order (p.343):

Di read a poem in the café last night.

The following clefted options are now available:
- It was **Di** who read a poem in the café last night.
- It was **a poem** that Di read in the café last night.
- It was **in the café** that Di read a poem last night.
- It was **last night** that Di read a poem in the café.

Not all elements take a clefted focus with equal facility. The verb cannot be used in this way – though we do find the occasional informal usage, especially in some regional dialects (such as Irish and South Asian English):

John taught Spanish for years.

→ It was teach Spanish that John did for years.

And focusing on the subject complement (Chapter 11) is also distinctly regional and informal:

You're very kind. → It's very kind that you are.

The cleft sentence is unusual in the way it straddles the divide between speech and writing. We might expect to find it in speech because of the way the prosody reinforces the grammatical movement. But it is also very common in all kinds of serious writing.

Academic clefting

Academic writing is very much concerned with the making of carefully focused statements, so the option of unambiguously highlighting an element is attractive. Here are two examples from entries in *The New Penguin Encyclopedia*, on 'aborigines' and on 'Louisa M. Alcott':

- In the 1950s they began moving into the cities of SE Australia and formed advancement groups; but it was not until the mid-1960s that activism became prominent.
- Some of her melodramas were produced on Boston stages. But it was her account of her Civil War experiences, 'Hospital Sketches' (1863), that confirmed her desire to be a serious writer.

The information in the subordinate clause is firmly in the background, enabling a single point to be highlighted.

It is not by chance that such sentences are often preceded by *but* or some other contrasting item (*however, in comparison, ...*). The focusing in a cleft sentence is usually part of an argument in which the semantic relationship with the preceding sentence is critical.

Other examples of academic clefting include such openings as *it is in this respect that* or *it is the case that*:

It seems to be the case that the findings of Jones and his colleagues are flawed.

Such phrasing is encountered when writers want to distance themselves from the content of what they are saying. The alternative version would be a little too uncompromising for many writers' tastes:

The findings of Jones and his colleagues are flawed.

The term **existential sentence** is an attempt to capture the meaning conveyed by the following type of construction:

There's a strange cat in the garden.

There were lots of people in town.

There weren't any apples on the tree.

There appeared a bright star in the sky.

The word *there* comes first, without any locative meaning or prosodic emphasis. It is then followed by the simple present or past tense (Chapters 23 to 24) of *be*, or a small range of 'presentational' verbs, such as:

appear   arise   ascend   come   emerge   erupt
exist   float   occur   spring up   stand

The noun phrase following the verb is usually indefinite (Chapter 35), as shown by such words as *a* and *any*.

EXPLANATION

The term 'existential' is appropriate enough, as long as we realize that this is not the only way of expressing such notions as 'existence' or 'occurrence' in English. We can, after all, say such things as *God exists* and *A waiter appeared*.

What the *there* construction does is highlight a clause as a whole, presenting it to the listener or reader as if *everything* in it is a new piece of information. It gives the entire clause a fresh status. In this respect, existential sentences are very different from the other ways of varying information structure, which focus on individual elements inside a clause.

The first part of the existential sentence can also be seen as a way of preparing the ground for the new information which is going to come later in the sentence.

Preparing the ground

To sense this preparatory function, we only have to say *There was* ... It is a common technique in story-telling, both spoken and written, and is the basis of the limerick:

There was this chap who had a boat with a hole in it ...
Once upon a time there was an old lady who lived in a house in the forest ...
There was a young lady from Glasgow ...

Painting a scene

Existential sentences are an effective way of building up a scene, as each sentence adds an extra feature to the overall description. The *there* construction is a way of distancing the observer. The effect is a little like seeing things through the eye of a camera, which moves about a scene pausing to focus on certain details. The technique can be seen in Chapter 3 of *For Whom the Bell Tolls*; Ernest Hemingway describes a scene at a sentry box:

There was a worn, blackened leather wine bottle on the wall of the sentry box, there were some newspapers, and there was no telephone. There could, of course, be a telephone on the side he could not see; but there were no wires running from the box that were visible. A telephone line ran along the road and the wires were carried over the bridge. There was a charcoal brazier outside the sentry box made from an old petrol tin with the top cut off and holes punched in it, which rested on two stones; but it held no fire. There were some fire-blackened empty tins in the ashes under it.

The use of verbs other than *be* is also typically literary:

There arose from within the lake a long thin hand.
There appeared parted tongues, as it were of fire.

Sentences make sense (p.8), and grammar is the study of just how they manage to do that. Each of the chapters in this book has dealt with a single mechanism, or set of mechanisms, which English makes available to us for the construction of sentences. The chapters summarized the form the grammatical mechanism takes, then investigated the meanings it expresses and the uses to which it is put. It is a finite task. Although grammar is complex, it is not infinitely complex. There are only so many mechanisms out of which a sentence can be constructed.

Once we have completed our survey of all the sentence-constructing mechanisms which are available, the study of grammar is complete. We can, if we wish, look beyond the sentence, and investigate the way in which larger units of discourse work, such as paragraphs, sections, and chapters, or genres such as poems, plays, and novels, but that is to enter a different linguistic world. It is a world in which a much wider range of mechanisms is available for creative expression, and where the rules governing their use are much more difficult to state.

These rules go well beyond grammar. They include our use of vocabulary and – the least definable of all – the way we use our knowledge of the world to construct linguistic realities. For speech, the rules include our use of prosody (Chapter 75); for writing, our use of punctuation (Chapter 76) and graphic design. We have to make sense of these domains too, if we hope to develop a full grasp of how language works.

A grammarian can make only a small contribution to the task of **discourse analysis** – in the broadest sense of that term, to include the study of spoken, written, and electronic texts. It transpires that certain mechanisms of grammar, which are important for the construction of sentences, are also useful ways of building up sentence sequences. And we can sometimes see combinations of sentence-connecting features which give an indication of how larger units of discourse are structured. These are certainly worth studying. Although grammar can never give a complete account of discourse structure, it can help to give definition to that structure. Most grammarians, therefore, devote at least a small amount of their time to looking (wistfully) beyond the level of the sentence.

DESCRIPTIVE SUMMARY

At various points in this book we have identified features which have a specifically connective role. Here they are illustrated in their role as connectors of sentences.

- Space and time adverbials (Chapter 54):
  I went to the library. **Afterwards** I went home.
- Abbreviatory devices (Chapter 62):
  I'll visit you tomorrow. I hope you **do so**.
- Determiners (Chapter 35):
  I gave Jo a chair. She sat on **the** chair.
- Comparative constructions (Chapters 51 and 68):
  Di ran her heat in 20.3 seconds. Jo was **faster**.
- Conjunctions (Chapters 64 and 65):
  The audience left. **But** Jim stayed behind.
- Conjuncts (Chapter 58):
  Jack volunteered to go. **Next** Jim did.

In addition, we can use the pattern inherent in the structure of a sentence to bring sequences of sentences into a semantic or pragmatic relationship. This leads to a consideration of structural balance and parallelism.

Sentences which are dependent

The clearest kind of sentence connection using grammatical means is when the structure of one sentence sets up a strong expectation that there must be another, preceding or following. Although they may be grammatically self-contained, such sentences are semantically dependent. It would be anomalous to begin a discourse with conjuncts such as these:

Moreover, the car will only hold three.

John decided to go anyway.

Or to end a discourse with these:

On the one hand, we'll get our money back.

That was why he made the following points.

We have already seen how some novels and poems do begin with an entity presupposed (pp.54, 213), and authors can reasonably expect us to string along with them if their demands are not too great. We can easily relate to the imagined conversation in which we find ourselves at the opening of Edward Thomas's 'Adlestrop':

Yes. I remember Adlestrop.

But an author would be asking too much of a reader if a text were to begin with a conjunct or conjunction:

However, nobody complained.

Sentences which balance

Sentences are most obviously in balance when their structures are parallel. But we have to notice the balance. It is not enough just to have, say, a Subject–Verb–Object structure repeated, for most clauses display that order. The parallelism has to extend to phrase level as well. And it will be especially noticeable if the sentences are very short or if they make use of some unusual feature, such as fronting or inversion (Chapter 71):

I came. I saw. I conquered. [Julius Caesar]

In Venice it was sunny. In Rome it was wet.

Who knows? Who cares?

Although there is no overt signal in these sentences that they belong together, we do not like to split them up. In this diary account of a trip to Europe, the writer has decided to wax rhetorical about the way their food ran out. He paragraphed it like this:

Our supplies didn't last. In France, we finished off the cheese. In Belgium we finished off the ham. In Luxembourg we finished off the fruit. In Holland we finished off the bread. It was time to go home.

There was a convenient boat leaving Rotterdam on the Friday morning ...

This makes rhetorical sense. We feel there is a coherence in the first paragraph, and a natural break before the second. By contrast, we would feel uncomfortable if we saw the following structure:

Our supplies didn't last. In France, we finished off the cheese. In Belgium we finished off the ham. In Luxembourg we finished off the fruit.

In Holland we finished off the bread. It was time to go home. There was a convenient boat leaving Rotterdam on the Friday morning ...

Sentences which cluster

Caesar's words make up a well-recognized rhetorical sequence – a cluster of three. Such clusters have their own internal semantic logic. They only work well if each item is a semantic development of its predecessor, and the final item achieves some sort of climax or resolution. Caesar's words work so effectively because they follow this rule – as can be shown if we alter the order. The result is bathetic:

> I conquered. I saw. I came.

Lists of three are a common feature of many styles of speech and writing. Lists of just two items somehow feel inadequate or incomplete. It seems much more natural to make a triad – 'this, that, and the other' – and many speakers and writers use this pattern. For example, when people are making political speeches, they often get their audience to applaud after a third sentence:

> We are united in purpose. We are united in strategy.
> We are united in resolve! [cheers]

And crowd responses regularly chant in threes:

> Leader: Maggie – Maggie – Maggie
> Crowd: Out – Out – Out

For pairs of sentences to cluster successfully, we need to link them semantically, such as through the notion of 'antithesis'. The first sentence sets up a point; the other reacts to it. The first point might be a rhetorical question which the speaker proceeds to answer in the second point. Or the two sentences might be linked by some internal point of comparison – as can be seen in this extract from a political speech by a Liberal politician at election time. Note the parallelism in the ellipsis after *one* and *other* (p.302).

> There are two conservative parties in this election. One is offering the continuation of the policies we've had for the last five years. The other is offering a return to the policies of forty years ago.

Longer structures

It is unusual to see sentences clustering in groups of four or more, unless they are identified as formal lists in writing, such as the clauses of a legal contract or the sequence of steps to be performed in an instruction manual. And in these longer sequences, parallelism – total or partial – tends to be missing. A long sequence of totally parallel structures would in fact feel extremely repetitive and boring. Experienced speakers and writers know when it is time to stop.

In writing, the notion of the **paragraph** has emerged as the structural unit within which longer clusters of sentences are organized. Paragraphs are identified by two characteristics:
- They display a relatively strong internal semantic coherence.
- They display relatively loose linkage with preceding and following paragraphs.

The operative word is 'relatively'. All writers revise their paragraph divisions at some time or another. From one point of view, they find sentence X belongs best as the last sentence of paragraph A; from another, it works best as the first sentence of paragraph B.

The first diary entry on p.359 is a case in point. There the writer ended his first paragraph with the sentence: *It was time to go home*. But this might equally have been the opening sentence of the next paragraph.

... In Holland we finished off the bread.

It was time to go home. There was a convenient boat leaving Rotterdam on the Friday morning ...

In the original case, the 'going home' provides a succinct conclusion to the chain of events reported in the paragraph. In the revised case, it provides a succinct start to a new theme. It is not a question of 'Which is better?'. The choice reflects how we want to tell the story.

Why have paragraphs?

We use paragraphs because without them writing becomes very difficult to process. Paragraph-less writing did once exist: it can be seen in Old English manuscripts, where whole pages continue without a break. And it still does exist, in some legal documents, where the writers avoid making paragraph divisions because of the possible risk of introducing new opportunities for disputed interpretation. We can also find 'pages' of unbroken text filling our screens in carelessly managed Web sites, such as many of the diary-sites known as Web logs. Nothing draws more attention to the importance of paragraphing than a screen filled with text in this way.

Paragraphs are there not just to help readers process text. They also help writers to create text. They are a device which we can use to impose structure on our thought. The different points we want to make, when we are creating a text, are each the basis of a possible paragraph. It is a widespread writing practice to jot down headings in advance. As we think further about these points, we will find ourselves revising our opinion. Some points will come together into a single paragraph. Others will break up further into separate paragraphs. But making a 'first approximation' to paragraph structure is always a useful creative strategy.

The process of revision which produces the best paragraphing has been much aided by word-processing technology. It is difficult to change our minds in the middle of a handwritten essay, where the task of rewriting a page is off-putting. Authors who write only in manuscript – and it is not so long ago since everyone did – and who get their paragraphing right at the first attempt deserve our greatest admiration. The skill takes time to mature, but it can be aided by being aware of the linguistic mechanisms on which good paragraphs rely.

Paragraph control

There are only so many ways in which a paragraph can evolve, if it is to be a successful piece of writing.

PARAGRAPHS HAVE TO BE COHESIVE

When we read a paragraph, we need to sense its unity. Two criteria need to be met for this to happen.

- There must be a single governing theme to which all sentences contribute. This might be found within a single sentence (what has been called the **topic sentence**), but it might be spread over two or more sentences.
- There needs to be grammatical consistency among the sentences in the paragraph. For example, the verb tenses (Chapter 23) should be compatible and the pro-forms (Chapter 62) should relate clearly to their antecedents.

PARAGRAPHS HAVE TO HAVE DIRECTION

There needs to be a detectable direction of semantic movement throughout the paragraph. Six such directions are widely encountered:

- The paragraph proceeds in a sequence of steps, one after the other, the progress being dictated by real-world logic. This kind of paragraphing can be illustrated from instructional language, narratives of chronological events, or closely-knit arguments. In this guide book, the paragraph structure and division is dictated by what happens in the real world:

  Finding the Transport Museum
  Turn left outside the station and follow the main road until you pass the town hall on your left. Cross the road and turn right into Arklow Street. After 200 yards you will find the Transport Museum on your right.

  The plan to create a museum of local transport can be traced back to a proposal made by a group of local engineers in 1880. They were concerned that ...

  Finding the museum is one thing. Telling us its history is quite clearly another.

- The first sentence of the paragraph states an issue which subsequent sentences develop. Here is the beginning of a paragraph in which travel-writer Paul Theroux introduces us to a new location (in *The Great Railway Bazaar*, Chapter 30):

    The Siberian port of Nakhodka in December gives the impression of being on the very edge of the world, in an atmosphere that does not quite support life.

    The claim is a general one, and requires illustration, which the rest of the paragraph provides. It continues:

    The slender trees are leafless; the ground is packed hard, and no grass grows on it; the streets have no traffic, the sidewalks no people. There are lights burning, but they are like lighthouse beacons positioned to warn people who stray near Nakhodka that it is a place of danger and there is only emptiness beyond it. The subzero weather makes it odourless and not a single sound wrinkles its silence. It is the sort of place that gives rise to the notion that the earth is flat.

    At the station ...

    And the new paragraph moves us on to an account of his train journey.

- The last sentence of the paragraph states the issue which previous sentences anticipate. Usually, it forms the trigger for the subject-matter of the next paragraph. This paragraph from Arundhati Roy's *The God of Small Things* (Chapter 1) begins with a sentence describing a house. But the paragraph is not really about the house. It is about who lives there.

    The house itself looked empty. The doors and windows were locked. The front verandah bare. Unfurnished. But the skyblue Plymouth with chrome tailfins was still parked outside, and inside, Baby Kochamma was still alive.

    She was Rahel's baby grand aunt ...

- The paragraph expresses its main issue midway. Such paragraphs are usually of some length, for we need preceding sentences to lead up to the issue, which acts as a turning-point, and subsequent sentences to see what follows from it. However, in this example, Oscar Wilde takes only two sentences to anticipate the dramatic climax, and two to describe its consequences. It is the point in *The Picture of Dorian Gray* (Chapter 8) when Dorian, after a paragraph in which he reflects on his frame of mind, finally decides to look at his portrait:

    He got up, and locked both doors. At least he would be alone when he looked upon the mask of his shame. Then he drew the screen aside, and saw himself face to face. It was perfectly true. The portrait had altered.

- The paragraph is a sequence of balanced sentences. When the whole of the paragraph is balanced in this way, the notion of a 'topic sentence' evaporates, as the unity lies in the contrast. This is the opening of Chapter 17 of Charles Dickens' *A Tale of Two Cities*:

    Never did the sun go down with a brighter glory on the quiet corner in Soho, than one memorable evening when the Doctor and his daughter sat under the plane-tree together. Never did the moon rise with a milder radiance over great London, than on that night when it found them still seated under the tree, and shone upon their faces through its leaves.

    Lucie was to be married tomorrow. ...

- The paragraph has no fixed structure of the above kinds, but meanders in various directions, reflecting the unpredictability of monologues in everyday conversation. Such paragraphs are only likely to be found in fiction where a real attempt has been made to reflect informal linguistic realities or to represent the randomness of thought processes. The illustration on the next page is taken from the opening page of David Lodge's *Thinks*:

One, two, three, testing, testing ... recorder working OK ... Olympus Pearlcorder, bought it at Heathrow in the dutyfree on my way to ... where? Can't remember, doesn't matter ... The object of the exercise being to record as accurately as possible the thoughts that are passing through my head at this moment in time, which is, let's see ... 10.13 a.m. on Sunday the 23rd of Febru – San Diego! I bought it on my way to that conference in ... Isabel Hotchkiss. Of course, San Diego, 'Vision and the Brain'. Late eighties. Isabel Hotchkiss. I tested the range of the condenser mike ... yes ... Where was I?

Notions such as paragraph and topic sentence cease to be relevant in such writing. This text goes on for nearly four pages before we get a paragraph division. Unusual punctuation is the norm. Indeed, in the extreme case, such as the long interior monologue at the end of James Joyce's *Ulysses*, there may be little or no punctuation at all.

Notions of elegance

Paragraphs are not only semantic units; they are aesthetic ones. A treatment can look unmanageable and off-putting if paragraphs are too long (even if the writing is clear). Equally, a treatment can look disjointed and superficial if paragraphs are too short.

It is partly a matter of page length and typesize, partly a matter of authorial intention. In the present book, the short page allows paragraphs of only three or four sentences to appear side by side without them appearing unduly short. The explanatory aim of the book also motivates the use of a length which avoids complex internal structure. The longest paragraphs in the book are in fact in the opening section of the present chapter, where a different 'overview' style is introduced. On p.357, there is a paragraph of thirteen lines – very long for me!

By contrast, a paragraph of thirteen lines would seem short compared with the large-scale units found routinely in, say, Edward Gibbon's *Decline and Fall of the Roman Empire* or in much of the writing of the eighteenth and nineteenth century essayists and novelists. A flick through any modern novel shows that shorter units are the norm for fiction these days. In academic writing, on the other hand, longer paragraphs remain usual.

The average length of a paragraph affects our sense of elegance; but it is the contrast in length between adjacent paragraphs which can create a semantic effect. All prose authors, whatever the length-norms within which they write, and whatever the genre in which they are writing, sense the need to vary paragraph length from time to time. The greater the contrast, the greater the impact, as in this example also taken (p.364) from *The God of Small Things*. The one-line paragraphs, after the gossipy preamble, provide maximum impact:

> The Government never paid for Sophie Mol's funeral because she wasn't killed on a zebra crossing. She had hers in Ayemenem in the old church with the new paint. She was Estha and Rahel's cousin, their uncle Chacko's daughter. She was visiting from England. Estha and Rahel were seven years old when she died. Sophie Mol was almost nine. She had a special child-sized coffin.
>
> Satin-lined.
>
> Brass handle shined.
>
> She lay in it in her yellow Crimplene bellbottoms with her hair in a ribbon and her Made-in-England go-go bag that she loved. Her face was pale ...

Such paragraph contrasts work well at intervals. The one-liners stand out because both preceding and following paragraphs are relatively long. Plainly, it is a device which would lose its impact if overused. (See another example on p.49.)

Overusing connectives

Overuse of *any* connecting feature within a paragraph is always to be avoided. A feature is overused when we start noticing its recurrence without being able to explain its use in terms of meaning or stylistic effect. Probably the most widely encountered example is the overuse of *and* in immature writing, as seen in this nine-year-old's story:

> One day I was walking along the road and I saw a little dog and it was whining because there was nobody taking any notice of it and so I went over to it and said you are my dog and then it took me to a small hole and it led to a cave and I thought I will follow him into the cave and I went inside with the dog ...

This use of *and* as a narrative connector is a natural extension of the usage which develops in children's speech at around age three (p.309). Because we tend to talk in this way, young authors instinctively write like it, and unless they are taught a more mature narrative style the habit can become entrenched. I have seen it – I am glad to say, rarely – in university-level essays.

Several grammatical notions need to be in place before a child can develop the more mature style. It is not enough just to make the sentences shorter by introducing full-stops, as this would not automatically eliminate the *ands*. Crucially, children need to have grasped the idea that adverbial connectivity at clause and sentence level (Chapters 57 to 58) offers a fruitful semantic alternative to the conjunction. The above author already uses a few connectives (*one day, so, then*), so the basic concept is there. The next step would be to motivate the use of semantically interesting connectives – time adverbials such as *after a while* and *soon*, and more dramatic items such as *at once* and *unfortunately*. For a child of nine, there are dozens to choose from. And if models are needed, authors such as Roald Dahl and J.K. Rowling use them all the time.

Above the paragraph

Everything which has been said about paragraphs applies to larger units. The kind of linkage we see between individual sentences can be used to join individual paragraphs. And just as we find clusters of sentences making up semantic units within paragraphs, so we can find clusters of paragraphs making up semantic units within sections of a text – as is routine in report writing, legal documents, and academic writing in general, where various grades of heading and subheading are introduced to highlight the semantic structure.

Higher-order semantic structure is especially noticeable in verse poetry, where the whole focus is on the structural manipulation of meaning. For example, some or all verses in a poem may display parallelism – beginning in the same way, or ending in the same way. In Tennyson's 'The Lady of Shalott', each of the nineteen verses repeats the resonance of the title, ending with the word *Shalott*. And in Edith Sitwell's poem about the 1940 air raids, 'Still Falls the Rain', each verse except the last recapitulates the words of its title:

Still falls the Rain—
Dark as the world of man, black as our loss—
Blind as the nineteen hundred and forty nails
Upon the Cross.

Still falls the Rain
With a sound like the pulse of the heart that is changed
  to the hammer-beat
In the Potter's Field, and the sound of the impious feet
On the Tomb:
                Still falls the Rain
In the Field of Blood where the small hopes breed and
  the human brain
Nurtures its greed, that worm with the brow of Cain.

Throughout this book, words have been taken as the minimal units of grammar. Only in a few cases have we looked into the structure of a word – where an ending (the **inflection** or **inflectional suffix**) has been attached to the **base form** of a word to express a grammatical contrast. This happened in relation to two areas of grammar:

- in the noun phrase: plurals, genitives, adjectives, and pronouns (Chapters 31, 34, and 48)
- in the verb phrase: person, tense, aspect, and contracted forms (Chapters 16, 18, 23, and 24)

Inflections do not change the lexical meaning of the words to which they are attached. In this respect, they contrast with a different range of affixes which do:

- **prefixes** precede: *mis-, hyper-, co-, ultra-*
- **derivational suffixes** follow: *-tion, -ment, -age*

English has about a hundred prefixes and suffixes which build up complex lexical items in everyday speech and writing. Several specialized forms are also used in science, such as *nano-* (10^{-9}) and *femto-* (10^{-15}).

In addition to **prefixation** and **suffixation**, there are two other main processes of word-formation:

- **compounding**, in which the base forms of two words are combined, using any of three graphic conventions – spaced, hyphenated, or solid:

    gold mine   city-dweller   headache

- **conversion**, in which a word changes its class without changing its form:

    I'll **text** you later. [noun → verb]

This chapter corresponds to *Rediscover Grammar* (3rd edition) Chapter 75.

Related issues

The primary purpose of prefixation, suffixation, and compounding is to pack meaning into a word — meaning which would otherwise take a much longer construction to express. A word such as *officialdom* is glossed by *The Longman Dictionary of Contemporary English* as:

> government departments or the people who work in them — used when you think they are not helpful

Certain other, less common types of word-formation also compress meaning in this way, notably:

- **abbreviations**: items pronounced as sequences of letters, such as *BBC* and *MP*; at least one, and usually all the letters are word-initial; an example where one of the letters is non-initial is *TB* for *tuberculosis*
- **acronyms**: items pronounced as ordinary words, such as *AIDS*, *radar* and *UNESCO*; in many cases, the original meaning of the letters is not recognized
- **blends**: *heliport, breathalyser, Eurovision*

Not all types of word-formation have the function of integrating meaning within a word:

- **Clippings**: shortened forms which show familiarity with specialized and usually polysyllabic words, used informally:
  - the end is dropped: *ad, doc, lab, deli*
  - the front is dropped: *bus, phone, cello*
  - both ends are dropped: *tec* (detective), *flu* (influenza)
  - additionally, sounds may be dropped: *bike, pram*
- **Familiarity markers**: add a suffix suggesting a close association with what is being referred to — usually intimate knowledge or extra affection:
  - **-y, -ie**: *daddy, drinkie, sweetie, telly, Susie, goalie*
  - **-er, -ers**: *rugger* (British), *starkers, shampers* [champagne]
  - **-o**: *ammo, aggro, weirdo, arvo* (Australian: afternoon)
  - **-s**: *Moms, Debs, Babs, fats*
  - **combinations**: *Momsie, fatso, the willies*

- **Reduplication**: compounds where the two bases are identical or only slightly different in form:

     goody-goody   helter-skelter   easy-peasy

  Reduplications have several functions:
  - Sound imitation: *tick-tock, ha-ha, bow-wow, rat-a-tat*
  - Intensification: *teeny-weeny, tip-top, goody-goody*
  - Disparagement: *wishy-washy, shilly-shally*
  - Alternating movements: *flip-flop, seesaw, ping-pong*

  They often provide an informal alternative to a standard word: *ping-pong* (table-tennis), *din-din* (dinner).

Affixation

Affixes provide us with the most flexible and diverse means of creating new words in English, but they are not used with equal frequency. Some items are very common (*re-, -ation*); others much less so (*hypo-, -dom*). Prefixes are less widely used than suffixes because prefixal meanings can be readily expressed in other ways, such as through adjectives or prepositional phrases – *afterthought* as 'later thought' or *tricycle* as 'cycle with three wheels'. It is much more difficult to paraphrase suffixes.

Affixation is relatively rare in conversation and very common in academic writing. The bias towards the academic stems from the fact that many prefixes are learnèd or technical, often deriving from Latin and Greek, and many suffixes express abstract meanings, which are at the heart of academic thought.

The different character of the two domains is suggested in these extracts (derivational affixes in bold):
- I asked Gerry to meet us outside the ground, but when we got there we couldn't see him – just too many people about – but fortunate**ly** Tony had his mobile ...
- The histor**ical** signif**icance** of this event is that the **anti**govern**ment** forces were **un**able to **counter**attack, and were forced to **re**group in the surround**ing** hills.

Prefixation

We can group prefixes into several semantic types.
- Negating:
  a- (amoral) **dis-** (disobey) **il-** (illegal) **in-** (indirect)
  ir- (irresolute) **non-** (nonsmoking) **un-** (undo)
- Reversing or removing:
  de- (defrost) **dis-** (disconnect) **un-** (untie)
- Something going wrong:
  mal- (malform) **mis-** (misfit) **pseudo-** (pseudo-art)
- Expressing size or degree:
  arch- (arch-enemy) **extra-** (extra-fit) **hyper-** (hyper-active)
  hypo- (hypoactive) **infra-** (infrared) **macro-** (macrocosm)
  maxi- (maxi-length) **mega-** (megabyte) **micro-** (microchip)
  mini- (mini-skirt) **out-** (outrun) **over-** (overeat)
  pan- (pan-African) **sub-** (subnormal) **super-** (superman)
  supra- (supra-national) **sur-** (surcharge)
  ultra- (ultra-modern) **under-** (undercut)
- Expressing a new orientation or position:
  anti- (antibody) **auto-** (autogiro) **be-** (bespatter)
  contra- (contra-flow) **counter-** (counteract) **en-** (encage)
  pro- (pro-Tory), **vice-** (vice-chair)
- Expressing time, space, and order:
  after- (afterthought) **ante-** (anteroom) **circum-** (circumpolar)
  co- (co-pilot) **endo-** (endoskeleton) **ex-** (ex-husband)
  exo- (exoskeleton) **extra-** (extra-mural) **fore-** (forearm, foretell)
  in- (infighting) **inter-** (interweave) **intra-** (intravenous)
  neo- (neo-Gothic) **out-** (outdoors) **sub-** (subsection)
  paleo- (paleolithic) **peri-** (perinatal) **post-** (post-war)
  pre- (pre-school) **proto-** (prototype) **re-** (recycle)
  super- (supersonic) **tele-** (teleport) **trans-** (transplant)
- Expressing number:
  bi- (bilingual) **demi-** (demi-god) **di-** (dioxide)
  mono- (monorail) **multi-** (multi-storey) **poly-** (polytechnic)
  semi- (semicircle) **tri-** (tricycle) **uni-** (unilateral)

Suffixation

We can group suffixes in terms of the word classes to which they relate (Chapters 21, 28, 30, 48, and 52). Only the most productive suffixes are given on this page.

- Forming abstract nouns from other nouns:
  -age (baggage) **-dom** (officialdom) **-ery** (slavery)
  -ful (spoonful) **-hood** (boyhood) **-ing** (carpeting)
  -ism (sexism) **-ocracy** (aristocracy) **-ship** (friendship)
- Forming abstract nouns from verbs:
  -age (wastage) **-al** (refusal) **-ation** (foundation)
  -ment (arrangement)
- Forming abstract nouns from adjectives:
  -ity (rapidity) **-ness** (happiness)
- Forming concrete nouns from other nouns:
  -eer (auctioneer) **-er** (teenager) **-ess** (actress) **-ette**
  (dinerette) **-let** (booklet) **-ling** (duckling) **-ster** (mobster)
- Forming concrete nouns from verbs:
  -ant (contestant) **-ee** (referee) **-er** (writer) **-ing** (building)
  -or (actor)
- Forming words which can be either nouns or adjectives:
  -an (republican) **-ese** (Chinese) **-ian** (Russian)
  -ist (socialist) **-ite** (socialite)
- Forming adjectives from nouns:
  -al (accidental) **-ed** (pointed) **-esque** (picturesque)
  -ful (useful) **-ial** (editorial) **-ic** (atomic) **-ical** (philosophical)
  -ish (foolish) **-less** (careless) **-like** (childlike) **-ly** (friendly)
  -ous (desirous) **-y** (sandy)
- Forming adjectives from verbs:
  -able (drinkable) **-ive** (decorative)
- Forming adverbs from adjectives and nouns:
  -ly (quickly) **-wards** (northwards) **-wise** (clockwise)
- Forming verbs from nouns:
  -ate (hyphenate) **-ify** (simplify) **-ise/ize** (hospitalize)
- Forming verbs from adjectives:
  -en (deafen) **-ify** (codify) **-ise/ize** (modernize)

Suffixal meanings

Suffixes express a wide range of subtly different meanings, which defy grouping into neat semantic classes. Several distinct nuances can often be detected within a single suffix. The groups below are therefore simply illustrative of the kinds of meanings which suffixes express.

- To do with quantity:
  bagg**age**   official**dom**   machin**ery**   spoon**ful**   care**less**
- To do with functions and activities:
  contest**ant**   sing**er**   bak**ery**   use**ful**   farm**ing**
- To do with manner of action:
  quick**ly**   north**wards**   clock**wise**
- To do with membership and types:
  republic**an**   veget**arian**   employ**ee**   engin**eer**   Dublin**er**
  Chin**ese**   Iraq**i**   Paris**ian**   Shakespear**iana**   Celt**ic**
  Dan**ish**   violin**ist**   social**ite**   child**like**   Scots**man**
  beat**nik**   aristoc**racy**   execut**or**   gang**ster**
  French**woman**
- To do with gender:
  actr**ess**   usher**ette**   aviat**rix**
- To do with attributes (of size, mind, behaviour, etc.):
  drink**able**   accident**al**   defi**ant**   vision**ary**   dogm**atic**
  point**ed**   wood**en**   absorb**ent**   roman**esque**   kitchen**ette**
  professor**ial**   aud**ible**   atom**ic**   horr**ific**   alp**ine**
  carpet**ing**   child**ish**   aut**istic**   attract**ive**   lamb**kin**
  book**let**   lady**like**   duck**ling**   friend**ly**   sens**ory**
  poison**ous**   whole**some**   sand**y**
- To do with causes and results:
  wast**age**   refus**al**   hyphen**ate**   deaf**en**   cod**ify**   build**ing**
  modern**ize**   arrange**ment**   depart**ure**
- To do with qualities and states of being:
  accur**acy**   disturb**ance**   vac**ancy**   found**ation**   employ**ee**
  emerg**ence**   dec**ency**   slav**ery**   boy**hood**   feel**ing**
  rac**ism**   rapid**ity**   kind**ness**   friend**ship**   cruel**ty**
  difficult**y**

Compounds

Thousands of compounds occur in everyday speech and writing, almost all consisting of two base forms. The vast majority are nouns and adjectives, with a few verbs (*babysit, outclass, cold-shoulder*) and the occasional other word class (*nowhere, everyone*).

It is possible to see some semantic patterns if we analyse compounds as if they were compressed versions of clause structures. (For the elements concerned, see Chapter 3.) Most compounds can be analysed in this way.

- The underlying meaning is: subject + verb:
    headache ['my head aches']   tugboat ['the boat tugs']
    Others: *daybreak, bee-sting, watchdog, firing squad*
- The underlying meaning is: verb + object:
    scarecrow ['scare crows']   haircut ['cut hair']
    record-breaking ['break records']
    Others: *songwriter, self-control, chewing-gum, tax cut*
- The underlying meaning is: verb + adverbial:
    diving board ['dive from a board']
    sun-bathing ['bathe in the sun']
    Others: *living-room, washing machine, home-made*
- The underlying meaning is: subject + object:
    water pistol ['pistol produces water']
    table leg ['table has a leg']
    Others: *motorcycle, bloodstain, TV screen*
- The underlying meaning is: subject + complement:
    girlfriend ['girl is my friend']
    goldfish ['fish is golden']   birdcage ['cage is for birds']
    Others: *killer whale, highchair, flowerbed, safety belt*
- The underlying meaning is: adjective + adjective:
    Anglo-Polish ['English and Polish']
    Others: *deaf-mute, socio-economic, psychosomatic*

Written varieties make full use of the semantic compression made available through compounds. They are much less common in conversation.

Conversion

This is an important process of word-formation, also known as **functional shift**, which has been in the language for centuries. It can be seen in such Shakespearian contexts as *he childed as I fathered* (*King Lear*, III.vi.108) and *I'll word it with thee* (*Cymbeline,* IV.ii.240). Most conversions operate between noun and verb, with other word classes sometimes involved.

Conversion is a different sort of word-formation from the others, as it has nothing to do with packing extra meaning into a word (p.371). Rather, it gives a word a fresh perspective.

CONVERSION OF VERB TO NOUN
- state of mind or sensation: *a doubt, love, taste, want*
- event or activity: *a search, laugh, swim, fall*
- recipient of an action: *a bet, catch, find, hand-out*
- doer of action: *a bore, cheat, coach, show-off*
- instrument of an action: *a cover, wrap, wrench*
- place of an action: *a retreat, turn, lay-by, drive-in*

CONVERSION OF ADJECTIVE TO NOUN
- *a daily* (*paper*)*, regular, perennial, comic, royal*

CONVERSION OF NOUN TO VERB
- put in or on: *to bottle, corner, garage, position*
- give or provide with: *to butter, grease, mask, muzzle*
- deprive of: *to gut, peel, skin, core*
- do something with: *to brake, elbow, finger, glue*
- act with respect to: *to father, nurse, pilot, referee*
- change or make into: *to cash, cripple, group*
- send or go by: *to mail, ship, telegraph, cycle, motor*

CONVERSION OF ADJECTIVE TO VERB
- make or become: *to calm, dry, lower, soundproof*

CONVERSION FROM OTHER FORMS
- *ifs and buts, a must, the how and why, to down tools, -ologies and -isms, also-ran, high-ups, has-been*

DESCRIPTIVE SUMMARY

At various points in this book we have had to refer to the way variations in pitch (**intonation**), loudness (**stress**), speed, and rhythm of speech – collectively called **prosody** – affect the way in which we analyse the structure of sentences. It is difficult to convey the effects in printed form, but the major semantic and pragmatic functions of prosodic features and other tones of voice can be readily summarized.

EXPLANATION

Prosody has four general communicative functions:

- It can convey attitude or emotion – as when we say something in an excited, sad, or insistent way.
- It can convey a personal or professional identity – as when we recognize a sports commentary or television commercial by the tone of voice.
- It can convey the structure of a spoken interaction – as when a public speaker elicits an audience reaction, or a speaker uses prosody to prompt a listener response.
- It can convey a grammatical contrast.

Although it is the last category which is the concern of this book, we have to note the relevance of the other categories, as the general way in which something is said can affect the way in which we try to write it down. Several of the controversies surrounding the use of punctuation (Chapter 76) – especially over the use of the comma – in fact result from the inability of early analysts to reconcile grammar with natural speech rhythm.

This chapter corresponds to *Rediscover Grammar* (3rd edition) Chapter 76.

Prosody expressing grammar

Prosody enables us to express contrasts of grammatical meaning which operate at all levels of structure. Not all of the possible grammatical functions of prosody are illustrated in this book, but the following contrasts have been noted in their appropriate place:

- At the level of the sentence
  - It helps form our sense of whether a construction is complete or incomplete (p.22).
  - It distinguishes a statement from a declarative question (p.63).
  - It conveys the contrast between the questioning and directive functions of tag questions (p.71).
  - It helps to signal exclamations (p.76).
  - It helps to signal echoes (p.80).
- At the level of the clause
  - It links clauses in the absence of a coordinating conjunction (p.310).
  - It is part of the spoken identity of a comment clause (p.330).
  - It reinforces semantic prominence when a clause is in final position (p.314).
  - It reinforces semantic prominence when a clause element is in final position (pp.100, 273, 314).
  - It marks the bringing forward of focus within the clause (p.344), especially in cleft sentences (p.352).
  - It identifies the vocative element in certain positions (pp.104, 108, 111).
- At the level of the phrase
  - It marks a contrastive relationship between restrictive and nonrestrictive relative clauses (p.233).
  - It highlights postposed adjectives (p.228).
  - It can add contrastive meaning to some auxiliary verbs (p.156).
  - It can give any word class a contrastive force (pp.25, 345).

DESCRIPTIVE SUMMARY

Prosody has sometimes been described as 'the punctuation of speech' – an interesting reversal of priorities, for the origins of punctuation lie in attempts to write down the way orators spoke, using a system of 'points', as an aid to reading aloud in public. It is not essential for a written text to be punctuated – and early manuscripts often lack any kind of graphic support (sometimes not even word spaces), as some legal documents still do. But since the Middle Ages, and especially since the arrival of printing, a punctuation system has evolved – and is still evolving.

Punctuation has an essential role to play in identifying grammatical structure in writing. A complete guide to the forms, publishing practices, regional variations, and rhetorical functions of punctuation would easily fill a book as long as this one. This final chapter can do no more than highlight areas where punctuation has semantic and pragmatic relevance.

EXPLANATION

Punctuation has four functions.

• Signalling a boundary
  This is its primary function, enabling us to identify paragraphs (through spacing and indention), sentences (through initial capital letters, full-stops (periods), question marks, and exclamation marks), functional elements within sentences (chiefly through commas, semi-colons, colons, dashes, and parentheses), and words (through spaces).

This chapter corresponds to *Rediscover Grammar* (3rd edition) Chapter 77.

Related issues

- Signalling grammatical function
  A capital letter identifies a proper noun (Chapter 29) – and in some earlier periods of English (especially during the seventeenth century) also other words felt to be semantically important. An apostrophe identifies the genitive case (Chapter 34). Quotation marks assign special status to the words they enclose. A question mark and exclamation mark signal two types of sentence – questions and exclamations (Chapters 5 and 7). Note that these marks (but not the full-stop) can be used within a sentence to signal an included unit:

  He argues – and do we not agree? – that we should go.
- Signalling an omission
  The apostrophe signals an omitted letter or letters, as in contracted forms (*we'll*), formal or colloquial elisions (*ma'am, fish 'n' chips*), and nonstandard spellings (as in *mos'* for *most*, p.341). The asterisk marks deliberately omitted letters in expletives and risqué forms (*f****).
- Signalling linkage
  At the end of a line, a hyphen signals a word continuation; in the middle of a word, it combines the parts of a compound form. A slash brings two (or more) items into a close semantic relationship (*yes/no*). In print, an en-dash (or 'long hyphen') links words in a relationship of 'between ... and' or 'from ... to' (§§523–5, London–Paris).

Other devices

Once we recognize the functions of the standard set of punctuation marks, we can see that other graphic devices can be used with similar function. A title of a book, for example, or an emphasized word, can be marked using quotation marks or through italics, bold face, underlining, small capitals, colour, or some other convention. Accents and diacritics (such as the diaresis in *Brontë*) are usually treated as part of spelling, indicating pronunciation.

Clarity

The overriding principle in the use of punctuation has to be semantic: the maintenance of clarity. We have to be able to identify grammatical units, otherwise our task of 'making sense' will be impaired. This means we may need to be flexible, upon occasion. Punctuation should always be in the service of grammar, not the other way round.

Even quite basic rules of punctuation may need to be adapted, when sense demands it. For example, there is a long-standing rule which forbids the use of a comma between the subject and the verb elements in a clause. We may not write:

Mary and John, can go to the meeting.

However, if the last word of the subject is the same as the first word of an immediately following verb phrase, then we *can* add a comma, to avoid confusion:

Anyone who can't make the meeting should let me know by six.
Those who can, can simply turn up.

Similarly, we may alter the rules governing where a hyphen may appear at the end of a line, to avoid a miscue. It is an unnecessary distraction if we see such line-breaks as *anal- ysis, the- rapist or sin- us.*

Clarity is the product of many factors. Whether to introduce a comma before or after an adverbial, for example, depends on a combination of issues, such as:
• the length of the adverbial – the longer, the more likely:
   Afterwards they caught the train.
   After a good night's sleep, they caught the train.
• the meaning of the adverbial (Chapter 56):
   She took the photograph naturally. [without artifice]
   She took the photograph, naturally. [of course she did]
• the prosody (Chapter 75) of the adverbial – whether the word would normally be spoken with separate intonation:
   Di soon felt better.   Di, soon, felt better.
   Di, however, felt better.   Di however felt better.

Levels of structure

An essential feature of clarity is ensuring that punctuation marks operate at the right level of structure. Many errors in immature writing occur when this principle is not followed. Here are two examples.

IN USING PARENTHESES
A parenthesis includes information which is in some way extraneous to that contained in the rest of the sentence. If we left the parenthesis out, we would still be left with a sentence which made sense. So, this first pairing of sentences is acceptable, but the second pairing is not:

- Mary and John (my cousins) are visiting next week.
  → Mary and John are visiting next week.
- ~~Mary (and John) are visiting next week.~~
  → ~~Mary are visiting next week.~~

IN USING SEMI-COLONS
The function of the semi-colon is to coordinate; in semantic function it closely resembles *and*. It can therefore be used to link units at the level of clause or phrase (even allowing single-word units, when some of the other units contain a comma):

- I had some tea; Sam had some coffee.
- The menu offered us juice; a boiled, fried, or poached egg; toast; and tea or coffee.

It is much more difficult to see the grammatical structure of such a list if only commas are used:

The menu offered us juice, a boiled, fried, or poached egg, toast, and tea or coffee.

It is, however, important to keep the coordination at the same level – all noun phrases, in the above example. It would be disturbing to use a semi-colon to add a clause to a list of phrases:

The breakfast menu offered us juice; a boiled, fried, or poached egg; toast; and I had some coffee.

Here a dash would be a more suitable connector:

... toast – and I had some coffee.

Medium differences

Different technologies permit the portrayal of punctuation in different ways, and also promote different conventions of usage. Traditional printing differs in several respects from other mediums such as the telex machine, typewriter, word-processor, mobile phone, and computer, offering a much wider range of graphic options. The oldest 'technology', handwriting, has its distinctive conventions too, especially when the writing is informal.

Among the more specific conventions adopted by traditional printing – at least in its classical typefaces – are the following:
- It routinely distinguishes between left-facing and right-facing quotation marks, which other mediums tend not to do.
- It makes a systematic contrast between a single dot and three dots (for ellipsis, p.21).
- It distinguishes between three types of horizontal mark: the hyphen, en-dash (or en-rule), and em-dash (or em-rule). (The terms *en* and *em* refer to the width of the two marks, equivalent to the respective width of N and M in typesetting.) All three types can be seen here:

  My co-driver—a man I've known for years—will be with me on the London–Paris run next year.

  These marks are not usually distinguished elsewhere, though a double-hyphen (--) is sometimes seen. The distinction is completely ignored in handwriting. And today em-dashes are usually replaced by en-dashes with spaces (as in this book).

Informal handwriting extends punctuation usage in several idiosyncratic ways, such as by the repeated use of the dash in multiple sentences (Chapter 63) or the repeated use of question and exclamation marks (*Really??, Yay!!!*) to express emotion. Typing in e-mails and chatrooms often extends these practices even further, notably by leaving out boundary marks completely (other than word spaces) and by inserting many more emotional indicators.

Fashion

Clashing to some extent with the semantic principle of clarity is the pragmatic principle of fashion. Punctuation practices change over time, in response to trends in graphic design and the emergence of new technologies. Pressure to maintain a coherent yet distinctive publishing identity fosters differences in usage between publishing houses and regions.

CURRENT TRENDS

The fashion to present a page which is as 'uncluttered' as possible (p.28) has led to a reduction in the use of full-stops in abbreviations (*Mr, BBC*), in the contrast between upper- and lower-case lettering (*adidas, vodafone*), and in the separating function of the apostrophe (*1990s, MAs*).

REGIONAL VARIATION

British and American practices differ in several ways. For example, American usage favours the use of double (as opposed to single) quotation marks, and tends to place the final quotation mark after all other punctuation at the end of a sentence. British practice is more varied.

PUBLISHING-HOUSE VARIATION

In some of my books you will find a 'serial comma' inserted before the word *and* in such sequences as:

... the terminology of politics, culture, and history.

In others there is no such comma. This is not a matter of personal inconsistency. It reflects only the house-style adopted by the individual publisher. Several punctuation practices are influenced in this way.

TECHNOLOGICAL VARIATION

Graphic functions are becoming even more diverse, as written language extends its realm to include computer and cellphone (mobile) communication. New conventions include the use of bicapitalization (*AltaVista*) and the asterisk as a means of emphasis (*the *real* issue*). Punctuation, it seems, continues to evolve.

Index

Further reading

Most of the research which provided the semantic and pragmatic information in this book is to be found in the relevant sections of three large grammars:

- Randolph Quirk, Sidney Greenbaum, Geoffrey Leech and Jan Svartvik, *A Comprehensive Grammar of the English Language* (Longman, 1985). This book provides the overall grammatical framework for the present work, as it did for *Rediscover Grammar.*

- Douglas Biber, Stig Johanseon, Geoffrey Leech, Susan Conrad, Edward Finegan, *Longman Grammar of Spoken and Written English* (Longman, 1999). This book provides detailed frequency data on grammatical structures with particular reference to the regional variation distinguishing British and American English and to stylistic variation as encountered in conversation, fiction, news, and academic writing. It regularly informed the semantic and pragmatic sections of the present work.

- Rodney Huddleston and Geoffrey K. Pullum, with other contributors, *The Cambridge Grammar of the English Language* (Cambridge University Press, 2002). This book provides a more advanced theoretical frame of reference for English grammatical description, permitting a greater level of depth to be added to the semantic and pragmatic discussion. It does however depart in a number of ways from the descriptive framework used in the present work.

Pearson Education
Edinburgh Gate
Harlow
Essex
CM20 2JE
England

ISBN 0 582 848636

First published 2004

Set in Bell Gothic
Printed in China
SWTC/01